COVENTRY

COVENTRY

November 14, 1940

FREDERICK TAYLOR

BLOOMSBURY PRESS

NEW YORK · LONDON · OXFORD · NEW DELHI · SYDNEY

Bloomsbury Press
An imprint of Bloomsbury Publishing Plc

1385 Broadway
New York
NY 10018
USA

50 Bedford Square
London
WC1B 3DP
UK

www.bloomsbury.com

First published in Great Britain 2015
First U.S. edition 2015

© Frederick Taylor, 2015
Maps by John Gilkes

ISBN: HB: 978-1-63286-197-9
ePub: 978-1-63286-198-6

Library of Congress Cataloging-in-Publication Data has been applied for.

2 4 6 8 10 9 7 5 3 1

Typeset by Newgen Knowledge Works (P) Ltd., Chennai, India
Printed and bound in the U.S.A. by Thomson-Shore Inc., Dexter, Michigan

I. M. Götz Bergander
b. Dresden 1927, d. Berlin 2013

These houses are deserted, felt over smashed windows,
No milk on the step, a note pinned to the door
Telling of departure: only shadows
Move when in the day the sun is seen for an hour,
Yet to me this decaying landscape has its uses:
To make me remember, who am always inclined to forget,
That there is always a changing at the root,
And a real world in which time really passes.

Philip Larkin, New Year Poem

Contents

Maps

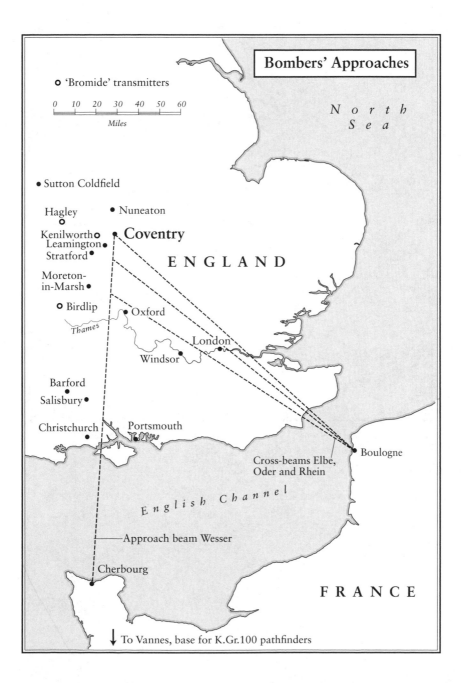

'Bromide' transmitters ○

0 10 20 30 40 50 60
Miles

Bombers' Approaches

N o r t h S e a

• Sutton Coldfield

Hagley ○   • Nuneaton

Kenilworth ○ ● **Coventry**
Leamington ●
Stratford ●

E N G L A N D

Moreton-
in-Marsh ●

○ Birdlip   ● Oxford

Thames

London

Windsor ●

Barford ●
Salisbury ●

Christchurch   Portsmouth ●

Cross-beams Elbe,
Oder and Rhein   • Boulogne

E n g l i s h   C h a n n e l

Approach beam Wesser

Cherbourg ●

F R A N C E

↓ To Vannes, base for K.Gr.100 pathfinders

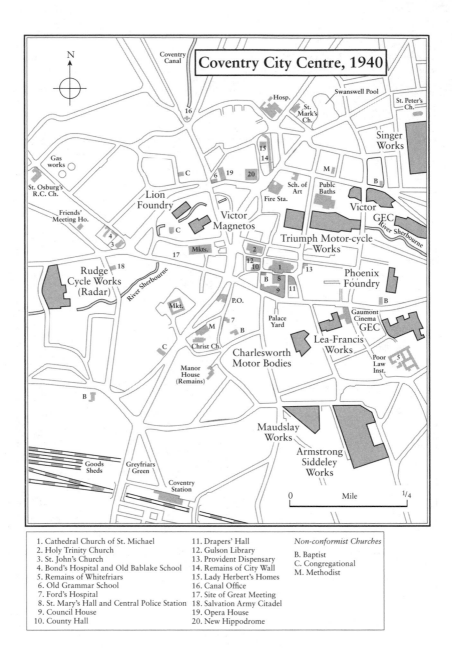

Coventry City Centre, 1940

N

Coventry Canal

Hosp.
Swanswell Pool
St. Peter's Ch.
St. Mark's Ch.
16
15
14
Gas works
Singer Works
St. Osburg's R.C. Ch.
C
6 19 20
M
B
Sch. of Art
Publc Baths
Fire Sta.
Friends' Meeting Ho.
Lion Foundry
Victor Magnetos
Victor GEC
River Sherbourne
4
3
C
Triumph Motor-cycle Works
17
Mkts.
2
12 10 1
13
Phoenix Foundry
Rudge Cycle Works (Radar)
18
B 8 9 11
River Sherbourne
Mkt.
P.O.
Gaumont Cinema GEC
B
M
7
Palace Yard
Lea-Francis Works
C
Christ Ch.
B
Charlesworth Motor Bodies
Poor Law Inst.
5
Manor House (Remains)
B
Maudslay Works
Armstrong Siddeley Works
Goods Sheds
Greyfriars Green
Coventry Station
0   Mile   1/4

1. Cathedral Church of St. Michael
2. Holy Trinity Church
3. St. John's Church
4. Bond's Hospital and Old Bablake School
5. Remains of Whitefriars
6. Old Grammar School
7. Ford's Hospital
8. St. Mary's Hall and Central Police Station
9. Council House
10. County Hall
11. Drapers' Hall
12. Gulson Library
13. Provident Dispensary
14. Remains of City Wall
15. Lady Herbert's Homes
16. Canal Office
17. Site of Great Meeting
18. Salvation Army Citadel
19. Opera House
20. New Hippodrome

Non-conformist Churches

B. Baptist
C. Congregational
M. Methodist

Introduction

The near-destruction in 1940 of Coventry, a substantial city in the English Midlands of both historical and industrial importance, ranks as one of the iconic events of the Second World War. Coventry's subjection to attack by the German Luftwaffe – its 240,000 inhabitants' own 'Blitz' – lasted, in fact, almost two years, from August 1940 until June 1942. However, for most of those many other people, all over the world, who still react to the name 'Coventry' by picturing a city's sudden destruction, their frame of reference is the massed, twelve-hour bomber raid during the night of 14/15 November 1940. Many are not even aware that the city was raided before and after that date, or that more Coventrians were killed in those other attacks than in the most famous – or notorious – one.

All the same, the November raid was, and remains, a central experience for the city's people and a central element in the consequent Coventry legend. That this legend was assiduously cultivated by the wartime British government's propaganda machine, to its considerable and lasting advantage, does not negate the shocking facts of the city's fate – especially shocking at the time, when bombing raids were still connected in the public mind, however tenuously, with the actual war being fought on the ground.

The Polish capital, Warsaw, lay under siege in late September 1939, when terrible destruction was visited upon it by the Luftwaffe. The levelling of the historic heart of Rotterdam the following May, dreadful as it was, occurred in the context of a German attempt to force the Dutch port's surrender. Even the sporadic raids on London during the first weeks of the 'Battle of Britain', and certainly those on air bases and individual factories, fitted into an existing framework of understanding. The ability of aircraft to inflict damage on enemy assets and installations from the air was well established. Indeed, during the First World War, especially its final couple of years and despite cases of terrible collateral damage to civilians, it had been recognised in principle as legitimate by both sides. Only improvements in military technology and armaments during the subsequent quarter-century changed the degree (and perhaps also thereby the moral sustainability) of aerial bombardment as a justifiable tool of attack.

The first great attack on Coventry, involving more than 500 German bombers and using advanced radar-guided techniques to approach and find their target, represented both a quantitative and qualitative change in the concept of aerial warfare. It raised this central issue: how much damage to civilian as well as military targets could be inflicted, on what scale, and how indiscriminately, without the supposed legitimacy of such a military method coming into question? After the big raid against Coventry, the function of aerial warfare was clearly shown to be not merely tactical and immediate but strategic and long term. The normally accepted military needs of the moment were no longer directly relevant. Against precisely which factories or installations the damage was inflicted was significant, but less important to an air bombing war that was starting to look like a process not of immediate knockout but of drawn-out attrition. In this process, the notional protection of civilians – always a somewhat dubious proposition – was inevitably all but abandoned.

The very shock, and sinister novelty, of the attack on Coventry helped give birth to a number of urban legends. The most stubborn of these holds that the city was 'sacrificed'; that at Churchill's behest no steps were taken to strengthen its defences because of an all-consuming need to protect the invaluable British ability to read secret German codes. These, so the story went, had provided the government with foreknowledge of the raid, but the information could not be used to prevent Coventry's destruction for fear that the enemy might realise his signals communications were compromised.

The government seems, in fact, to have known in advance (albeit at very short notice) of the impending attack. The problems with the 'sacrifice' theory are nevertheless many. First, as we shall see, the government did not really learn of the planned attack on Coventry through reading German secret codes, but through basic human intelligence of the traditional kind. Second, the government did take steps to protect the city, but they were neither obvious nor successful. Third, the government did decide against 'warning' Coventry of the attack. However, this decision almost certainly had nothing to do with protecting the famous 'Ultra' secret and everything to do with a hard-headed calculation that balanced humanitarian concerns against risk to public order.

Stubbornly durable legends are a common legacy of major catastrophes of all kinds, and especially of devastating bombing raids. As I learned when researching my book on the bombing of Dresden, it is very hard to gainsay such stories once they have achieved purchase in the collective consciousness of the survivors. The disorienting shock of such events, irrupting into the peaceful daily lives of their civilian victims, most of whom have no previous experience of the horrors of war, certainly plays a role. In fact, for a historian to present an alternative account can be seen by survivors as insolent, even offensive.

As was also true in the case of the population of Dresden, so for Coventrians, the even tempo of everyday modern life, with its taken-for-granted securities and its deceptive predictability, provided little preparation for the destruction that came so suddenly from the sky. In earlier centuries, cities at war at least had news of the enemy's approach, giving time for psychological and physical preparation. Also, of course, for surrender or escape. The modern air war granted the individual civilian no such comforts, however cold they might prove, and the level of destruction it could inflict was instant and terrible. It is always fascinating, if grimly so, to be permitted insight into the feelings of human beings at war, and in the case of civilians, for all the reasons outlined above, especially so. It is also instructive.

Growing up in decent but humble circumstances on the outskirts of a prosperous English town in the 1950s, I experience a shock of recognition when I read or hear the many vivid accounts by urban and suburban victims of the bombing of Coventry. The interrupted life they describe resembles, with a few but unimportant differences, that of my own early childhood, a post-war Britain that was little different from their pre-war Britain, before the near-universal spread of television and the advent of the age of the motor car and of 'you-never-had-it-so-good' consumerism.

The bombing of Coventry reveals, therefore, not just another city exposed to and devastated by new and ever more deadly military technology. There were many of those in Europe, and particularly, as time went on, in Germany. No, the raid reveals a way of life caught at the instant of dissolution. Tradition-rich historic city and rapidly growing armaments-industry boom town in one, Coventry represented a quite particular, and rare, place. It would, in fact, despite the destruction, remain a boom town for another quarter of a century after the war, before the chronic symptoms of British manufacturing finally succumbed to the terminal economic ailment they had for so long masked. What Coventry once had been, however, and after 15 November 1940 could no longer boast of being, was 'genuinely old and picturesque'. These were the words of a famous British writer of the time, J. B. Priestley, who had visited Coventry in 1933, the year Hitler, the city's nemesis, came to power in Germany. Priestley continued: 'I knew it was an old place, but I was surprised to find how much the past, in soaring stone and carved wood, still remained in the city.'[1]

Despite fine intentions on the part of its modernist planners, the post-war city would become a byword for brutal and soulless redevelopment, further underlining the horror of what happened in Coventry's Blitz.

It will be seventy-five years in November 2015 – more than a biblical life span – since the worst night of Coventry's two-year martyrdom to the twentieth-century's most savage military innovation – aerial bombardment. In the decades since then, we have had the pilotless flying bomb, the missile, the atomic and the hydrogen bomb. Now we have the computer-guided drone. 'Pilots' sit in warm rooms in front of computer screens, hundreds and thousands of miles from their victims. Once, men braved flak and night fighters while risking their lives to pour destruction on their fellow humans, and often the attackers paid that ultimate price. This provided perhaps a modicum of moral balance in the equation. The end result, however, is the same. Death from the sky, sudden and merciless, liable to take the life of civilian or soldier, innocent or guilty, young or old, with equal lack of discrimination. For all that worse – and far worse – has since been visited on innocent humanity since, Coventry remains an exemplar and a warning.

I

Wool, Buttons and Magnetos

There are not many historic cities, especially in northern Europe, whose early identity is defined by nudity. Coventry is one.

The story is well known.[1] In the eleventh century, the lady Godiva, wife of Earl Leofric of Mercia – the part of Anglo-Saxon England covering the midlands of the country – took the part of her husband's subjects when they protested against oppressive taxes. The Earl, presumably in jest, then said that he would remit the taxes if she would ride through the city of Coventry naked. Godiva agreed, but issued a proclamation demanding that none of the citizens looked at her while she did so. The citizens respected their virtuous lady's wishes when she rode through the town, her nakedness covered, so it was said, by her long, golden hair. However, one young man, overcome with curiosity, drilled a hole in the door of his house so that he could spy on her. He was supposedly struck blind as a result, and became known as 'peeping Tom', a phrase still in common use in the twenty-first century to stigmatise voyeurs. The Earl, meanwhile, kept his word, and reduced the burden of taxation – this last element in the story being one of the reasons why a whiff of legend clings to its telling.

The legend itself seems to originate from around two hundred years later, in the thirteenth century, and despite its antiquity is almost certainly fiction (especially the 'peeping Tom' part, which seems much more recent in origin). However, Lady Godiva definitely existed, though the name itself is a Latinisation of the original, very common, Anglo-Saxon female forename 'Godgifu' (God-given One). Renowned, it seems, for her piety and beauty, she came from a prominent West Mercian family and was a large-scale landowner in her own right, making extensive donations to the Church and founding a number of religious institutions. She outlived Leofric and even seems to have survived the Norman conquest of England, which took place towards the end of her life.

It is not clear whether pre-Conquest Coventry was a really substantial town, even by the standards of the time. The only firm evidence is that a religious house, a richly endowed priory devoted to St Mary, was established there by Godiva and her husband in 1043. A population certainly began to accrue around this place, which, like most medieval foundations, was a centre of economic as well as religious activity. Coventry's entry in Domesday Book (1086) recorded a population of less than three hundred, though for bureaucratic reasons this may not have included the existing urban area, if such there was.[2] By the fourteenth century, however, it had certainly become an important walled town, a bishop's see, with a cathedral priory, a thriving market and a population of between 5,000 and 10,000. This made Coventry, by some measurements, the fourth largest town in the entire kingdom of England, surpassed only by Bristol, Norwich and London.[3]

A major part of Coventry's rapid growth and consequent prosperity came from the River Sherbourne, which ran through the middle of the town, there forming a large lake that is still memorialised in the Bablake district and one of the city's well-known historic places of learning, Bablake School. The river and lake provided a source of water and power for mills. There were plentiful supplies of timber nearby, especially in the Forest of Arden, for fuel and building purposes. Building stone – a distinctive red sandstone – was quarried mainly at nearby Whitley and Cheylesmore. There were good arable land and extensive commons all around Coventry, making excellent grazing for sheep. Its central location in England and proximity to the ancient Roman roads of Watling Street and the Fosse Way, still important routes in the Middle Ages, made it ideally situated for trade.

Coventry would repeatedly, in its history, find itself classed, in whatever form of words was current, as a 'boom town'. The first time it acquired prominence on the industrial landscape was in the four-teenth century, when Coventry became famous as a centre of cloth dyeing (hence the importance of the river). Specifically, it became the best-known producer of a fine-quality, wash-proof azure dye, synthesised from woad, in turn a product of the leaves of the plant *Isatis tinctoria*. By the high Middle Ages, this expensive 'Coventry Blue' cloth was exported all over Europe and brought, while the trade lasted, great prosperity to the town. So much so that the actual chemical make-up of the dye was said to be a closely guarded secret. A seventeenth-century book of English proverbs linked Coventry to the expression 'true blue'. In fact, the phrase ran in its full form: 'True as Coventry blue'.

Even centuries later, with the wool trade a thing of the distant past, the famous dye itself remains lodged in the city's memory through the sky-blue playing strip of the local football team, who are still known as 'the Blues'.

Although medieval and early modern Coventry became a city of well-endowed churches – its 'Three Spires', the tall steeples of St Michael's, Holy Trinity and Christ Church, dominating the sky-line, became a famous landmark associated with the city – it was nonetheless always a place of practical work and industry. In the Eng-lish Civil War, Coventry was a hotbed of Parliamentary sentiment. A Royalist siege was resisted by a joint force of Parliamentary troops and townspeople in August 1642, after which Coventry remained stoutly loyal to the Parliament and later to the Protector, Oliver Cromwell. In fact, the phrase 'to send to Coventry', meaning to shun or wilfully ignore, may have originated from the coldly monosyllabic treatment awarded by its inhabitants to Royalist prisoners unlucky enough to be kept captive there. After Charles II was restored to the throne in 1660, as a punishment for its former dissidence he ordered the city's expensive and prestigious two miles of high and sturdy walls to be demolished, leaving only a few sandstone gates and some short sections in place.

Of course, once Charles II and his brother James had gone, and the eighteenth century's 'era of liberty' dawned, no English city needed walls anyway. In 1707 came the union of England and Scotland. It was time for the newly constituted Great Britain to get rich, and Coventry along with it. After the decline of the dyeing industry in the 1500s, the city had languished, certainly compared with its earlier prosperity. Now the tradition of Protestant, Nonconformist hard work and domestic virtue that had so irritated the Stuart monarchs became a driver in Coventry's renewed rise.

There had been some silk weaving in Coventry since before the civil war, and by the beginning of the eighteenth century, assisted by the skills of Protestant Huguenot refugees from France, ribbon weaving had become established. In 1705 William Bird, a 'silk man', served as Mayor. The silk trade grew rapidly, aided by the building of a branch waterway connecting Coventry with Birmingham on the one side (with northwards connections to the Trent/Mersey Canal) and Oxford on the other. Soon it was the mainstay of the city's economy. After the Napoleonic Wars, there were around 5,000 hand looms and 3,000 engine looms working in Coventry, and 10,000 of its citizens were occupied in the trade. Forty years later, in 1857, with a rail connection also established that enabled even more rapid transport of Coventry products all over the country, that number had risen to 25,000.

The eighteenth century also saw the growth, less spectacular but vital to the city's future development, of watch- and clockmaking in Coventry, which, alongside Clerkenwell in London and Prescot in Lancashire, became a centre of this precise and highly skilled craft.

By the middle of the century, a couple of thousand specialised workers were employed in making watches. The heyday of the trade was relatively brief. After 1880, American and Swiss manufacturers would begin to undercut Coventry's factories, but the watch trade did provide the town with a pool of highly skilled workers, for which the city became famous. These human resources proved vital to the new mechanical-engineering industries that soon replaced watchmaking. The manufacturing of sewing machines and bicycles flourished towards the end of the nineteenth century.

Then, in 1897, the first British motor car was produced in Coventry. It used the petrol engine developed in Germany by Gottlieb Daimler and Wilhelm Maybach, and carried the Daimler name. Already, by 1907, by far the largest industrial employer in Coventry was the cycle and motor manufacturing industry, maintaining an exclusively male workforce of some 5,400 (a quarter of the entire working population of the city).[4] As the twentieth century progressed, Coventry became famous for its motorcycles, motor cars, machine tools and, finally, aircraft manufacturing. Singer, Daimler (dependent on a German patent), Triumph (founded, as it happened, by two immigrant Germans, Moritz Schulte and Siegfried Bettmann), Standard, Alvis, Humber, Armstrong Siddeley and Rootes, all became internationally known automotive brands. The city also developed as a centre for the manufacture of chains (drive-chains, that is, for cycles, motorcycles, and motor vehicles).

In 1901 the population of Coventry was still a little under 70,000, having quadrupled in the course of the previous century.[5] Victorian and Edwardian suburbs, mainly terraced, spread out quickly from the historic core and its immediate environs, where the old craft masters had established themselves a hundred or a hundred and fifty years before. Here, they often maintained work spaces on the uppermost floors of their houses, known locally as 'top shops'. Skylights were cut into each roof, the extra light facilitating their employees' precise and often minute work. Coventry became known for its factories, workshops and housing remaining all mixed in together.

Even when the new engineering industries expanded in the twentieth century, this pattern continued. A number of major motor industry factories were very close to the old city centre. The suburban growth continued apace, with workers' houses grouped around the rapidly proliferating car, machine tool and aircraft production complexes. Even the silk industry, no longer the city's chief industry but still important, had gone 'high-tech' with the building of Courtaulds Silk Works in the outer suburb of Foleshill in 1904. Here the first artificial fibres, including nylon, would be produced in Britain.

According to the 1911 census, in a mere ten years the city's population had increased by a further 50 per cent and now totalled 106,349. Then came the First World War. The European catastrophe brought death and suffering for tens of millions, but for Coventry, like many other manufacturing centres on both sides of the conflict, it meant unprecedented wealth. Its consumer industries could easily be retooled for war purposes, producing guns, munitions and vehicles – and from 1916 also aero engines – for the world war.

Soon Coventry had more work than it could handle. There was a massive aerodrome at Radford, two miles north of the city centre. At Whitmore Park, just down the road, White and Poppe's small-engine design and production factory switched to making munitions components such as aluminium fuse bodies and shell sockets on a tremendous scale, increasing its workforce from 350 in 1914 to 12,000 at the end of the war.[6] In Red Lane, around three miles north of the old city centre, the Ordnance Works expanded so rapidly that an entire major housing development, Stoke Heath, was built to accommodate the labour force. In all, by 1918 some 60,000 workers were engaged in war production in Coventry. Half of them were recent incomers.[7]

The wartime boom did not benefit the factory-owning and share-holder classes alone. Labour shortages developed. Wages inevitably rose. Women, previously employed mainly in the textile and silk industries, or in domestic service, now entered munitions factories, where the work was appreciably better paid. This excited, on the one hand, the envy of workers in less favoured consumer industries, which often suffered under wartime priorities; and, on the other, distaste from the war workers' social 'betters'. As one chronicler of Coventry put it:

> Countless stories circulated in polite drawing rooms about high wages, extravagance and revolutionary tendencies among the men, and the way in which the 'Guinea Girls', employed in shell filling, squandered their money on grand pianos which they could not play.[8]

Similar widespread resentment of supposedly feckless, unpatriotic munitions workers, showered with money they could scarcely spend fast enough, was also not uncommon on the other side of the wartime divide, in Germany.[9]

The First World War led to a big increase in factory building and in the workforce throughout Britain, but especially in the Midlands, and most remarkably in Coventry. The mechanical-industrial industries that had been established in the city, even before the war, were attuned to changes in a rapidly modernising British society. Moreover, they could be rapidly retooled from war to peacetime production, from military vehicles and equipment back to motor cars for the middle classes and to consumer goods of all kinds, including the profitable new electrical goods. This meant that Coventry, though not unaffected, avoided the worst of the slump which hit heavy industry, shipbuilding and coal mining immediately following the end of the First World War.

This sense of immunity from the decline suffered by other, more traditional, sectors of the British economy continued in the 1930s. The Great Depression laid waste to the economy in great swathes of northern England and Scotland, and led to a flight from the old heartlands of the Industrial Revolution. Coventry's population, after an initial blip coinciding with the end of war production, increased by more than 90,000 over the level of 1921, from 128,000 then to 220,000 at the outbreak of the Second War. Between 1936 and 1938 alone, the population of Coventry leapt by almost 20,000. Many of these new arrivals came from the country's depressed areas, including South Wales, and from Ireland.

Since the nineteenth century Coventry had been a popular emigration destination for the Irish, and now more than ever, for so far separation from Great Britain had brought priest-ridden social and economic stasis, rather than the bright new future that the heroes of the country's war of independence had promised. To many observers, this rapid increase in population, in great part because of immigration, lent Coventry a certain impersonal quality. In boom towns, there is always the suspicion that people are only there for the money. J. B. Priestley, in his 1933 visit, remarked that the young man who had guided him round the Daimler factory was 'not a Coventry man and did not like the place'.

> Here he was in entire agreement with the head porter of my hotel, also not a Coventry man – perhaps there are no Coventry men – who answered my questions about a possible evening's amusement with the most sardonic negatives.[10]

Priestley was generally not much taken with what might be called the 'soul' of 1930s Coventry, though he found its industry impressive, and the city centre itself surprisingly appealing, accurately representing Coventry's ability to change trades with the centuries and somehow 'come out on top':

> In the centre of the city, I found ample remains of the cutlery, cloth, button, clock and ribbon periods scattered about, now oddly mixed up with Lyons, cheap tailors, Ronald Colman, cut-price shops, berets,

and loud speakers. It is genuinely old and picturesque: the cathedral of
St. Michael's, St. Mary's Hall, Ford's and Bablake Hospitals, Butcher
Row, and the old Palace Yard. You peep around a corner and see
half-timbered and gabled houses that would do for the second act
of the *Meistersinger*.* In fact, you could stage the *Meistersinger* – or
film it – in Coventry.[11]

However, this was not why Coventry was such a prosperous place
in 1933:

These picturesque remains of the old Coventry are besieged by an
army of nuts, bolts, hammers, spanners, gauges, drills and machine
lathes, for in a thick ring around the ancient centre are the motor-
car and cycle factories, the machine tool makers, the magneto
manufacturers, and the electrical companies. Beyond them again
are whole new quarters, where the mechanics and fitters and turn-
ers and furnace men live in neat brick rows, and drink their beer
in gigantic new public houses and take their wives to gigantic new
picture theatres.[12]

There was an extra reason for the abrupt increase in the city's
population during the latter half of the 1930s. The Conservative-
dominated coalition government of Prime Minister Neville
Chamberlain (scion of a Birmingham industrial and political
dynasty) had decided in 1936 that, with an aggressively nationalistic
government in power in Germany, steps must be taken to strengthen
and secure Britain's neglected war industries. This applied especially to those supplying the air force, which was expected to play
a decisive role in any new war.

The government accordingly offered energetic support through
grants and loans for engineering companies to produce the aircraft,
aero engines, weaponry, instruments and spare parts required for

* Richard Wagner's famous music drama, set in mid-sixteenth-century Nuremberg.

a strong RAF. These new, quasi-governmental facilities, known as 'shadow factories', were to be kept strictly separate from the commercial businesses concerned. In effect, though managed by powerful private companies on a fee basis, and supposedly free of everyday bureaucratic interference, they remained ultimately under the ownership of the government, their priorities decided from London and their production audited by officials.

In Coventry, the change in occupation patterns among the working population caused by the big rearmament push after 1936 is reflected in official figures, which show a dramatic shift towards war-related production:[13]

Industry	1932	1938
Engineering	4,165	8,937
Iron Founding	1,420	1,989
Electrical Manufacturing	4,935	3,093
Vehicles and Aircraft	29,658	41,825
Electrical Communications	41	6,376
Metal Industries	4,932	5,919

Between 1914 and 1918, Coventry had grown to become one of Britain's great centres of armaments manufacture. By 1938, with many, if not most, Britons expecting the country to be at war again soon, the city was tooling up for a similar role in the coming conflict.

During the First World War, while the old Europe tore itself apart, Coventry's arms and munitions businesses had run at full heat. Since Coventry lay far inland, munitions workers had lived safe from attack, too. The Germans had made a few attempts to send their high-altitude Zeppelin airships to bomb the city. However, lacking target-locating technology, the bomber crews of this nascent German air force seemed unable to actually find Coventry. They had still not found it when, in 1916, a new anti-aircraft ammunition that combined explosives with phosphorus came into production. This powerful incendiary bullet, invented – as it happened – at a workshop on Spon Street, in the historical centre of Coventry, finally made the Zeppelin vulnerable, all but eliminating it as an effective weapon of war.[14]

Any new war would be different, however. This was a fact of which the majority of the population was all too aware. War-related factories, and the residential districts surrounding them that housed their labour forces, would this time be vulnerable to a novel mid-twentieth-century terror: the long-distance bomber aircraft and its deadly payload.

2

'The bomber will always get through'

The first civilian victims of bombing in Coventry died, in fact, more than a week before war broke out.

On Friday, 25 August 1939 at 2.32 in the afternoon, a 5-lb bomb exploded in the carrier of a tradesman's bicycle parked against the kerb outside Astley's, a well-known hardware store in Coventry's main shopping street, Broadgate.

Friday was market day in Coventry, and the streets in the city centre were busy. Five passers-by were killed, twelve seriously injured and forty or more needed treatment.[1] Two of the victims were shop assistants on their lunch breaks. One, twenty-one-year-old Elsie Ansell, had been so terribly injured as to be identifiable only by her engagement ring. She had been due to marry in September. John Arnott, at sixteen the youngest of those killed, worked as a sales assistant at a nearby branch of WH Smith, the newsagent. He was, by all accounts, a cheery young man. Newspaper reports described him as a 'curly-headed lad who wore glasses and must have served thousands of Coventry people with their papers and magazines'. Rex Gentle, thirty-three, one of a pair of identical twins from mid-Wales, had been in Coventry just two weeks, also working at WH Smith on a summer holiday relief basis. He had changed his lunch hour so as to spend it with Arnott. He, too, was engaged to be married. Gwilym Rowland, fifty, a street sweeper for the city council, happened to be doing his job in Broadgate when the bomb went off. The oldest victim, James Clay, was a well-known local figure, former President of Coventry Co-operative

Society, and a spry eighty-one-year-old who still worked part-time as an accountant. He had been lunching with an old business colleague at a café in the area but had left early because he felt unwell. After the explosion, the friend told reporters that this was the first time, in six years of meeting regularly for a meal, that he and Mr Clay had not left the café together.[2]

It was immediately assumed that the attack had been mounted by the Irish Republican Army, which, for the entire previous eight months, had been 'at war' with Britain. In January 1939, the IRA, now under the control of a group of hard-liners led by Sean Russell, had announced a new 'campaign' against what was left of the British occupation of Ireland, including attacks against the British mainland. The operation was known as the 'S' (for Sabotage) Plan. The IRA leadership commissioned new and existing groups of its activists on the mainland to carry out acts of violent sabotage against public services and utilities, mostly using explosives and incendiary packages (the latter often sent through the mail) but also including arson as well as the severing of telephone wires.

Dozens of actions were carried out all over Britain during the first eight months of the year, mostly to no great effect.[3] Counting pinpricks such as wire cutting or small incendiary attacks, Coventry experienced a couple of dozen that were probably part of the campaign. In June 1939, an unexploded bomb was found near a petrol dump in the city. At the beginning of July 1939, there was an explosion in the cloakroom of Coventry station, one of a coordinated series of outrages across the LMS rail network in the English midlands. One person was actually killed by a similar bomb at King's Cross Station in London towards the end of that month. On 13 August, an explosion destroyed an allotment shed occupying waste ground behind some suburban houses in Coventry. Police suspected (rightly, as it turned out) an accident at an IRA arms dump.

It cannot, therefore, have come as a particular surprise to the authorities when a bomb went off in Coventry less than two weeks later, on 25 August. What may have been genuinely unexpected was the fact that it was set to explode in a much-frequented public place and cause inevitable heavy loss of life. Until now, no bombs of such destructive power had been laid. Indeed, the IRA had publicly announced earlier in the year that it intended no civilian casualties.

Within hours, it was known that the bomb had featured a timer. Although the explosion had blown off the entire front end of the bicycle, sending fragments hundreds of feet into the air, forensic experts rapidly started to make sense of the mess. The bicycle, it seemed, had been left, parked directly behind a car, for between three-quarters of an hour and an hour before the detonation. But who had placed it there? Probably Irish terrorists, but then there were thousands of Irish people in Coventry.

The hunt for more evidence soon revealed not just traces of the timer but also a registration number on the frame of the bicycle, which proved that the bicycle had been bought at a shop in Coventry just three days previously and collected just after noon on 25 August. The purchaser, an Irishman who gave his surname as Norman, handed over £5 to reserve the item, with the balance to be paid on collection. However, it was a different Irishman who had picked it up three days later, handed over the rest of the money and ridden it away. Less than two hours later, its carrier now packed with a home-made explosive charge of potassium chlorate, the bicycle exploded, killing and maiming innocent civilians enjoying their Friday lunch hour on Broadgate. The address the original purchaser of the cycle had given was a false one, as was his name, but by that same evening the police had a description of him.

It was the existence of a parallel plot in London that led to the unravelling of the mystery. On 25 August, Special Branch police raided a flat in Leinster Gardens, Paddington, which they had been watching for some time. The tenants, Irishmen described as 'labourers', had been observed taking possession of a tradesman's tricycle in the East End and having other tradesmen's cycles at their west London address. The men scattered and fled over the rooftops. After a chase, four were arrested and the flat searched. Large quantities of explosives were found in hat boxes. A ticking timer clock was set for 2:31 that after-noon (one minute before the Coventry bomb's setting). Questioning revealed that New Scotland Yard, Westminster Abbey and the Bank of England had been their planned targets, using the cycles currently parked outside the address.

That evening, when he arrived back at his lodgings nearby, a man named Peter Barnes was visited by Special Branch officers. Barnes was the IRA transport officer suspected of having couriered the explo-sives from Liverpool to London and – as evidence in his room indi-cated – to Coventry also. Police also found an incriminating letter, unposted but addressed to a certain 'Jim Kelly' In Ireland, which strongly implied Barnes's role in and expectation of an imminent IRA 'spectacular' bombing. When asked to confirm if he had visited Coventry recently, Barnes replied: 'I have been to Coventry, but coin-cidences can happen, can't they?'4

Meanwhile, in Coventry the murders of the passers-by in Broadgate had caused uproar, accompanied by intense anti-Irish sentiment. At the weekend the London *Sunday Times* reported that the police were looking for a Belfast-born Catholic Irishman by the name of Dominic Adams, a nationalist activist known to have lived in Coventry for some years.5

On the Monday after the outrage, some 2,000 workers from the Armstrong Whitworth aircraft works at Baginton (on the edge of what is now Coventry airport) left their work and marched several miles into the city centre to protest against having to 'cooperate with Irish labour'. Others joined them along the way. At the Council House (as Coventry Town Hall is known), they were addressed by their chief shop steward and then by the city's Mayor, Sidney Stringer. Stringer, a strong Labour man, reminded the protestors that the overwhelming majority of Coventrians of Irish nationality or heritage (of which there were many) were equally appalled by the atrocity. The crowds eventually dispersed after passing some urgent resolutions, but it took some time for anti-Irish feeling to die down.

Threats were made against Irishmen lodging in the city, and many left, at least temporarily.[6] The Chief Constable of the city, Captain S. A. Hector, had meanwhile felt forced to issue a curious statement disclaiming suspicions about his own background: 'Stupid rumours have reached me that I am of Irish extraction. I am a Somerset man. I am not Irish, and had had no Irish connections, and I have never even been in Ireland.'[7]

One of the houses searched by the police during the days after the bombing was at 25 Clara Street, in the outer district of Stoke Heath (where homes had been built for munitions workers during the First World War). A young Irish-born couple, the Hewitts, who lived there with Mrs Hewitt's mother, Mrs O'Hara, were said to have an Irish lodger, recently arrived in England, who went by the name of James Richards (actually, as it transpired, born James McCormick). Moreover, rumour had it that they, too, harboured republican sympathies.

A suitcase found on the premises retained traces of potassium chlorate. Mrs O'Hara, it turned out, had purchased some flour bags, along with a suitcase, at the request of a man who turned out to be Peter Barnes, the IRA transport officer already arrested in London. He was known to have been in Coventry on 24 August, the day before the bombing. Thoughtfully, and possibly because, like all bureaucracies, the IRA demanded proof of purchase before it paid expenses, Barnes had kept the receipt for the suitcase. Soon the whole matter became clear. He had supplied the explosives. He may have bought the bicycle. Richards had collected the bicycle from Halfords on the day of the atrocity and ridden it to Clara Street, where he had parked it out the back of the house.

Another conspirator, always referred to only as 'the strange man' (his identity was never clarified – at the consequent trial all the accused refused to name him) had appeared at 25 Clara Street on the morning of 24 August, carrying tools. He had worked for some time in the front sitting room on a mysterious project. He reappeared when Barnes

dropped off a suitcase containing 'white powder' that he had brought
up from London. On the morning of the next day, 25 August, after
the Hewitts had gone to work, the 'strange man' came back once
more and seems to have finished off and packaged up the bomb,
possibly with Richards's help. After Richards had fetched the bicycle
from Halfords and parked it out the back of the house, the 'strange
man' took possession of it. The bomb was placed in the carrier. The
'strange man' then rode the bicycle into the city centre and left it
outside Astley's, before disappearing from the story and, so it seemed,
from history.[8]

At Birmingham Assizes, five people were eventually tried for
the murders: the Hewitts, Mrs O'Hara, James Richards and Peter
Barnes. Only Richards and Barnes were convicted. They were
hanged in February 1940. The others, despite being found not
guilty, were deported to Ireland under government emergency
powers.

There were widespread protests against the executions in Irish
Nationalist circles. Some of the responses were of the reflex sort
mounted when any IRA operatives were subjected to the death
penalty; others concentrated on the particular fact that neither of
the two convicted men, though accessories to the plot, had actually made, or indeed planted, the bomb. Barnes, in particular, had
merely (in his view) supplied the potassium chlorate, and seemed
genuinely surprised to find himself on a murder charge. Both
claimed that they had not believed the bomb would be used to kill
(though this is not a defence in English law where a potentially
lethal conspiracy is concerned). The fact that almost identical
bombs, found in Leinster Gardens in London, had been planned
to be set off at the same time that same day in busy locations in
the capital would also have tended to negate the plea that no harm
was meant to innocent life.

By the time the sentences were passed and carried out, it was
February 1940. If the IRA murder plot had grabbed the city's attention during the crisis that was already looming over Europe in the

final days of August 1939, soon there were even more terrible things to think about.

At 11:15 a.m. on 3 September, following Hitler's invasion of Poland, Mr Chamberlain, the Prime Minister, speaking in a radio broadcast from Downing Street, informed his fellow countrymen that they were at war with Germany.

Unlike in 1914, no one was under any illusion as to the horrors a new European conflict would entail. As early as November 1932, when Hitler was not yet Chancellor of Germany and there was still some hope of disarmament, the prominent Conservative politician Stanley Baldwin had gloomily declared in parliament that 'the bomber will always get through', and so, should the international situation deteriorate, British society must brace itself accordingly. And deteriorate the situation certainly did. By the time war came, plans had already been put in operation to evacuate children, pregnant mothers, the disabled and the blind from major population centres, especially London and the industrial towns considered likely targets for the enemy air campaign that was imminently expected. Coventry did not feature among the cities given initial priority.

London, Birmingham, Manchester, Liverpool and a group of other northern towns were the first to be affected by the evacuation scheme. It was only after the Coventry civic authorities put pressure on central government that the more thickly populated parts of the city were approved as 'evacuable'. School-age children whose parents registered them for the scheme would be billeted in private homes outside the city. During the autumn term that was just starting, they would also be taught locally in their new environments, in part by teachers who had accompanied them from their own city-centre schools.

Although *The Times* triumphantly reported that in the United Kingdom as a whole more than 1.3 million, mostly children, had been evacuated with 'not a single mishap',[9] this could be slightly misleading. In Coventry, at least, the scheme was not a roaring success.

Only a fifth of children's parents registered them at all. The large majority of these registered children were assigned to allegedly safer destinations more or less in the vicinity of Coventry and therefore quite convenient for parental visits – Kenilworth, Wellesbourne, near Stratford-upon-Avon, Leamington, Meriden, and so on. All the same, a mere 3,200 of the 8,625 children initially registered (that is, not all that much more than a third of what was already only a fraction of those eligible) appeared at the assembly points on 4 September, ready to begin their 'holiday' in the country. Sometimes the reasons for going or not going – and finding or not finding a fitting temporary home – were complicated. As one Coventry woman, Mary Evans, touchingly recalled:

> I was evacuated on 3 September 1939. Well, I knew why I was going, because my father was very ill, and my mother had lost a little boy just before I was born. And I think I was a bit special to them. Otherwise, I don't think I would have gone.
>
> I can remember getting on the bus at 11 o'clock in the morning. On the way, we stopped at a place called Fenny Compton, and we were given a bar of chocolate and some biscuits. And we sat in the school all afternoon, and I was one of the last ones to be taken to my new home, which was only across the road. Mrs Freeman only lived in a little cottage and she said to the people, if there's a little girl on her own, she said, I'll have her. but I can't have a boy, she said, because I've only got one bedroom and I've got a little girl.[10]

As it turned out, Mary was lucky. 'Mrs Freeman was a lovely person,' she said. 'She taught me how to darn. She taught me to turn heels on socks too. We didn't really know the war was on.'

In the following weeks, the press did its best to encourage nervous parents to part with their children. 'NO DESIRE TO COME HOME. PLENTY OF ROOM FOR MORE YOUNGSTERS. SCHEME A SUCCESS – APART FROM THE NUMBERS' declared the *Coventry Herald* not altogether convincingly a little less than three weeks after the war had begun. It printed pictures of groups of smiling evacuee children from Coventry schools, frolicking in the greensward, to prove its point.[11] However, within weeks, when the immediate and devastating German air raids that had been expected failed to occur, many of those allegedly happy migrants had returned home to the city.

Mary Evans was an exception. She stayed with her host family for a long time and a strong mutual affection took root. Her father, already seriously ill with tuberculosis when war broke out, died shortly after Christmas 1940. When the news arrived of her loss, the little girl of her host family 'sort of looked at me, and said, if you haven't got a daddy of your own, she said, you can have half of mine. And he was always half my dad, all over the years.'

Like many other local government bodies, in 1935 Coventry Council had instituted an Air Raid Precautions Committee. Early in 1937, it appointed a Major Yiend as 'a full time executive officer for the organisation of air raid precautions', at a salary of £400 per annum (upwards of £20,000 today). Initially, however, the council, whose left-wing majority tended towards pacifistic views, proved reluctant to put real energy behind the enterprise.

By the end of 1937, when a new Air Raid Precautions Act, arising from new and much more alarming estimates of German air power, passed through the British Parliament, the system in Coventry still stood at only 44.86 per cent of its authorised establishment. A pamphlet published by the National Peace Council and the Peace Pledge Union mocked the obsession with gas bombs and gas masks and attacked the new law as 'a further stage in the organisation of the country on a militarised basis'.[12] All the same, in February 1938 Major Yiend was awarded a pay rise to £500 and authorised to employ two general assistants, an additional shorthand typist, and a general labourer.[13]

In the autumn of 1938, after the Munich Conference, Hitler annexed the German-speaking areas of Czechoslovakia known as the Sudetenland. In March 1939, in flagrant disregard of the previous year's agreements, he occupied the rest of the country, which was overwhelmingly not German-speaking at all. That same month, Coventry, along with other large local authorities, received a set of sealed War Orders from the Home Office, to be opened in case of a conflict that was beginning to seem inevitable. By then, all but the most committed pacifist must have been persuaded that Hitler had to be 'stood up to', and that the public would have to be protected from the consequences of the conflict that would almost certainly result.

When war finally came, and the seals on the War Orders were broken, the Civil Defence Service was at one stroke put under command of the Chief Constable. The Council's Policy Advisory Committee became a 'National Emergency Committee'. A third element had been added with the creation by London in April 1939 of a nationwide network of so-called Regional Commissioners, who would take over the administration in given areas if the usual functions of central government were disrupted by enemy action.

The man nominated for the West Midlands post, including Coventry, was the Earl of Dudley. This was less a token establishment appointment than it might at first seem. The Ward family, of which the Earl was head, had been heavily involved in the industrial world of the Midlands for generations. Before he inherited his peerage, the Earl had been an MP and a junior minister. As Commissioner, he proved, by consensus, competent and able to get on with most local worthies, even the hard-bitten Labour Party grandees who ran Coventry and the other industrial towns of the Midlands conurbation.[14]

Under the Air Raid Precautions legislation, a system of ARP (Air Raid Precaution) wardens, based at Air Raid Posts throughout the city, had been established to carry out immediate rescue operations in case of air attack, aided by volunteer organisations such as the Red Cross and the St John Ambulance Brigade. A volunteer Auxiliary Fire Service swung into action to support the regular Fire Brigade, with street fireguards patrolling individual neighbourhoods. Employees were put on nightly 'fire watching' rotas in factories. Such vital activities, along with gas drills and air raid drills, now became an integral (and exhausting) part of everyday life. As elsewhere in the country, black-outs were instituted and enforced, lasting from sunset to sunrise. Factories and other key transport facilities were camouflaged – in the case of Baginton airfield so effectively that early in the war several pilots flying the Armstrong Whitworth aircraft produced nearby couldn't find it and were forced to land elsewhere.[15]

There were clear insufficiencies, all the same, even as the city awaited the worst that modern war could inflict. Some were not specific to Coventry, although the effect would be keenly felt there. In the case of fire watchers, for instance, the failure to introduce an element of conscription meant that the task remained voluntary. So, instead of there being one watcher per street, as was intended, the service was considerably more thinly stretched. The same was true for the auxiliary fire stations.[16] Other problems seem to have been locally determined. Recalling the nationwide pre-war campaign for war readiness, one of Britain's most senior fire officers was scathing about Coventry Council's tendency towards parsimony:

In their instructions to authorities before the war [the Home Office] had told them in the form of a memorandum, you will consider the importance of water supplies, find as many emergency water supplies as you can to augment the water that's in the mains . . . Now Coventry was always a difficult authority. They'll probably resent my saying this, but when they were told by memoranda to provide these things – they would get refunded by the Home Office afterwards – they wanted to say, well, who's going to pay? And the Home Office in effect said, these things will be settled later, you get on with the job. And we'll argue about who's going to pay and what proportion later on. And Coventry refused to provide any water supplies until they knew who was going to pay for it.[17]

Curiously, and whether relevantly or not seems impossible to judge, the Coventry City Treasurer, and presumably therefore one of the key local officials responsible for this short-sighted decision, was Sydney Larkin (father of the Coventry-born British poet Philip Larkin). Since his son later became one of Britain's most respected post-war writers, and the subject of several searching biographies, we know more about Larkin Sr than might normally have been the case for a relatively obscure city official. From these biographies it seems that Sydney Larkin, a highly competent but otherwise rather arrogant and intimidating self-made technocrat, was also a keen admirer of Adolf Hitler. He even attended several Nazi rallies at Nuremberg before the war. As his son confided to his friend, the novelist Kingsley Amis, during their time at Oxford: He [Sydney] even had a statue of Hitler on the mantelpiece which at the touch of a button leapt into a Nazi salute.'[18]

Moreover, Sydney also decorated his office in the council building with Nazi regalia, including a swastika. This remained on full display until, on the outbreak of war with Germany, he was commanded by the Town Clerk to remove it. The Treasurer's deputy later told a biographer that, although his immediate superior toed the line regarding office furnishings thereafter, he did not desist from expressing his admiration for Germany and its 'efficient administration'. Nor did he hide his dislike of Winston Churchill. The new Prime Minister might well have been a hero to everyone else, but Sydney Larkin personally considered him to possess 'the face of a criminal in the dock'.

The city was served by reservoirs on its outskirts with a capacity of twenty million gallons, under normal circumstances ensuring a plentiful supply for everyone's needs, including those of firefighters. But, then, war was not 'normal' circumstances. Static water supplies had to be created for emergency use. The Coventry Fire Brigade's plans for an emergency water supply in case of air-raid-related fires initially consisted of the Coventry Canal. After the outbreak of war, the River Sherbourne was supplied with 'dams' – at first temporary, then reinforced with steel sluice gates – to provide a series of static water tanks in case of emergency. In April 1940, the

Home Office recommended a huge expansion of capacity through batteries of such steel dams in all populated areas, giving accessible capacity of between 100,000 and 200,000 gallons, but this was not acted upon in Coventry. Part of the problem was that, at least before the outbreak of war, no one had anticipated widespread use of incendiary bombs. In the Spanish Civil War and in the Italian campaign in Abyssinia use of these had been rare. Even Home Office advice, issued widely in June 1939, merely stated that an air attack 'may bring numbers of small incendiary bombs . . . water is the best means of putting out a fire started by an incendiary bomb. Have some buckets handy.'[19]

Far more urgent, so far as the authorities were concerned, seemed to be the threat of poison gas. Gas, released from pressurised containers or fired in the form of shells, had constituted one of the terrors of the trenches during the First World War and could well, it was assumed, be dropped from aircraft on to civilians during the second. Such a use of gas, on a massive scale, had quite specifically, indeed enthusiastically, been proposed in a notorious book published in the 1920s, *The Command of the Air*, by the Italian General Giulio Douhet. In it he wrote:

It has been calculated that it would be possible, using 80 to 100 tons of poison, to swathe great cities such as London, Berlin or Paris in a cloud of lethal gas, such that they could be annihilated by high explosive, incendiary and gas bombs, since the presence of the gas would prevent the fires from being extinguished. A system of attack has also been conceived which bears the name 'cloak of gas'. This consists of producing an invisible cloud of poisoned gas above the city, one heavier than air. As it slowly sinks to earth, it annihilates all things that it encounters, be they in the basements of dwellings or on the roof gardens of skyscrapers . . .[20]

Douhet had been appointed Under-Secretary for Air when Mussolini first came to power in Italy. Although forbidden under the 1925 Geneva Protocol, chemical weapons (in the form of both

mustard gas and phosgene, the latter an odourless toxic gas proc-
essed from carbon monoxide and chlorine) had also been used
by Mussolini's invading forces against Abyssinian troops in the
mid-1930s, as well as against insurgent groups in other parts of
Italian-occupied East Africa.[21]

In late August and early September 1939, adults and children, military and civilians alike, were much more preoccupied with gas mask
distribution and testing, and gas drills, than with other aspects of air
raid protection. We know now that, although at that time all the major
world powers possessed reserves of poison gas, the mutual deterrent
effect proved sufficient to ensure that such substances were not fired
from artillery or dropped from the air on to towns and cities during
the war that broke out in September 1939 (although the Japanese did
use gas shells in China on many occasions; like the Italians in Abyssinia, they presumably considered their enemies racially inferior and
themselves immune from retaliation).[22] In 1939, however, the population in Britain in general and Coventry in particular could not know
that gas would not be used.

With hindsight, the population should have been much more
urgently prepared, not just for high-explosive bombs, but for fire-
bombing from the air. Although incendiary bombs had not been
used in great quantities in previous wars, it would quickly become
apparent that they would play an important role in this one. As
early as mid-September 1939, the Polish capital, Warsaw, had been
subjected to massive attacks by German bombers, dropping a mixture of high-explosive and incendiary bombs. Shortly before Warsaw
surrendered, towards the end of the month, it was reported that the
crews of German Junkers 52 aircraft could be seen literally shovelling
incendiaries through their cargo doors to rain fire on the city below,
including the historic Stare Miasto, or old town, which was almost
completely destroyed.[23]

While the danger from incendiary bombs was underestimated,
terrifying reports of the bombing of Spanish cities with high explosives during the recent civil war meant that the fundamental need

for shelters was well understood. The difficulties arose when it came to questions of responsibility and cost. In September 1938, when the Munich crisis put Britain on real notice of war for the first time in twenty years, trenches were dug in open spaces in Coventry (to provide basic protection against blast and bomb-splinters), gas masks distributed and trial evacuations of school children begun.[24]

However, there remained a serious shortage of public shelter provision, even after the outbreak of war. The notion that the public should be protected through government-provided shelters still failed to win the day, despite vocal and influential agitation by the well-known scientists J. B. S. Haldane and J. D. Bernal (both members of the Communist Party) criticising the inadequacy of air raid protection measures. Haldane, in particular, considered this a class issue, accusing the Conservative-dominated government of indifference to the fate of the urban working class.[25]

The politics of shelters was complicated by the fact that after the signing of the Nazi–Soviet Pact in August 1939, which allowed Hitler to occupy Poland, Stalin's Soviet Union had become a *de facto* ally of Germany. The official line of the British Communist Party, which had hitherto been vehemently anti-Hitler, quickly switched to one of awkward neutrality in the recently declared war, which was now defined as simply a fight by one set of imperialists against another. In part as a consequence, the agitation for more adequate air raid shelters became a way in which the Communist Party could criticise the government without appearing openly disloyal, while at the same time underlining its message that the war did nothing to benefit the British worker (on the contrary, in fact). In the late summer of 1940, a Communist front organisation, the People's Vigilance movement, led by Denis Pritt, a Marxist lawyer who had recently been expelled from the Labour Party, was founded to pursue this line.[26] It was mirrored in the agitation of the small but noisy Coventry Communist Party during the whole of the period leading up to Hitler's invasion of the Soviet Union in June 1941 – after which time, of course, the

Communist Party became an enthusiastic, indeed unconditional, supporter of the war effort.

The practical result of all this was mixed. In London, popular complaints about shortage of deep air raid shelters (as opposed to basements and home-built constructions) forced the government's reluctant decision to open the underground stations at night. During the London Blitz, up to 120,000 civilians would take refuge there every night.[27]

No such facilities existed, or could be created, in a middle-sized city such as Coventry. Plans to build an underground car park that could double up as a secure bomb shelter were approved by the council's ARP Committee, but shortly before the outbreak of war the Home Office in London vetoed the plan.[28] Shelters were built to protect the workforces of major factories. These varied in their effectiveness but were generally better than the public provision. One employer, Sir Harry Harley of the Coventry Gauge and Tool Company, by 1939 a major supplier of aircraft instruments, sank a very deep shelter near his works, a refuge for his workers that was also, at various times, used to accommodate civilians, especially children.[29] Other public buildings also converted their basements for public shelter use, including department stores such as the Liverpool-based Owen Owen, a large and seductively up-to-date branch of which had opened in Coventry shortly before the war. However, all safety was relative, as those who took refuge in such places were to discover when the bombs began to fall.

The local authority was granted powers to construct public shelters. Some were underground – usually in parks and on waste ground – and some were brick constructions, as blast-proof as could be managed, entirely or partly above ground. A somewhat panicky building programme led to just about any quote from local builders receiving council approval. The vulnerability of the shelters that were built was a matter of common sense, and common knowledge, for which reason they proved unpopular with the public. The absolute number, moreover, remained seriously inadequate. By the autumn of 1940, the Ministry of Home Security was asking for a third of all cement production to be used for the construction of shelters, but the actual allocation ended up at around 12 per cent. With invasion considered imminent, steel and cement were urgently required for war production and for military construction. These needs had to take priority, however unpopular the government might make itself in the process.[30]

The truth was, in any case, that the government would rather the public stayed home and provided for their own safety. This official encouragement of domestic shelters was in good part due to the government's conviction, not that they were safer than public provisions, but that they were more hygienic and less of a danger to public order than larger, more crowded public shelters.[31] The question was, how could this be done?

Although cellars and basements were, on the whole, rarer in Britain than, for instance, in Germany, many older houses did contain underground spaces that could provide shelter in case of air raids. And if they existed, they generally were used. However, in more modern homes, including those in the extensive suburbs surrounding the centre of Coventry, many of which had been built during or after the First World War, basements had been omitted for reasons of cost.

In the latter areas, so-called 'Anderson shelters' (named after David Anderson, the government engineer who had designed them) came into their own. These government-approved corrugated-iron constructions were supplied in the form of a 'kit', comprising straight panels for the walls and curved for the roof, all to be bolted together, giving a hut 6 feet (1.8m) high, 6 feet 6 inches (2m) long, and 4 feet 6 inches (1.4m) wide. They were reckoned to be large enough for up to six people. Available free to any family whose income was less than £5 a week, and for £7 to the better-off Briton, Anderson shelters were supposed to be capable of being assembled and installed by the head of an average household. Ideally they would be sunk into a hole dug 4 feet (1.2m) into the earth, leaving 2 feet remaining above ground (and allowing for an entrance). This extraneous part would then be covered by a mound of earth, which in turn could, according to taste, be planted with flowers or such like to improve the aesthetic impact of the structure. One and a half million were distributed before the outbreak of war, and a further 2.1 million afterwards. Though often cold and damp, they were reasonably effective in minimising the effects of a neighbourhood bomb blast, though not much proof against direct or near-direct hits (nothing but the deepest, strongest purpose-built shelters were).

There would always be an element of chance, and hence a pervasive sense of fear and inadequacy, when it came to air raid protection of all kinds. It was, however, a fact that 45 per cent of people who responded to a public survey carried out in vulnerable areas said they had no domestic shelter provision. Since it was reckoned that public shelters had space for only 10 per cent of the population in those areas, it becomes clear why so many stories of death and loss during the coming horror would centre around lack of any real air raid protection at all.[32]

Meanwhile, in Coventry, with existing companies swamped with orders and new war-related factories being built at speed, labour poured in from other parts of the country (and Ireland). Wages increased in leaps and bounds. Just as it had in the First War, the old city on the River Sherbourne became a centre of the armaments effort and a byword for full employment. The munitions boom bred labour shortages and high wages, with all the fortunate – and in some critical eyes unfortunate – consequences that such sudden prosperity brought with it.

Autumn turned to winter, and winter to spring 1940, and still the 'phoney war' persisted. After September's fear of devastating German bombing raids proved wrong, Britain's cities relaxed somewhat. And their workers had money to spend.

3

Boom

In early 1936, with Hitler's Germany re-arming at speed, the British Cabinet recognised reality and accepted a plan known as 'Scheme F', according to which the RAF would increase its number of front-line aircraft within three years to 8,000. This alone would necessitate the building of numerous new factories and the recruitment of a skilled workforce beyond that which was then available. It would not, so the government and its advisers supposed, be possible to do this within the existing framework of government-controlled ordnance industries.

In May 1936, service and government representatives met leading Midlands motor manufacturers to discuss how they could help to achieve this dramatically increased production. The consequence was the so-called 'shadow factories' scheme. The government hoped that these industrialists, their management teams and workforces could play a key part in their belated plan to quickly expand British air power by supplying the experience in mass production from which such a project would clearly benefit. The actual technical peculiarities of aircraft and armaments production, especially aero engines and aircraft frames, were, it was assumed, something that could be learned with time by people already experienced in making cars and motorcycles and trucks, even though the machinery required would be new and different.[1]

Across the country, 225,000 people would eventually be employed on airframe construction, and 120,000 on aero-engine manufacture.

Some of these 'shadow factories' came to Coventry, or its outskirts. They had to be built, equipped and then staffed within a remarkably short time. Even the existing factories and industries in Coventry expanded rapidly.

Roughly a couple of months after his motor industry colleagues had met with the government, on 23 July 1936, Sir Alfred Herbert of Alfred Herbert Ltd., established in Coventry almost half a century earlier and now Britain's largest machine tools manufacturer, was told by representatives of the defence services that the planned rearmament drive would require almost 18,000 new machine tools, costing in the region of £10,000,000 (at least half a billion in modern pounds).[2] This meant a huge expansion of Herbert's existing, already massive, works in Edgwick, north of Coventry city centre. It would eventually occupy 22 acres and employ nearly 4,000 workers.[3] Herbert clearly saw war as inevitable. The factory had, on his instructions, been blacked out since the Munich crisis in September 1938, and a night shift added to the schedule.[4]

It was after Munich that the pace really accelerated everywhere. Part of the problem, not just in Coventry, was the service chiefs' insistence that, instead of expanding production of existing aircraft, new designs were needed.[5] The logic of this would be ultimately confirmed (it gave Britain the Spitfire, the Hurricane and the Blenheim and Whitley bombers), but it did require time-consuming, expensive design and test work. It meant also that new tools, machines and production lines customised for the new models had to be built and installed before the big production push could become a reality.

The speed-up in aircraft and weapons production, accompanied by the loosening of financial restrictions on government investment, came not a moment too soon. When war broke out in September 1939, a huge construction project was still under way at Banner Lane, five miles west of the city. Here the Standard Motor Company, already making 50,000 cars a year for the civilian market, was to run a shadow factory producing Bristol Hercules engines for military aircraft, especially bombers.

So quickly had the Banner Lane project been approved and progressed (despite Coventry City Council's protests that the factory
was being built in a protected area of green belt[6]) that the 88 acres
of farmland upon which it would come into being had been sown
with summer crops that same spring in all innocence of what was
about to happen.[7] The largest shadow factory in Coventry, it occupied
some thousand construction workers, seven days a week, for a year.
Apart from office and administrative buildings, it housed three huge
machine shops, each covered with a roof spanning 250 feet. When
opened, it employed more than 6,000 workers. At the height of the
war, at least 25,000 workers would be employed in or near Coventry
in shadow factories that had not existed before 1938.[8]

Nor was it only the government-controlled shadow factories that
powered Coventry's latest industrial transformation.[9] From 1939,
Daimler's existing factory in Brown's Lane on the north-western
outskirts of Coventry (part of the BSA Group) began making the
highly successful 'Dingo' scout car for the British forces. Dunlop Rim
and Wheel in Holbrook Lane made tyres, wheels, barrage balloons,
and anti-gas suits, among other things. Coventry Gauge and Tool
expanded until it was making three-quarters of the gauges used in the
country's armaments. The Standard Motor Company made thousands
of light-armoured cars. BTH (British Thompson-Houston, a subsidi-
ary of the huge General Electric conglomeration), based in Rugby
but with a large plant in Alma Street, close to the centre of Coventry,
supplied the RAF with hundreds of thousands of magnetos* and
dynamos. Wickman's, founded and run by Axel C. Wickman (originally von Wichmann), the London-born son of German parents,[10]
was another prominent machine-tool company, based in Coventry,
which held British rights to import the tungsten carbide powder
invented by the German armaments giant Krupp. This additive gave
a diamond-hard, extremely durable edge to metal tools and machine

---

* A small generator that uses permanent magnets to create an alternating current,
most often used in car or aircraft ignitions.

parts. Wickman's manufactured tungsten-carbide-tipped machine tools and, later, also armour-piercing shells.

Not least, there was the VHF (Very High Frequency) Radio Link, equipment developed and made by GEC at its Copsewood telephone and radio works, three miles east of the city centre. Using this advanced airborne communications device, while in flight, commanders could stay in constant touch with their formations as well as with their bases. By the autumn of 1940 this had been introduced widely, though not universally, into Fighter Command. It would be some time before the Luftwaffe could match this, and superior VHF technology remained a crucial British advantage throughout the war.

During the lull that extended through the first winter of the war, *The Times* in London published a series of occasional articles, appearing under the heading, 'Great Britain in War-Time', about how different towns and regions of Britain were contributing to the war effort. The fifth of these was entitled 'Coventry's Task', and appeared on 8 February 1940. 'Coventry,' the article reminded its readers, 'is also a great centre of the machine tool industry, which in war-time might almost be termed a master key industry. Coventry makes the machines that make the munitions. It is therefore contributing to the production of war supplies not only directly, its own munition factories, but by equipping engineering shops all over the country with precision tools.' Then came the paragraph on the shadow factories:

> The principal war task allotted to Coventry is to turn out aeroplanes, aero-engines, and aircraft accessories, besides machine tools. The so-called shadow factories for aircraft construction are to-day things of substance; the eight which are in or near Coventry will all be in full production within the next few months.[11]

Prominently positioned as it was in the British establishment's newspaper of record, widely read abroad (including in German government circles), this 1,200-word article, highlighting Coventry's rapid and continuing expansion and its crucial importance to British wartime armaments production, reads (certainly with hindsight) practically like an invitation for the Luftwaffe to bomb the city with all its might and main.

In the late spring of 1940, with production dramatically stepped up to cope with the threat from the German successes in the West, the population of Coventry was growing at a rate of a thousand a month. Unemployment afflicted, so *The Times* said, less than 2 per cent of the insured population. There was already a shortage of accommodation for the newcomers, with the city authorities forced to set up a lodgings exchange service, but this did nothing to deter eager job seekers. Operatives in the factories boasted of in the *Times* article were working long hours with a lot of overtime. They were also making what was, by normal standards, very good money, and some earning very good wages indeed.

A social research organisation, Mass Observation – best known for its massive collection of individuals who recorded the details of their everyday lives – took the financial pulse of Coventry during the months when the phoney war was turning into a real war. More precisely, in May/June 1940 it carried out a survey on behalf of the National Savings movement, concentrating on two areas of the country. The survey compared income, standards of living and attitudes towards money and saving, first in Coventry (described as 'a town which has seen a very definite boom through the expansion of arms manufacture'), and second in what was then considered a typical working-class area of London: the borough of Islington.

'Apart from rationing,' the report remarked, 'Coventry is maintaining its pre-war standard against the rise in prices . . . Smart clothes in the streets, prosperous looking homes, busy public houses, crowded shops, long queues outside cinemas, gave an air of vitality and affluence . . .'[12]

In stark contrast to what would be expected in early twenty-first-century Britain, average incomes in 1940 for social categories rated as 'working class' were much higher in Coventry than in London. The survey reported that the per capita income (i.e. including non-working family members and children) of 94 per cent of such families in London was less than £2, whereas in Coventry this was true of only 33 per cent; for 41 per cent in Coventry, earnings averaged between £2 and £3 9s 11d (6 per cent in London); and for 25 per cent in Coventry they were £3 10s and upwards (as against zero per cent of the same social group earning more than this amount per capita in London).[13]

Above all, the wartime prosperity, coming on top of already good wages because of the pre-war expansion in war-related manufacturing, was a phenomenon of the hourly paid worker, who could dramatically increase his or her (but mainly his) earnings through overtime pay. Even the unskilled or semi-skilled could do well in Coventry, which was what attracted so many incomers from other parts of the British Isles. A cinema manager interviewed for the survey complained of an Irish employee who had recently gone to work in an aircraft factory:

He earned £10 9s in his first week, though he knew nothing about machinery. He told his former employer he did only 35 minutes work a night. He hoped to avoid income tax by sending £6 to his mother at Belfast.[14]

There were the seeds of real resentment here. 'Staff' employees such as clerical and supervisory grades, on the other hand, received a fixed salary (and often enjoyed greater status and more comfortable working conditions) but did not benefit from overtime and therefore, despite relatively small annual bonuses, felt their standard of living either stagnating or even declining, given wartime price inflation and tax increases.[15]

The white collar and supervisory section of the working population was not the only group to be left behind by the armaments wages boom. A Coventry bus driver's wife complained:

Money doesn't go far. The rates have gone up. My husband's wage of £4 doesn't alter much even when he works on his day off. It isn't much for a wife and child. And others in the factories are getting £10 a week and throwing it away, not saving. They don't value it.[16]

Even more resentful, with even better reason, were the wives of men serving with the forces, who found themselves forced to survive on meagre military allowances. The lowest ranks in the army, for instance, were paid only 2s (around £4 today) per day, and the wife of such a soldier, with two children, received an additional allowance of only £1 5s (just under £60 today) per week.[17] A female factory worker in Coventry could earn at least three times that amount, a youth (under twenty-one) roughly the same.[18]

The practical result of all this was that, for most working-class Coventrians, both those born there or more recent arrivals, life in wartime could seem, as the survey began by pointing out, quite comfortable. Old traditions were certainly being upended. Age, social background and experience no longer brought the rewards they once had. Particularly shocking to many was that young people of both sexes were suddenly flush with cash. The Mass Observation survey identified 'the young earner, boy or girl, who is making a lot of money and only handing in a small part of it to his family'. While many girls gave their wages to their parents and received an allowance, about half the girls, so the head of the city Probation Service said, paid their family a fixed amount for board, so that they had money to spend on clothes and other non-essential items. Moreover, they could get the boys to 'treat' them and so enjoyed even more disposable income than the bald figures would indicate. Sales in the perfumery section of the department store surveyed (unnamed, but almost certainly Owen Owen) had apparently doubled since the outbreak of hostilities. Coventry's thirty cinemas were also thriving, with one of the largest theatres taking 'record sums'.[19]

Ordinary working-class people were earning the kind of money that had hitherto been the privilege of the middle class, a phenomenon that would continue beyond the wartime emergency. And, especially with its large proportion of 'opportunistic' incomers, Coventry could seem to the disgruntled members of that formerly privileged class even more of a cold, materialistic place than it had when Priestley had cast a gimlet eye over the city seven years earlier. A department store manager haughtily remarked of his customers: 'Coventry people are a selfish lot, out to get what they can. Before the war a man would often shift round six factories in a year, just to get a few extra pence per hour.'[20] 'A bit of the Hitler regime would do the Coventry worker good,' said the secretary of the Coventry Employers' Federation. 'He's an undisciplined blighter. That's my sorry opinion after twenty years' contact with him. Competent, but no soul. No interest in the town or his country.'

Of course, what to their social superiors could look like selfishness, from the perspective of the average worker and his or her family felt more like self-preservation. The cost of such relatively high wages were working weeks of seventy or even eighty hours. The men and women on the production lines were under permanent pressure from the 'rate fixer', a fellow worker promoted above his colleagues from the bench. The rate fixer's job was to constantly retime their work and thus ensure that the piece rate could, where possible, be reduced, so that men would have to work even harder to make the same money. Workers were permanently tired. There was little time for leisure activities, or even simple pleasures such as going to the pub. Rents were high. Many also felt a generalised insecurity, an anxiety both for their own long-term employment prospects (few, especially the older generation, had forgotten the depression that followed the 1914–18 armaments boom) and the prospects of the country in general.

By the early summer, while there had been none of the expected air raids, a German invasion of England seemed likely in the near future. One Coventry toolmaker told Mass Observation that many people he knew shared the same thought: 'If Hitler gets here, the money will be no good, so let's spend it all.'[21]

4

Waiting for the Luftwaffe

On 10 May 1940, Winston Spencer Churchill, the eternal prophet of war and, many would say, chief driver of rearmament, finally became Prime Minister. The maverick aristocrat loner, Churchill, replaced the bourgeois machine politician, Neville Chamberlain, who had finally resigned after the failure of British efforts to defend Norway from German invasion.

The existing Chamberlain administration had been a Tory-dominated 'national' coalition that had won a big majority at the last general election, in November 1935. This had occurred in part thanks to an unfair electoral system that favoured the government. Although the Labour opposition had won almost eight million votes, little more than two million fewer than the ruling Conservatives, it had gained only 25 per cent of the seats in Parliament, against the Conservatives' 63 per cent. New elections were due before the end of 1940. Chamberlain's fall had resulted from his inability to persuade the Labour Party to serve under him in an inclusive coalition government behind which, with the war situation in crisis, the whole nation could unite.

It was thus Churchill who now invited the Labour Party to share in power, with its leader, Clement Attlee, as Deputy Prime Minister. Labour's trade union strongman, Ernest Bevin, took the key post of Minister of Labour. The former dockers' leader would now be responsible for ensuring that the British workforce gave its all. Labour's other major powerbroker, Herbert Morrison, became Minister for

Supply and in October 1940 Home Secretary, an important figure in the organisation of home defence and air raid protection. The normal five-year term of parliament was extended indefinitely.

This was a genuine government of national unity, and unity was what Britain urgently needed. Within weeks, beginning on the very day Churchill took power, the Low Countries and the Channel ports were occupied. Catastrophe followed catastrophe. Almost 340,000 British and other Allied troops were evacuated from the besieged Channel port of Dunkirk over a period of nine days between 27 May and 4 June 1940. Although Paris had not yet been taken, it was clear that the Germans had victory in sight. There was for a while serious reason to believe that Britain might also come to an arrangement with Hitler. Nazi Germany dominated the Continent, from the Channel coast in the west to the River Bug that now formed a direct border between the Reich and its new, if temporary, eastern ally, Stalin's Soviet Union.

For some days at the end of May 1940, the British War Cabinet was split. The question was, should Britain join France in what was beginning to seem like an inevitable accommodation with all-conquering Germany – Mussolini had offered still-neutral Italy's offices as mediator – or should she fight on alone? It was a close-run decision, but once it had been made, the better part of the nation united behind the call for continued resistance.[1] Aided by skilful government propaganda spin which turned Dunkirk from a forced evacuation into a victory, the mood in Britain rapidly turned into one of fierce defiance. This in turn fuelled the dramatic rise in military production that further fed Coventry's boom.

The new Prime Minister, Winston Churchill, made this renewed determination perfectly clear in a radio broadcast to the people on 14 July 1940. He was heard by almost two-thirds of the British population – a significantly larger audience than for his famous 'Finest Hour' speech the previous month:[2]

We shall defend very village, every town and every city. The vast mass of London itself, fought street by street, could easily devour an entire hostile army; and we would rather see London laid in ruins and ashes than that it should be tamely and abjectly enslaved. I am bound to state these facts, because it is necessary to inform our people, and thus to reassure them.[3]

Perhaps the British people were indeed thus 'reassured'. Hitler, however, was not. The Führer had travelled down to the Berghof, his mountaintop residence near Berchtesgaden in the Bavarian Alps, where he was spending a great deal of time drafting and redrafting a speech that he would make on his return to Berlin. Hitler was outraged at Churchill's stubborn refusal to recognise what he regarded as reality.[4] Nonetheless, along with the rest of the Nazi leadership, the Führer continued to hope that, despite all this big talk of resistance, the British government could, perhaps under pressure from public opinion, in the end be persuaded to come to some kind of arrangement with victorious Germany. Since the beginning of the month, Propaganda Minister Goebbels had been directing the tame German press to direct no insults against the British people but only against 'Churchill and his clique'.[5] His propaganda attack dogs would be kept on their temporary leashes for some weeks.

True, on 16 July, only two days after Churchill's statement of defiance, Hitler ordered his somewhat reluctant generals to make plans for the invasion of Britain that autumn, but it was clear that he saw this in good part as a form of pressure on the London government. The Führer still hoped that an actual cross-Channel assault (rather than the threat of one) would turn out to be unnecessary.

On 19 July the Führer, having arrived back in his capital from Berchtesgaden earlier that same day, made a triumphant two-hour speech to his rubber-stamp Reichstag. After trumpeting his victories, announcing rich rewards and promotions for his generals, and lambasting the Allied 'warmongers', Hitler insisted on his good intentions and appealed once more for the British to 'see reason':

In this hour I feel compelled, standing before my conscience, to direct yet another appeal to reason even in England. I believe I can do this as I am not asking for something as the vanquished, but rather, as the victor! I am speaking merely in the name of reason. I see no compelling reason which could force the continuation of this war. I regret the sacrifices it will demand. I would like to spare my people too. I know that the hearts of millions of men and boys are aglow at the thought of finally being allowed to wage battle against the enemy . . .

[tumultuous agreement] . . . who has, without any reasonable cause, declared war on us a second time!

However, I also know that at home there are women and mothers whose hearts, despite their willingness to sacrifice to the last, hang onto this last with all their might. Mr. Churchill may well dismiss this declaration again, crying that it is nothing other than a symptom of my fear and my doubt of final victory. Be that as it may, I will have eased my conscience with regard to what is to come.

[tumultuous applause][6]

The speech was long on triumph but short on detail, especially regarding what Goebbels described as Hitler's 'generous peace offer',[7] It was also delivered with a curious mix of bombast and conciliation that may have gone down well with the Nazi faithful, but was unlikely to appeal to the British public in general or to their Prime Minister in particular. Repeated references to 'Jewish warmongers' and insulting references to Churchill as a 'practised liar' and a 'blood-covered dilettante' hardly sounded, to British ears, like the kind of words a statesman would use when offering the olive branch. Sure enough, the initial, unofficial reaction from London was negative.

All the same, the evidence seems to show that at this time Hitler expected something to come from his speech. He was certainly still vacillating about his immediate future plans. According to the diary of the Italian Foreign Minister, Count Galeazzo Ciano, who was in Berlin at the time, when the British rejection of any accommodation with the Reich became clear, 'a sense of ill-concealed disappointment spread among the Germans'.[8] The next day, 20 July, Ciano had a meeting with Hitler, during which the Führer told him that 'He would like an understanding with Great Britain. He knows that war with the English will be hard and bloody, and knows also that people everywhere today are averse to bloodshed.'⁹

Hitler was more positive in a conversation with his old comrade-in-arms Goebbels. He chose not to accept the British rejection at face value. Instead, he would wait a little longer. His appeal had been directed, after all, not at the British elite but principally at the British people. Perhaps Hitler hoped that Churchill would be overthrown before he could fully convince his cabinet colleagues and the British people of the need for continued war *à l'outrance*. In any case, he told the Propaganda Minister, Germany's military and logistical position was favourable. Why not wait a few more days? Germany could afford it.¹⁰

The formal British rejection of Hitler's last peace offer came on 22 July 1940, and was delivered not by the Prime Minister (who insisted that he was 'not on speaking terms' with the Führer) but – at Churchill's insistence – by his Foreign Secretary, and former rival for the premiership, Lord Halifax. Hitler had appealed to 'reason' in his speech, and Halifax had indeed been the leader of the 'peace camp' in late May/early June 1940. The latter's delivery of the British government's refusal made it clear that even 'reasonable' British politicians rejected the Führer's terms.¹¹

Hitler was once more away from Berlin when the news of Halifax's reply came through – at Bayreuth, in northern Bavaria, where he attended a performance of Wagner's *Götterdämmerung* at the opera house (the last time he saw a Wagner opera) and met up (also for the last time, as it happened) with his old boyhood friend from Linz, August Kubizek. The dictator was furious, especially at the double insult conveyed by Halifax's role as messenger, but it made little concrete difference to Germany's immediate military intentions.¹²

So, for the meantime, while the war of words continued, the mighty German Luftwaffe continued to be held back from targets on the British mainland. That did not mean that Göring's squadrons remained idle. From mid-July, shipping in the English Channel was systematically attacked from newly established German bases on the coast of conquered France, forcing the British to confine their ships' passage through this key transit route to the hours of darkness. There were some bombing raids against key ports on the south coast of England, most destructively against the naval dock-yard at Portsmouth. Only in retrospect would this be recognised as the initial stage of the great aerial conflict known to history as the Battle of Britain.

At home, Germany was, in truth, suffused with a strange, ambiva-lent atmosphere. On the one hand, the population was exultant. Even those who had previously doubted the Führer were now con-vinced of his genius, even his infallibility. Victory in Europe had been achieved – a victory beyond the wildest dreams of 1914 – and the British driven back to their island. There they now appeared to be at bay and, despite loud protestations of defiance, unlikely to launch any attempt to recover the European mainland any time soon. Surely some kind of peace deal was inevitable?

Thirty-five Wehrmacht divisions were demobilised by a Führer-Order of 13 July 1940, representing a reduction of around 20 per cent in the strength of the army (though Hitler insisted that the troops could be recalled at short notice at any time). There had been a grand victory parade in Berlin on 6 July, of the kind that usually signals the end of the war rather than a mere pause for breath. Hitler's open-topped Mercedes carried him in a roundabout route through streets lined with ecstatic, cheering crowds, from the Anhalt Station, where his special train had arrived from his Bavarian retreat, through the Brandenburg Gate and finally back down towards the New Reich Chancery on the Wilhelmsplatz.

Victory parades were held in other major cities during July and August, though without Hitler's presence. In Dresden, for instance. On 19 August 1940, the Fourth Dresden-Saxony Regiment, returning from France, marched through the city's streets in blazing sunshine, cheered on by enormous crowds. It was, as a local historian has writ-ten, 'an absolute high point in the life of the city . . . hundreds of thousands of onlookers – young and old – stood cheering on the pavements. They, like the soldiers, hoped that the war was now as good as over.'[13]

A certain increased bitterness against Britain had been apparent, however, ever since its leaders had refused to follow the French into surrender after the military defeats of May–June 1940. It was now only the treacherous Anglo-Saxons who stood in the way of a final peace settlement that would give Germany the leadership of Europe it had so long deserved but been denied.

Hitler seems to have lagged, for once, behind his own supporters in his apparent reluctance to strike a swift, fatal blow against Britain. London's rejection of his 'peace offer' of 19 July had nurtured further doubts among the German masses. With doubt came anger at the stubborn British, a 'widespread desire . . . for the total destruction of Britain', as the secret public opinion reports of the *Sicherheitsdienst* put it at around this time.[14] Goebbels, across whose desk copies of these reports passed, drew on them to declare that public opinion 'burned' to destroy Britain. The next day, after a meeting with Hitler, he predicted 'massive air attacks . . . the English will really experience something'.[15]

Then finally, on 31 July, back at the Berghof once more, Hitler summoned a group of his paladins and announced that his patience with the British was at an end. Plans for an invasion had been prepared but put on hold. Now he told his naval commander, Admiral Raeder, to prepare for a cross-Channel attack. Raeder insisted that this could not happen before mid-September, and Hitler agreed.[16]

On 1 August the Führer issued Directive No. 17, in which he announced: 'I have decided to carry on and intensify air and naval warfare against England in order to bring about her final defeat.' The destruction of the RAF on the ground and in the air headed his list of priorities; without this, no invasion could be successful. After that came the destruction of the British armaments industry, especially those parts serving the anti-aircraft defence effort and fighter aircraft production.[17] London itself could be attacked only on the Führer's personal instruction. The document ended with the statement, underlined by Hitler for emphasis: 'Terror bombing as reprisals is a matter to be decided by me'.[18]

August 1940 was to be the month in which Germany seized control of the skies over southern England. Only once this had been achieved, at least on a decent temporary basis, would the planned cross-Channel invasion have a serious chance of success.

Since Hitler had scheduled the landing in England for mid-September, his air force commanders had five to six weeks to carry out this task. During this limited time, the Luftwaffe had to crush the British air defences while keeping its own capabilities more or less intact. As one distinguished historian of the Battle of Britain has put it: 'This meant achieving a favourable kill ratio high enough to reduce Fighter Command to ineffectiveness within five weeks and leave the Luftwaffe fighter force sufficiently intact to protect the invasion against British bombing attacks.'[19]

To perform its allotted task, the Luftwaffe could call on 1,438 bomber aircraft (949 of them currently serviceable) and 1,479 fighters (1,198 serviceable). The Germans had no separate 'commands' for bombers and fighters as the British did. Instead, their air force was divided into three air fleets: 2, 3 and 5. Each included both sorts of aircraft. Air Fleet 5, based in Norway, was considerably smaller than the other two (only six squadrons, two of fighters and four bombers). Fleet 5 faced long flight times, which also meant that its planes had no fighter escort, as well as having to face the dangers of the notoriously stormy North Sea. It played no major role in the latter part of the campaign.[20] Against these forces, the British could put into the air, at the beginning of August 1940, sixty operational fighter squadrons amounting to 715 serviceable aircraft. Seven of these squadrons were converted bombers adapted to a night-fighter role (none too successfully, it seems).[21]

The Luftwaffe's attacks against the British mainland had been authorised to begin any time after 5 August. Some small attacks occurred in the few days following this date. Mainly due to unfavourable weather conditions, the first large-scale offensive operations, however, did not take place until 13 August – so-called 'Eagle Day' – and even these were disrupted by further bad weather and disorganisation. Coordination between bombers and their escorts was inadequate.

It had been hoped in Berlin that on 'Eagle Day' the Luftwaffe would repeat what it had achieved in Poland and France by surprise attacks in force – the destruction of substantial parts of the enemy's air force on the ground and the decisive dislocation of his command and control system.[22] This was not what happened. Though ground installations were damaged and British personnel killed and wounded, no targets were so badly damaged as to be put out of action. The Luftwaffe lost forty-five aircraft, against thirteen British losses. 'Eagle Day' was something of a flop.

It was seven weeks since the end of the Battle for France and ten weeks since Dunkirk. Partly because of Hitler's hopes that Britain could be coaxed into a peace settlement, the country had enjoyed an unexpectedly long period of freedom from direct attack in which to strengthen her air defences. Moreover, although Hitler had ordered the invasion of Britain, the debate about the feasibility of the project, codenamed Operation Sea Lion, was still continuing in German military circles. Matters were further complicated by the fact that, on Hitler's orders, preparations had also begun for an invasion of Germany's alleged ally, the Soviet Union, the following spring. German energy was diffused. The British had only one thing to think about, and one thing to devote their efforts to – the prevention of German control of the air over southern England – while German strategic priorities were still not entirely clear.[23]

An important, perhaps even key, element in British preparedness was the chain of radar stations that existed by the early autumn of 1940, half of them on the south and east coasts. The stations stood ready to track the attacking Germans well before the Luftwaffe's aircraft crossed the coastline, thus enabling commanders to make an informed decision about where to send their defensive fighter formations (or, indeed, whether they would choose to intercept a particular attack in the first place, or preferred to conserve their forces).

The radar chain was not perfect, and many of the crews operating the stations were not yet adequately trained. All the same, combined with the work of the Observer Corps (which took over the task of spotting enemy aircraft and relaying their strength and depositions once the Luftwaffe arrived over the British mainland) and a well-functioning telephone system that drew all the information together and fed it into Fighter Command headquarters for processing and relaying to commanders of individual groups and sectors, the British defensive system was considerably more coordinated (and more flexible) than the Germans believed.

German intelligence about British capabilities was, on the whole, poor. The Luftwaffe neither understood the British system nor knew from where it was controlled. Throughout the battle, it was assumed that British command and control was completely local to each base rather than, as was actually the case, highly centralised and coordinated. Poor intelligence was also the reason why the Germans underestimated both the combat-ready strength of Fighter Command and the British aircraft industry's ability to replace any RAF losses.[24] The British, curiously, consistently overestimated the forces ranged against them on the German side. Did the enemy but know it, Britain's problem was not so much that of replacing fighter aircraft but of replacing the men (especially the experienced men) who flew them. Almost a third of Fighter Command's strength had been lost during the battle for France;[25] training of replacements took time.

The first stage of the German air offensive was aimed at a range of radar stations, individual industrial targets and British fighter bases. Also included in the plan was a constant stream of small so-called *Störangriffe* (disturbance attacks) on urban targets all over the country, calculated to spread fear and keep the British population from their beds due to air raid alarms. These all involved a combination of medium-distance bombers and fighter-bombers and – at least in the attacks over the southern counties – relatively short-range fighters such as the Messerschmitt Bf 109.

Unlike the British, who had always planned to use their island bases, in case of war, to strike from a distance at ground targets on the Continent, and built planes that could do this, in 1940 the Germans had no long-range heavy bombers. All Luftwaffe aircraft were constructed so as to be able to act as ground support when the occasion demanded. Ever after, its former commanders and its historians have agreed that in August and September 1940 the Luftwaffe was asked to do too much, further increasing the nagging background sense that energy and purpose were spread thinly.[26]

German losses overall were worrying during the early stages of what was supposed to be a swift, triumphant stab into the heart of Britain. So, on 15 August, for instance – the 'busiest' of the entire battle – more than 500 bomber-type aircraft and almost 1,300 fighters were involved on the German side. Fifty-seven were shot down, making losses of more than a hundred since 13 August.[27]

Among a number of other discomfiting revelations for the Germans during the early days of this campaign was the realisation that the notorious Junkers 87 dive-bomber, known as the Stuka, though highly effective during the ground campaigns in Poland, the Low Countries and France, was pretty much useless in conditions where the Luftwaffe did not control the air space in which it operated. Elsewhere, it had struck terror into civilians and ground troops alike, in part through the terrifying, howling sirens that accompanied its attack dive. However, the Ju 87, it turned out, was both very slow compared with the defending British aircraft and, because of its method of bombing, swooping down to 2,000 feet or so before its load was automatically released and then climbing again at the alarmingly low speed of 120 mph, very vulnerable to attack. This way of operation also made it very difficult (and dangerous) for fighter escorts to provide close protection. The grim picture was completed by the Ju 87's reputation for disintegrating when hit by enemy gunfire.[28] Losses on 'Eagle Day' had been disproportionately heavy. The downing of seventeen Ju 87s in one single afternoon on 18 August, caught by British fighters while attacking Coastal Command bases at Gosport, hammered home the message. The aircraft were promptly withdrawn from service.[29]

On 18 August, the Luftwaffe raided the important Fighter Command station at Biggin Hill, near Bromley, in Kent, for the first time. From the air, the damage looked extremely impressive. The German press claimed that it had been 'completely destroyed . . . wiped out of existence'. German pilots who had taken part in the raid, so it was written, shook their heads at the ease of it all and asked: 'Has it gone so quickly? Is England already finished?'[30] In fact, the vital sector operations room there was put out of action for just a few hours, and two other stations managed to cover for it while the damage was repaired.[31] One incidental piece of knowledge gained by the RAF from the Biggin Hill raid was especially useful. Some officers' fear that female personnel (WAAFs) would go to pieces under fire proved wholly unjustified. Their calm was exemplary. One WAAF received the Military Medal for her work 'flagging' unexploded bombs, a perilous task.

As a result of a conference on 19 August, held on Göring's estate at Karinhall, near Berlin, the Reich Marshal reframed the escort rules to give more protection for the German bombers, whose losses had made up an unnervingly large part of the 300 aircraft he had lost during the past week alone (compared with only 200 in the whole of July).[32] Glory-hungry young fighter aces such as Mölders and Galland were promoted, and the Luftwaffe was ordered to concentrate on putting the British defences, on the ground and in the air, out of action.

For the next two weeks, Fighter Command was, accordingly, the main target of the renewed German attacks. Some of these, like the first raid on Biggin Hill, seemed very impressive. Again, the Germans overestimated the damage done, both to the actual bases and installations, and to the number of aircraft that the British could continue to put up against them. One more heave, so it seemed, and the British air defences would be rendered useless. The Luftwaffe intelligence appraisal which formed the basis of Göring's decision-making at Karinhall claimed that the British had only 300 serviceable fighters left, whereas the actual figure was 855. The total number of fighters on the Command's strength, including those in storage and those being used for training, was 1,438 – twice the number available at the beginning of July.[33]

The Luftwaffe did indeed chalk up some real successes – on 31 August, Fighter Command suffered its greatest ever losses in one day – but the Germans' own casualties were also heavy. Moreover, yet again the Luftwaffe consistently overestimated its own achievements and underestimated both British strength and the speed at which British fighter losses could be replaced. At the end of August, German Air Intelligence estimated that eighteen Fighter Command stations had been completely physically eliminated and the rest rendered useless. In fact, though from the air these bases may have looked like complete wastelands, none had been destroyed, and most had never been out of action for more than a few hours at a time. Operations rooms were often transferred to other premises in nearby villages, as at Biggin Hill. At Kenley, even before the station was seriously attacked, a backup facility had been established in a butcher's shop in nearby Caterham. In the space of just a week, between 12 and 19 August, so the Luftwaffe intelligence's fantasy continued, 624 British aircraft had been downed against 174 German. Monthly fighter production in Britain was estimated at 280 (it was, in fact, 450). And so on.[34]

The reality was, of course, clear every time the Luftwaffe appeared over England and found British fighters swooping from the sky to oppose it. The official line may have insisted, in public at least, that the British were within an ace of defeat, but Goebbels, ever a shrewd interpreter of events, was already proposing changes in the tone of his ministry's propaganda to prepare the German people for a longer war against a formidable opponent. 'The people should gradually be familiarised with the possibility that the war might drag on through the winter,' he told his underlings at the Propaganda Ministry's regular weekly conference on 23 August 1940. Mockery would no longer be the weapon of preference: 'The toughness of the English determination to wage war [should be] placed in the foreground and we should report on the ridiculousness of everyday English life only in exceptional cases.'³⁵

More proof of imminent failure in the great push for air superiority was provided by the comments of his newly promoted senior officers when Göring ventured to the Channel coast in early September. Despite complaints that the Bf 109 was peculiarly unsuited for close-escort commitments (the Messerschmitt light fighter was excellent at 'bouncing' enemy fighters in free pursuit, but not good at dogfights), the Reich Marshal excoriated his fighter commanders for lack of aggression. Afterwards, seeking to placate them, he asked what he could give them to make their job easier. Mölders asked for better engines for the Bf 109. The waggish Galland suggested he could use a squadron of Spitfires. As a recent historian of the battle has said, 'Göring's sense of humour failed him at this point.'³⁶

A turning point had, however, already been reached. In the last week of August, the Luftwaffe had dropped its first bombs on London, and the RAF had raided Berlin. Attacks on British military targets continued, but the Luftwaffe's emphasis had begun to switch from their island enemy's air defences to its civil and industrial infrastructure.

As late as 24 August 1940, a directive of the Wehrmacht High Command reaffirmed that no attack could be mounted on London – then confined to the relatively small London County Council (LCC) area* – without the Führer's express permission. That very same night, however, at around ten o'clock, German aircraft dropped bombs in London proper. The attack spread destruction over the

---

* From 1889 to 1965, London was much smaller than it is now. It officially consisted of the County of London (302.77 square km) and was administered by the London County Council (LCC). This was the area reserved for Hitler's decision. In 1965 London was hugely expanded by the inclusion of suburban areas that had once been part of the surrounding shire counties. 'Greater London' (1572 square km) came under the jurisdiction of the Greater London Council (and remained as an entity even after the abolition of the GLC in 1986). The former county area became known as 'Inner London'.

East End, including damage to the church of St Giles, Cripplegate, at the heart of the historic City of London, in what is now the Barbican complex. Supposedly the actual target had been the Thames Haven (later dubbed Shell Haven) oil terminal, almost thirty miles to the east of the City of London.[37]

It is not entirely clear whether this was a mistake. The same source says that Göring sent a telegram to the bombers' HQ demanding the names of the crew responsible so that they could be transferred to the infantry. Other authorities seem to imply this was more a case of inevitable 'mission creep'.[38] There was nothing accidental about the British response, however. The next night, two squadrons of Hampden and Wellington bombers of the RAF attacked Berlin. In this first attack, there were no fatalities. The blow to morale was what counted, however. Early in the war, Göring had made a fatal public boast that if British aircraft managed to bomb the Reich, then 'my name is Meier' (the equivalent of saying that if such-and-such happens, 'I'm a Dutchman'). Another RAF attack on the night of 28/29 August hit the main Görlitz Station in central Berlin and spread into the surrounding residential area of Kreuzberg/Friedrichshain. This time ten people were killed and twenty-one seriously hurt. When Hitler, who was back at the Berchtesgaden, heard about it, he immediately returned to the capital.

The British attacks were flagged by Churchill's cabinet as retribution for the first German bombs on London. If they were also intended as provocation, however, they succeeded. According to his air adjutant, von Below, Hitler saw them as 'a calculated insult' which called for an appropriate response, which could only be against London.[39]

Mass attacks on the British capital had always been planned for later in the course of preparations for Operation Sea Lion, but now they were brought forward and presented to the German people as overt 'revenge attacks'. The day after the second RAF incursion, instructions were issued for the Luftwaffe to proceed within days to a devastating campaign against London. On 4 September, addressing the mass meeting that launched the 'Winter Relief Fund' (*Winterhilfswerk*) charity appeal for 1940/41, Hitler also escalated his accustomed verbal aggression to new heights, declaring to a noisily appreciative crowd:

And if the British air force drops three or four thousand kilograms of bombs, then now in one night we shall drop 150,000, 180,000, 230,000, 300,000, 400,000, a million kilograms. If they declare that they will launch large-scale attacks on our cities – [then] we shall obliterate their cities! We shall settle the hashes of these night-pirates, so help us God. The hour will come when one of us cracks, and that one will not be National Socialist Germany![40]

Hitler's audience leapt to their feet. 'Never! Never!' they cried.[41]

5

Blitz

The Luftwaffe's bomber force was finally unleashed against London, on a massive scale, during the late afternoon of Saturday, 7 September 1940. The attack continued well into the night. Ever since, historians have debated whether this was a disastrous mistake, a miscalculation, that cost Germany the battle for Britain.

The story goes that when the Luftwaffe switched its attention to London, it was within a hair's breadth of reducing Fighter Command to impotence by completing the destruction of its command infrastructure and air defences. Had the Germans continued with attacks on the fighter stations and the radar systems, which they carried out until the end of 6 September with a good deal of success, the RAF must have succumbed. Or so it was thought. German intelligence estimates at the time support this idea and undoubtedly encouraged the Luftwaffe to see Fighter Command as a spent force, enabling it to move on to city targets.

But, then, it is impossible to prove a negative, in history as in anything else. With hindsight, the change in strategy relieved the strong, arguably lethal, pressure that the Luftwaffe's attacks on the defence infrastructure and the fighter stations had continued to exert. What is clear without hindsight is that from the German point of view, the beginning of the systematic bombing of London, eight-million-strong megalopolis and capital of the British Empire, felt like a new beginning, a crucial relaunch of the fatal assault. This campaign must, it was keenly felt, represent the end for Germany's remaining enemy.

The commencement of German attacks on London undoubtedly created a refreshing new clarity of purpose for their planners and air crew alike. The last three and a half weeks since the near-fiasco of 'Eagle Day' had seen many successes and at least an equal number of failures. These had been spread over a disconcertingly wide variety of areas and often radically varied targets, making clear conclusions difficult. Moreover, they had been accompanied by a constant drip-drip of German losses in aircraft and men – in a service that was supposed to be preserving its strength for a crucial support role in the big cross-Channel invasion, now postponed until 21 September.

Göring's campaign against London even had its own codename, *Loge*, named after the devious demi-god of fire who features in Wagner's opera *Das Rheingold*. His men's big night over the British capital was meant to light fires that would, so to speak, not go out until Britain surrendered. However, unlike their big day back in mid-August, this performance was indeed a success. The Reich Marshal had declared himself in personal command of the new campaign. He had royally wined and dined his senior commanders the previous evening aboard his luxurious, armour-plated private train in a siding between Boulogne and Calais. Göring then appeared the next afternoon – splendid uniform, diamond-encrusted marshal's baton and all – at the forward observation post on the cliffs at Gris Nez, opposite Dover, to watch the beginnings of the mighty attack that he hoped would bring the Luftwaffe – and Germany – final victory in the air.

Three large waves of bombers duly crossed the Channel. The first, consisting of 348 aircraft, took off in the late afternoon, when it was still light. It reached London around 5 p.m. The second wave arrived over the target area at 8 p.m., with a third continuing the assault in darkness until the small hours of the next day. On this first day, the population of London was under attack for around eight hours.

The Luftwaffe bombers had one big advantage: unaware of a major change in German tactics, most of Fighter Command remained on the alert for dispersed attacks on its own installations, rather than expecting a concentrated aerial bombardment of one, huge urban area. The first attack wave was closely accompanied by 607 fighters as it swept in over southern England. A very big incursion but, unlike earlier Luftwaffe swarms, this one did not disperse to launch a series of attacks. Unexpectedly from the British point of view, it headed straight for London en masse. One of the British fighter pilots who witnessed this recalled: 'Ahead and above a veritable armada of German aircraft . . . *Staffel* [squadron] after *Staffel* as far as the eye could see . . . I have never seen so many aircraft in the air at one time. It was awe-inspiring.'[1] Another was even more awestruck:

> One German bomber formation stretched from over London right out to Southend, twenty miles or more, I suppose, about a quarter of a mile wide. And with an escort of fighters above. It was a breath-taking sight.[2]

The first formations approached London through the south-eastern suburbs in fine, clear and warm weather, ending up at the docks and the Woolwich Arsenal. They dropped some 300 tonnes* of bombs, with damage recorded from Blackheath and Plumstead on the way into the main targets on the river. The second wave, three hours later, came in through the south and south-west of the London suburbs but also ended up at the docks, as did all the aircraft that night. It was part of the plan. Another 330 tonnes of bombs fell on a swathe of London, from Clapham and Kensington to the East End. The aim of attacking in this way was to give the succeeding waves the opportunity to bomb without too much interference. The Luftwaffe planners calculated that any British fighters going up to meet the first wave would, meanwhile, have been forced to land and refuel. Once it was dark, after around 7:30 p.m., the British fighters were more or less useless in any case.[3] And so the destruction

* 1 metric tonne = 1.10 'short' (US) or 0.984 'long' (UK) tons.

continued. The docklands were indeed severely affected, with some massive fires started.

Four hundred and forty-eight Londoners died, two-thirds in Inner London, the remaining third in the suburbs.[4] Substantial areas of the East End and the docks, as well as individual houses and streets in the suburbs, were destroyed or badly damaged. The mix of the bomber fleet's destructive loads was around 50 per cent high explosives, 30 per cent delayed action high explosives (to hinder fire-fighting efforts) and – peculiarly suited to setting large fires among the masses of warehousing in the docklands areas – 20 per cent so-called *Flammenbomben*, large incendiaries filled with oil. The Luftwaffe lost forty aircraft, around 4 per cent of the thousand or so involved, two-thirds of them bombers. The Luftwaffe lost fourteen fighters and the RAF twenty-eight.[5]

It could not be said that this was explicitly 'terror bombing', though it was not strictly confined to military objectives, either. Goebbels certainly saw the new concentration on London as political. He also knew, of course, that the RAF's 'cowardly' attacks on Berlin had actually been little more than pinpricks in the military sense. He therefore admitted during a meeting at his ministry on the very day that *Loge* was launched:

The air raid last night [6 September] on Berlin had not, against expec-tations, led to effects that would be necessary, so far as the world is concerned, for us to cry outrage and so justify a massive escalation of our attacks on London. We should be clear that the destruction of London would amount to the greatest human catastrophe in history, so that this measure ought also to appear somehow justifiable to the world. One would therefore hope that such an opportunity will be provided by one of the English air raids as soon as possible.[6]

Goebbels was insistent, as a result, that, however much damage was caused, and whatever political motives were actually present in Ger-man planning, the attacks on London had to be portrayed as strictly military operations. It was an instruction he repeated two days later to his officials with a typical mix of cynicism and cunning:

> We have to reckon with the possibility that because of bad weather our attacks on London will temporarily diminish in power. This in no way alters our determination to destroy London in the event that the English do not yield in a timely fashion. Our reporting should therefore keep up its strong tone, even if for a while there are no new developments to report. It should, however, beware of over-emphatic statements (such as: 'London in flames'). In principle, now as before, the emphasis should be that we are attacking only military targets.[7]

It was, in any case, true that the Luftwaffe's pilots were attempting, at this stage, to hit industrial and dockland areas, whose importance to the British war effort was clear. However, as Goebbels' remarks show, there was not too much worry on the Germans' part if residential areas were hit and large numbers of civilians killed as a result. Damage to British civilian morale was a beneficial side effect. Who knew but that if the experience of the Luftwaffe proved horrific enough, Churchill would yet be overthrown and replaced by a man ready to negotiate with the Third Reich?

The fact was that Operation *Loge* amounted to very serious bombing indeed, on a scale and with a deadly effectiveness (and discipline) that no British bombing raid had so far been able to muster. Yet more proof that the Luftwaffe had established something close to control of the air space over England. Its positive effect on morale both within the Luftwaffe and the rest of the Wehrmacht, and among the civilian population at home, was very considerable. At last, the capital of the hypocritical British Empire was forced to swallow a taste of its own medicine!

Meanwhile, the weather had indeed turned bad. More big raids on London followed, on 9, 11 and 14 September, but they were neither as spectacular nor as successful as the 7 September triumph. Air superiority on one day was one thing, but unless the enemy had been completely annihilated it was something that had to be fought for with each new morning.

While the Germans still did not have their victory, the tally at the end of the first week of the offensive against London was not one to gladden British hearts. Between 7 and 15 September, Fighter Command lost 120 aircraft, the German fighter units 99. Despite this, however, there were still 656 operational fighters available to Fighter Command four days later, and some 1,500 trained pilots. On the German side, however, the Luftwaffe had begun the month of September at 74 per cent of its pilot strength (700–800) and then proceeded to lose 23.1 per cent of their pilots during the course of the month. Another factor acting against the Luftwaffe was that, whereas British pilots who survived combat and managed to land or bail out found themselves in friendly territory, and thus able to return to the fray (wounds allowing), their German equivalents (around a thousand men) ended up as prisoners and so taken out of the war altogether. So far as German fighter strength was concerned, availability of serviceable aircraft consistently remained at the level of five hundred. So much for the myth of the 'few' of Fighter Command versus the giant German Luftwaffe.[8]

By the beginning of the third week of September 1940, another element was impinging on the Luftwaffe's planning. The German attacks continued to wreak havoc and destruction, and the Luftwaffe's air crews' courage and determination was impressive. On the other hand, there was no diminution in the capacity of the British to take to the air to oppose the bombers and their escorts, albeit with varying degrees of success. Moreover, the RAF's Bomber and Coastal Commands continued to conduct damaging raids on the Channel ports and estuaries where the mass of German barges and ships intended for Operation Sea Lion were awaiting the order to set sail for England.[9] The whole question of the viability of 21 September as the date for the cross-Channel invasion was starting to loom large once more. General Jodl, Hitler's Chief of Operations, wrote that the invasion would take place only 'if it is a matter of finishing off a country already defeated by the air war'.[10]

In mid-September, as the cloud began to clear over southern England, Göring determined on what he saw as one more, surely decisive, roll of the dice. The fourteenth of the month had brought more cause for optimism. No great bomber attack, but a lot of fighter duels over the coastal areas in which, once more, the Luftwaffe had won the numbers game by eleven kills to eight.

This second great attack on London would be clearly different from the first. This time, the Reich Marshal would send his bombers in two daylight waves straight across Kent, accompanied by at least three times their number of fighters. The first attack would begin at noon, the second two hours later. The British would be forced to put all their strength – which, of course, on the basis of faulty intelligence reports, Göring and his commanders crucially underestimated – into the air to defend the capital, and his teeming fighters would then go in among them. His Messerschmitt 109s, not confined to close escort of the bombers as they had been a week earlier, would be allowed a 'free hunt'. They would massacre the RAF's last reserves of Hurricanes and Spitfires, thus finally ceding Germany the prize of control of the air.

Hitler had held a major meeting with his commanders the previous day, at which he considered postponing Sea Lion but decided to hold on at least until 17 September. A lot depended on how successful (or otherwise) this latest raid on London would be.

The 15 September attack became known in the United Kingdom as 'Battle of Britain Day', supposedly the juncture at which the aerial contest for control of the skies was won by the RAF. There is evidence that it was somewhat more complicated and less epoch-making than that. Put in terms of figures, it seems that, over the course of the day, out of 158 aircraft that reached the target, the Luftwaffe lost 56 altogether – 30 bombers and 26 fighters – and Fighter Command 28.[11] Göring's hope that his fighters would massacre the British as they rose to meet the attack was certainly disappointed.

Freak headwinds from the north-west, up to 90 mph, and low cloud, also slowed the bombers. This gave Fighter Command, in the shape of 11 Group, operating from stations in Kent and Sussex, extra time to plan for their approach and dispose its resources based on up-to-the-minute information. The weather also reduced visibility, such that damage inflicted on London was nowhere near what it had been on 7 September. It was, of course, also true that the same headwinds then blew the Germans back to France at speeds high enough to avoid what could have been an even more deadly harvest for the British fighters than proved to be the case.[12]

The wildly inflated British claim at the time was of 185 German planes downed, a figure that was not revised until after the war. It was nevertheless a definite victory, though not as spectacular as the (highly successful) propaganda of the time would have the British people believe.

Göring called a conference of his commanders the next day, Monday, 16 September. Addressing them, he continued to fantasise that the raid had been a success, because the RAF had been forced to use its entire fighter strength to protect London. In fact, for both engagements against successive waves of German attackers, less than a half of Fighter Command had been committed to the battle. This meant that even in the wildly improbable event of every single British aircraft being destroyed, the next day would have seen more Spitfires and Hurricanes confronting the new enemy assault. Even the appearance of the massed formation known as 'Big Wing', part of 12 Group, which had intervened from its stations to the north of London during the latter stages of the battle, 'spooking' many of the German bomber crews, was seen as a sign that the British were unable to work out how to handle the German attacks. Göring welcomed this as a further opportunity for German fighters to kill masses of British aircraft. Most importantly, he concluded that, even after the previous day's losses, the initiative remained with the Luftwaffe. Round-the-clock bombing of London, and the consequent rapid attrition of the RAF's fighter force, would eliminate British air power as a consideration

within a matter of days. There would be no pause in attacks on the
British capital.

Despite Göring's bombast, what 15 September 1940, so-called
'Battle of Britain Day', showed, yet again, was that the Luftwaffe
could not keep its promise to the Führer. It could not convincingly
show that it controlled the skies over Britain – at least, for more
than a few hours, perhaps a day or two, at a time. For the success
of an operation on the scale of Operation Sea Lion, that was simply
not enough.

On 17 September, copies of a new Führer-Order, 'Nr. 00 761/40
g.Kdos. Chefs', were sent from Hitler's Supreme Headquarters to the
Army, Air Force and Naval High Commands, postponing the invasion
of Britain until further notice. The invasion barges and the support
systems were to be left in place, however, just so that the British would
not be able to relax.

Göring never had much faith in Sea Lion in the first place. He was
happy to concentrate on bringing Britain to its knees through air
power alone. As a report written by an aide, General Wilhelm Speidel, stated on 23 September, it was time for a third phase, attacking
London mostly by night, with fighters prowling southern England
by day. 'Our own forces,' Speidel announced, 'still feel themselves
to have the upper hand over the enemy, and are completely confident that the air war can be prosecuted successfully.'[13] The 'Battle of Britain' may have been over, but the battle *for* Britain was
continuing.

There was still talk of needing just a few days more to bring the
enemy to his knees, but, tellingly, the Luftwaffe units stationed in
northern France began to move into winter quarters. Phase three of
the air offensive against Britain was suddenly looking less like a *coup de
grâce*, more like a war of attrition. This was fine by the Reich Marshal,
who still thought he could cover himself and the Luftwaffe in glory,
albeit of a less instant kind. As for Hitler, he issued no new directives
for the Luftwaffe for another ten months. By then, the postponed

conquest of Britain had been superseded by an even more vast and perilous invasion project – against Stalin's Russia.

However little faith Hitler had in air power, unlike Göring, it was clear that the bombing of Britain had to continue into the winter of 1940 for the same reason as the preparations for Operation Sea Lion had to appear to be still in hand: first, because despite everything a massive air campaign might yet break the British will to resist; second, for internal morale reasons, given that the German public still expected huge things of their much-lauded Luftwaffe; and third, to convince Stalin that Britain was still Germany's principal enemy, and thus to mask the preparations that had already begun for the invasion of the Soviet Union in the early summer of 1941.[14]

From 7 September, the British capital was bombed for fifty-seven successive nights, with nuisance raids during the day, too, to keep the already exhausted Londoners in their shelters, or in the Tube stations which, after some government resistance, became a popular refuge. Between the beginning of the bombing campaign and the end of October 1940, 13,685 tonnes of high explosive and flame bombs, and 13,000 incendiary canisters were dropped on London.[15] If the suburbs are included, almost 20,000 Londoners would die during the autumn and winter at the hands of the Luftwaffe.

London was still the Luftwaffe's main target after 16 September, but in place of the myriad 'disturbance attacks' on other towns and cities by individual and small groups of German bombers that had been a feature of the past few weeks – sideshows for the main events – the Luftwaffe would now begin serious, larger-scale strategic raids against military-industrial centres. In particular, it would target the Midlands, where many factories producing aircraft and aircraft parts were concentrated.

Within the staff of the Luftwaffe, its intelligence apparatus, and the interdepartmental committees in Berlin, there was continuing, lively discussion of what the exact aims of the coming strategic bombing offensive would be. A blockade of supplies to Britain, especially from America? Destruction of infrastructure and public services? Damage to war production, especially the crucial aircraft industry? Or a wearing down of British civilian morale – in short, sheer terror?

The ordering of 'terror-bombing' was, of course, something the Führer had reserved explicitly for himself. He would not give a direct order to unleash that for another eighteen months. The way plans were evolving in certain areas of the military-political bureaucracy were, however, moving close to terror by any meaningful definition.

The 'England-Committee' (*England-Ausschuss*) of the German Foreign Ministry stated on 20 September that 'any propagandistic misgivings as regards terror attacks against the English civilian population no longer exist', since both the British and the American press were anyway in the habit of presenting all German bombing as directed against civilians, and particularly the working population. The England-Committee was of the opinion that, in fact, such attacks on the working-class residential areas would be particularly effective, since the proletarians would flee to the more exclusive districts of west London, leading to 'a clear . . . break in the social alignment' and a dislocation of food distribution networks. Furthermore: 'If the poorer section of the population is exposed to a level of real want, it will exercise on the Labour Party sufficient pressure that this will force the government to call an end [to the war].' It also recommended bombing broadcasting studios and the 'newspaper quarter' (presumably Fleet Street) since 'without newspapers there is no politics of any kind in England'.[16]

The mildly bizarre elements of this report, complete with its surely unintended tribute to the power of a free press, helped make it one of the most extreme to be found in surviving German records. Terror was the word being used, though as a possibility rather than a current reality. Discussions among the Luftwaffe staff officers engaged in further planning for the air offensive against Britain spoke of 'a terror-effect on the entire London area' being most efficiently achieved by the crippling of all public utilities. The goal, one report said, should be to hit the people who were in a position to bring about a 'legal' change of government: 'Since for these influential people (civilians), this is in the final analysis a matter of all or nothing, the fate of some hundreds of thousands of their compatriots is a matter of indifference. What they are not indifferent to is their own ruin.'[17]

The other main priority was the destruction of the British aircraft industry and its supply chain. This, wrote staff analyst Major von Dewitz, could be 'paralysed in a very short time, the effects of which would be decisive for the war'. On 28 September he demanded attacks on Coventry and Sheffield, as key centres of this industrial sector.[18] Another discussion document a week earlier had pointed out that attacks on Coventry, in particular, could be devastating:

> The effects on industry [in Coventry] would be especially amplified, due to the fact that the work force, which lives in immediate proximity to the factories, would suffer along with them. As a consequence of the flimsy construction of the factory and residential buildings, and the close concentration of the built-up areas, an especially powerful effect could be expected when incendiary bombs are used.[19]

6

Raiders

In the spring of 1939, with war against Germany now considered all but inevitable, a report for the Directorate of Home Operations within the British Air Ministry had classified the cities and regions of the United Kingdom according to perceived risk of heavy German attack from the air.

After a brief discussion of strategic alternatives, the document graded various areas of the country by likelihood of a major German attack. Only central London and the innermost suburbs seemed, it was felt, likely to face the entire might of the German air force, which in April 1939 was reckoned at 650 aircraft a day, with 800 predicted for April 1940. This most at-risk area was proposed as Grade I. Grade II, where substantial but less than total concentration was expected, began with the outer London suburbs, which were supposedly likely to receive the attention of 50 per cent of German air capability at any given time. After that came the Birmingham/Wolverhampton area, Manchester, Liverpool, and then Coventry. All also at 50 per cent. Leeds/Bradford and Sheffield/Rotherham were reckoned at 33 per cent, and so on, down to 10 per cent against Plymouth (this last a prediction that turned out to be a painful underestimate).[1]

The authorities had expected massive German air raids against London and other major cities in the first week of war. Instead, it took almost a year for bombing on anything like that scale to become a reality. Coventry may have been graded near the top of targets

against which the Germans would send very substantial forces, but at
first aggression from the air was highly intermittent and minor. 'Disturbance attacks', as the phrase went. All the same, they were lethal
enough if you were on the receiving end, as two young Coventrians
experienced at the beginning of that fatal English autumn:

> I worked at the Radiator for a while, and I was leaving. My sister
> came with me. We crossed the highway and there was a plane coming
> over, and it was going to the Standard painting shop across the field
> by Henry Parkes* school. We both had to duck down quick.
>
>   Well, he machine-gunned us, and all the machine gun bullets were
> on the pavement. We flew across to the air raid shelter in the middle
> of the field. When we got there, the ARP wardens were there to greet
> us, they said, oh my God, you're as white as snow.[2]

The date was 26 September 1940, the time around 5:30 p.m. Coventry was in the process of experiencing its first daylight raid, by a
lone German aircraft that was, as its pair of intended victims realised,
about to drop a devastating load on the painting shop of the Standard
Motor Company at Canley, four miles south-west of the centre of
Coventry. The two eyewitnesses who survived to give this account
were sisters, Doreen and Kathleen Tucker, respectively almost sixteen
and eleven years old. The 'Radiator' Doreen referred to (Coventry
people often refer to specific factories or production facilities as 'the
X' or 'the Y') was the fairly modern (late 1920s) Standard Radiator
and Pressing Works.

    This was Luftwaffe staff work made violently concrete, Major von
Dewitz and his colleagues' suggestions about how to bring Britain
to its knees simplified down to an attack on a factory paint shop and
an attempt to kill two young girls. Young Doreen was, of course, an
employee of a company engaged in war production – in Standard's

---

* (Sir) Henry Parkes (1815–96), Canley-born Australian politician (emigrated 1839).
Several times Premier of New South Wales and promoter of a united Australia.
Knighted 1877.

case, air frames for fighters and trainers, and armoured cars – and so arguably a legitimate target, despite her youth (which a Luftwaffe pilot could hardly be expected to judge at that distance and under those circumstances). Her sister, however, was a child.

The first raid in the Coventry area had been on the night of 25 June 1940. A small group of German aircraft attacked Ansty aerodrome, five miles east of the city, which was the base for an RAF training squadron. There were no casualties. On 22 August, in the small hours of the morning, bombs were dropped on the Tile Hill district, north of the city centre.[3] Again, there were no casualties.

On 25 August came the first serious raid, when German bombers, arriving just after dusk, scattered some incendiaries around the newly built Rootes shadow factory at Ryton, nearly six miles south-east, damaging the contractor's yard but leaving the plant itself unharmed, before heading for Coventry and swooping in over the city centre. It was around 9:45 in the evening. This time they caused substantial damage to the area around Bond and Corporation Streets. In particular, the modern, self-styled 'super-cinema', the Rex, in Corporation Street was all but demolished.[4] With its grand Wurlitzer organ, 'first class' restaurant and fashionable snack bar, the 2,500-seat picture house had been given a spectacular gala opening, complete with speech by the Mayor of the city, in February 1937.[5] Fortunately, there was no show at the theatre that Sunday evening, but in a coincidence that has enjoyed lasting appeal for fans of the dry local sense of humour, the film due to premiere the next day was *Gone With the Wind*.

On 26 August, according to a schoolgirl diarist of the time, bombs were dropped on the functioning but still not fully built Daimler shadow factory in suburban Browns Lane. Then 'incendries' (sic) fell at Exall, out to the north towards the town of Nuneaton, and further on 28 August, more bombs on the city, landing in Swanswell Street and Cambridge Street, just north-east of the centre.

When there were no bombs on Coventry, there were often German planes over Birmingham, twenty-five miles to the west. Since

Coventry was on the approach route, this meant alarms, night-time scuttles to the shelter and broken sleep. In one case there was simply the unexplained note of 'planes over all night (no warning)'. Coventry was getting used to the developing new German strategy, and to the fact that the Luftwaffe knew where the city was. As the diarist noted: 'The Air Raid Shelters which stood [i.e. presumably stood empty] for nearly a year were crowded every night.'[6]

There were only two serious incidents during September. The Luftwaffe was concentrating on London. On 16 September, shortly before 11 p.m., came eight bombs on Wallace Road, a little more than a mile from the big Daimler shadow factory, which may have been the raider's target. The diarist notes that the attacking plane got tangled in a balloon barrage (tethered with cables that were expressly positioned to get in the way of enemy aircraft) and came down at Shilton, about seven miles due east. After that, there were air raid warnings most nights but no incidents, until in the late afternoon of 26 September that dive bomber attacked the Standard Motor Company (and shot at the Tucker sisters). Daylight alarms became more frequent for the next couple of weeks, though there were no attacks. Each page of the diary, covering seven days, had written at the bottom during this time: 'RAIDS ON LONDON ALL THE WEEK'.

It was in the second week of October 1940 that Coventry once more started to feel heat from the air. On the early evening of Saturday, 12 October, a sizeable formation of bombers, apparently around twenty, came over Coventry, during a period of about two hours dropping a swathe of incendiary and high-explosive bombs, some of the especially dangerous delayed action variety. They hit several areas in the city centre, as well as the Daimler Works, the Prince of Wales cinema, a skating rink and a gas works. At least one incident reportedly involved an oil bomb.[7]

The 12 October raid forms at best a footnote to most accounts of the Coventry Blitz. Yet for those Coventrians involved it was every bit as horrifying as what happened later. Michael Logan, then six and a half, came from a family of Irish immigrants. He, his parents and two

brothers lived near the centre of the city, in what can only be called
slum conditions. There was no question of his feeling invulnerable,
as so many better situated children seem to have done. His memory
of the first stage of the raid, which hit the cramped, ancient centre
of Coventry, remains grim and terrifying:

There were all little houses in a court. And they didn't have toilets or
anything like that, and we had to go into the yard to get water. We
didn't have electricity either.

When the planes come over, we were all dragged down into the
shelter, crying. And my mother was screaming, because she was a
bit scared. They only had three of us, you know. Three boys, and
we were all very young. My father was up the road in a pub, and
someone rang up the pub from the area and told him, and he come
running down and joined us. So we sat on a wooden bench in the
shelter. We had no beds or anything, just wooden benches we had
to sit on.[8]

Moments later, quite early that night, in his spartan place of refuge
beneath the street, little Michael Logan became an orphan. Soon after
the family had crowded into the shelter with their neighbours, hoping
to sit out the danger, they suffered a direct hit from a high-explosive
bomb. The concrete roof of the shelter collapsed.

I don't know how long we were there for. I just don't know. A man
that went to help the ARP warden – she lived next door to me – he
held the concrete slab up on his back while the wardens went in to
put people out. I was conscious. I wasn't hurt badly at all. I just had
a scar on my leg. But my brother, Patrick, who was a year older
than me, he had a very serious head injury. He was out. I wanted
to know where my parents were. My father was killed immediately.
And Frank was killed immediately. And my mother, they took her
to Coventry and Warwickshire Hospital, and she died there within
a couple of hours.[9]

Many years later, Michael Logan found out that his mother had been heavily pregnant at the time. No one had told him. His solitary surviving close family member, Patrick, was so badly affected by his head injuries that he was taken to Ireland to stay with relatives, leaving Michael alone in a children's home.

The national newspapers were not at this stage of the war allowed to state which cities outside London had been bombed, and so the official account read:

> In a Midland town considerable damage was done to houses, commercial, and other premises, and a number of fires caused. Particularly fine work was done by the fire services in this area, and all the fires had been extinguished or brought under control by an early hour in this morning. A number of casualties, some of them fatal, was caused in this district.[10]

There were warnings all the way through Sunday, from early afternoon to the small hours of the morning. Then, on Monday, 14 October, came Coventry's biggest raid yet. German aircraft swept over in three waves during the course of the evening and dropped bombs on the historic centre of the city, including the Barracks Market, the Opera House and the Owen Owen department store, whose basement housed one of the largest air raid shelters in the town. Ford's Hospital, a half-timbered sixteenth-century almshouse for women on Greyfriars Lane, near the Barracks Market, was part demolished by a high-explosive bomb. The warden of the institution, a nurse and six of the residents were killed.[11] Towards the outskirts, several factories, including Herbert Machine Tools, Courtaulds, the Humber Motor Works and the Triumph Works, as well as residential streets, were also visited by the Luftwaffe.

The *Manchester Guardian*, because of censorship once more referring only to 'a Midlands town', reported the casualties at Ford's Hospital ('a home for aged women') and Owen Owen ('a departmental store') and added that 'some houses were demolished and people believed to be trapped under the wreckage. Office buildings and commercial premises were slightly damaged.'[12] This was, quite literally, the city's emergency services' baptism of fire. The diarist recorded that the Fire Brigade had responded to some 200 calls.

There was a lull for the rest of the working week, but it was deceptive. Some high-explosive bombs were dropped on Friday evening near London Road, to the south-east of the city, probably by aircraft heading for Birmingham. Then, on Saturday, 19 October the centre was hit again, plus the greyhound track, the Herbert Machine Tools factory and Armstrong's. The next night it was Courtaulds (again), the Hey Engineering Works, Sterling Metals, the Riley Motor Works and the Ordnance Works, as well as residential streets. Monday, 21 October saw another night raid, with extensive damage. As did Tuesday.

The regularity of the raids was beginning to tell on the civilian population. As it happened, the time between 22 and 27 October saw only alerts, but by now it was quite possible, in most Coventrians' minds, that their city could be the target, and so nights were broken with trips to the shelter at the end of the street, or in the garden, or in the improvised hiding places under the kitchen table or the stairs.

It was also at this time that the habit of leaving the city at night-time became common among many people in Coventry (as was the case in other cities). Tens of thousands began, in the course of October, to leave the city routinely before nightfall (the German raids now came overwhelmingly at night), to stay with friends and relatives, or in begged or rented rooms outside the urban area. Local bus companies began running special services taking nervous Coventrians out to local small towns and villages.

Local authorities at nearby towns, including Warwick, Kenilworth and Leamington Spa, allowed people from Coventry to sleep on the floors of council halls. Nervous city-dwellers with cars drove out into the countryside, parked them in secluded lanes and slept in them before returning to the city in the morning to go to work. On the night of 24 October, when serious raids were hitting Birmingham and it seemed Coventry might also be on the Germans' target list, the crowds at the main station for local trains out into the country became unmanageably large. Hundreds had to be turned away. They were directed to sleep in the public shelter on the common at Greyfriars Green.[13]

The air war had not, so far, turned out to be the cataclysm many in the urban centres of Britain had expected, but it had already killed well over a hundred people in Coventry as well as causing damage, by official estimates, to over 2,000 houses.[14] Moreover, as many locals had come to fear, Coventry was one of the places where it was about to get a great deal worse.

The Luftwaffe's strategy was evolving to fit new circumstances. The British military aircraft industry, of which Coventry was a famous – from the German point of view, infamous – centre, was becoming an ever more important preoccupation of policy-makers in Berlin. Throughout October, there were growing disagreements within the military leadership. The intelligence team that worked out of Göring's personal command train, 'Robinson', was still hawking a version of Germany's air war that was near enough all excellent news. Their report on 10 October claimed that 50 per cent of the British aircraft industry's capacity had been eliminated; 1,770 British aircraft had supposedly been destroyed since 1 July 1940, leaving the British air defences with just three to four hundred serviceable aircraft. And as for the London docks, these had been 'for the most part extensively destroyed', with deaths amounting to at least 10,000 and injuries 20,000. It added hopefully:

> The constant air raid warnings, the nightly stays in air raid shelters, which have now been going on for almost 5 weeks, the dislocations in food distribution and the endangering of important infrastructure associated with utilities and sanitation must lead to a strong accumulation of manifestations of ill health, which could easily grow into epidemics.[15]

A better illustration of the tendency of intelligence services in dictatorships to tell their masters what they wanted to hear, it would be hard to find. The situation was exacerbated by the relentless, brutal positivism that was a peculiar feature of both political and martial thinking in Nazi circles. Ever onward, ever upward, and ignore the contrary evidence.[16]

In Berlin, however, Major von Dewitz, who had earlier belonged among the chiefs of the positive thinkers, was beginning to back-pedal. He criticised colleagues, including the 'Robinson' team, for over-optimism and pointed to a shortage of photographs of the damage. Evaluating the current situation a week later, on 17 October, Dewitz ventured that the situation in London was, in fact, 'stationary'. It had not proved possible to paralyse London's public utilities, as the planners had hoped. Aircraft attacking by night could not find such targets with any accuracy, and in daylight the British defences were sufficiently effective to prevent the low-altitude approaches by German aircraft that might have enabled accurate bombing of electricity and gas mains, gasometers and power stations, telephone networks, and so on.

Based on this less rosy assessment, Dewitz put forward three main suggestions: first, shift the burden of the Luftwaffe's attacks to the suburbs and residential areas; second, divert larger numbers of bombers to attack the aircraft industry in central England (Coventry, Birmingham, Sheffield), with the added advantage of forcing the British to split their defensive effort, currently concentrated on London; third, after a while, catch the British by surprise by unexpectedly bombing central London once more in force. This last, with the defences temporarily unprepared, might enable the Luftwaffe to go in close and hit the utilities as well as shattering urban lives that by now would have started to return to normal, and thus delivering a severe blow against morale.[17]

These suggestions found special favour with the Political Section of the Luftwaffe High Command, which saw the Midlands as the homeland of 'conservative, stubborn-dour Englishness' and therefore of the British will to resist. The Midlands were also the place, so the Political Section believed, where the physical wealth of classic British industrial capitalism was to be found. Both Stanley Baldwin and

Neville Chamberlain, the last two prime ministers before Churchill, had been powerful business figures from the Midlands. Baldwin's money had come from a flourishing family-owned iron founding concern, based near the Worcestershire town of Kidderminster. Chamberlain, son of the Victorian Lord Mayor of Birmingham and cabinet minister, Joseph Chamberlain, had become independently wealthy as managing director of Hoskins & Sewell, a successful Birmingham manufacturer of finished metal goods, ranging from bedsteads to ships' berths. Wealth such as these men's, unlike the mobile capital of the London financial elite, could not be transferred out of the country in case of defeat. Destroy the productive capacity, and with it the morale, of the Midlands, and England was lost. Or so the theory went.

It was not all theory. By the end of October 1940, parts of the British north and Midlands, as well as the south coast ports and Liverpool, were beginning to feel themselves as much under attack as London, and to make vocal protests to the central government about it. People in Coventry seem to have felt especially strongly on this matter. Ernest Bevin, Minister of Labour, an old trade union warrior not known for his nervous disposition, was moved to write personally to Churchill on Thursday, 7 November about the situation in Coventry, enclosing a letter he had received from the local employers' federation. He described the state of things in worrying terms:

> I was in the Midlands last week-end and I found the position very serious indeed. It was so serious that on Sunday night I left a message for the Secretary of State for Air, through his Private Secretary, and also mentioned the matter when I returned on Monday, to Air Marshal Portal.* I found the output was down by over 40% and the most serious matter I think arose from the undefended state of the town on Saturday morning, to which attention is called in the letter.

* Charles Portal (1893–1971), senior RAF commander, recently (25 October 1940) promoted from C-in-C Bomber Command to Chief of the Air Staff.

I mentioned this to the Minister of Home Security as well.

Now something must be done to restore the morale of Coventry
and of the Midland Area generally. I realise the great strain on the
Forces but no amount of talking can recover the position unless
something is done in the way of defence.[18]

The letter from the Coventry employers' organisation to which
Bevin referred highlighted the fact that they were losing workers in
key industrial sectors because of lack of confidence in the military's
ability to defend the city. Workers, it said, had 'left their lodgings or
billets and . . . returned home to other parts of this country and to
Ireland, Scotland or Wales as the case may be, without any intention
of returning to work'. The same went for some householders, who had
been bombed out of their homes. These, too, had taken themselves
and their families off to safer towns, with no intention of returning.
Others, though not yet affected by bombing, had 'had their morale
shaken' and 'have . . . left the City to return to their native parts or,
alternatively, have evacuated themselves into the surrounding country
districts – and here again these people are endeavouring to get work
in the districts that they have evacuated themselves to and . . . have
no intention of returning to work in Coventry'. Many workers were
also beginning to demand the end of night shifts so that they could
be back home with their families before 5:30 p.m. and the beginning
of the blackout.[19]

The sense in Coventry was that the anti-aircraft, barrage-balloon
and fighter defences were wholly inadequate. It was clear from the
employers' letter that an interestingly disproportionate (and negative)
psychological effect had been created by the intrusion of a single
German raider into the air space over Coventry at dawn on Saturday, following a night-time raid that had ended some hours earlier.
The sense in the city was that this raider had managed to penetrate
unopposed to Silver Street, just north of the city centre, where it had
bombed and strafed before making good its escape, again without
interference from the ground or air defences.[20]

Bevin made it clear to Churchill that he considered the situation 'disastrous'. The result of his initiative was a meeting of the Chiefs of Staff Committee, which issued a confidential report on 10 November. It was a measure of the role of Coventry as a centre of war production, especially the aircraft industry, that its complaints and problems were discussed at such a high level. The conclusions of the report were unsentimental, even cold, but commensurate to the city's importance.

Among other things, the report raised a theme which would reoccur frequently in official judgments of Coventry's morale and capability to keep going under pressure:

The morale of the workers in Coventry has unquestionably deteriorated as a result of enemy air attacks. War production has attracted a large population from other parts of the country. These people naturally are not imbued with the same civic patriotism, and consequently do not have the same anchors, as the long-established inhabitants of other provincial towns or of London. Coventry, moreover, is a small town, and the effect of bombing is therefore more concentrated than in the case of large towns.[21]

Whether Coventry was a 'small town' (with a population of around a quarter of a million) might be moot, but, as the report also maintained, there were forty anti-aircraft guns in the city as against 232 defending London (although, as it does not say, London proportionately had far more newer, heavier and therefore more effective guns). This meant, if we are to believe these somewhat slanted figures, that Coventry had over five times as many guns per head of population as the capital. The number of barrage balloons was fifty-six, with sixteen more about to be deployed. So far as airborne defences went:

Fighter protection of Coventry is concerned with daylight attacks from which, with the single exception of the raid on 2nd November, Coventry has not suffered. If a mass daylight raid were delivered against Coventry, the present Fighter sector organisation is such that

it would be difficult to repel. Even so, it may be said that some of
the enemy would be intercepted on the way in, and more on the
way out. Meanwhile the Fighter sector organisation is being pressed
forward on the highest priority. Furthermore, the decision was taken
to-day by the Air Ministry to increase the fighter protection of the
Midlands area, of which Coventry forms part, by the equivalent of
half a Fighter squadron.*[22]

Concealed within this are two half-admissions. First, that fighter
defences for the area were inadequate. Because of this, it would be
impossible to repel even a substantial daytime attack. Second, by
observing what the report omits, we can conclude that in the autumn
of 1940 fighter defence against night bombing was non-existent. Under
conditions of darkness, and especially if it avoided known anti-aircraft
artillery concentrations, the German bomber would always (or very
nearly always) get through.[23] This last, conspicuously unmentioned
reality was one good reason why the Luftwaffe had switched almost
exclusively to night bombing by the time the Chiefs of Staff's report
was written.

So far as threats to industrial production were concerned, the report
rejected the estimate of a 40 per cent drop in output, and once more
returned to the conventional official narrative about the particular
unreliability of Coventry's largely immigrant population. 'There is
no doubt,' it said, 'that the morale of the workers in Coventry leaves
a good deal to be desired, owing to the fact that their heart is not so
staunch as elsewhere.'

The tone of things, from the point of view both of people in Coventry and other industrial cities, which were now being subjected to
increasingly constant attacks from the air, and of the powers that be in
London, was becoming a little sourer and a little less self-consciously
heroic. The Battle of Britain was over, the nation saved from invasion.
What now lay ahead of Britain was a war of attrition, of indefinite

* Standard strength of a fighter squadron was sixteen aircraft, so this meant eight
extra aircraft for the entire region.

duration, in which there was an enormous uphill military struggle to be won, at home and in other parts of the world. The country also faced an air war in which her factories and the homes of her urban population would be equal targets.

Of course, the problematic nature of the new war situation was also a factor so far as the Germans were concerned. Some in Berlin still hoped that, as the State Secretary at the Reich Foreign Office, von Weizsäcker, noted on 3 November, 'the East End of London will suddenly get tired of this, and that negotiations with Germany and perhaps even a new cabinet will be demanded'.[24] The alternative was very unattractive, especially when measured against the euphoric expectations of the period immediately following the fall of France.

For German pilots, worn down by months of gruelling, repetitive combat missions over enemy territory – unlike the RAF, the Luftwaffe allowed its men very little time for rest or recuperation – the challenge of keeping alight the flame of motivation was not an easy one. On 25 October, the Luftwaffe headquarters staff found it necessary to admonish all commanders of the bomber fleet to emphasise to their air crew the importance of this new kind of air war and so to reassure them that their sacrifice was not being made in vain.

Above all, with the Blitz on London continuing to prove spectacular but indecisive – in part because the megalopolis of the empire was just too big to destroy – Germany needed a big success. A truly devastating attack on a major British provincial city might just provide the overwhelming evidence of German air power.

A later age would use the phrase 'shock and awe' to describe the required phenomenon. It had to be one that would buoy up morale in the Luftwaffe and at home in the Reich sufficiently to carry the nation through the war's second winter – a season that millions of Germans had hitherto fervently hoped would be the first of a victorious peace.

7

Knickebein

One of the crucial meetings of the air war took place shortly after the evacuation from Dunkirk, just before the fall of France. On 12 June 1940, a brilliant twenty-eight-year-old Oxford physics graduate walked into the office of a sixty-five-year-old RAF group captain and took a seat.

The younger man was Dr R. V. Jones and his original area of specialisation had been infra-red waves. For four years he had been working for the Air Ministry on measures to protect Britain against the German air force, initially by developing infra-red aircraft detectors. Though these last had not proved sufficiently effective to satisfy his superiors, his combination of a fine brain, dogged patriotism and wide-ranging knowledge led to his being assigned as a scientific adviser to British intelligence. After the outbreak of war, his job was to study new German weapons, real and potential.[1]

Jones's senior, in both rank and age, was Group Captain L. F. Blandy. Blandy had begun his military career with the Royal Engineers in the reign of Queen Victoria, almost twenty years before the First World War, later transferring to the Royal Flying Corps and thence the RAF. One of the outstanding signals officers of that era, although of pensionable age he had now been recalled to active duty as head of the RAF's 'Y' Service (DDSigsY), whose task was to intercept German radio signals.

Blandy opened his desk drawer, took out a sheet of paper and handed it to the young physicist. 'Does this mean anything to you?' he asked. 'It doesn't seem to mean much to anybody here.'[2]

The message read: KNICKEBEIN, KLEVE, IST AUF PUNKT 53 GRAD 24 MINUTEN NORD UND EIN GRAD WEST EINGERICHTET. ('Crooked leg, Cleves, is established at point 53 degrees 24 minutes north and one degree west').

It did indeed mean something to Jones – a very great deal, in fact. Then and there, he told Blandy why. This message revealed that the Germans had a radar beam transmitter set up in the town of Kleve, near the Dutch border, known in its anglicised form to most Britons as the home of Anne of Cleves, Henry VIII's last-but-one-wife and allegedly referred to as the 'Flanders Mare'.

Jones had been on the track of this German technology for months, because he knew the threat it represented for Britain's cities and industries. The transmitter was built to send a radio beam that could be followed by specially equipped German aircraft. Another transmitter, further north, would likewise send a beam. The target would be the point at which these two beams met, and their signals became one, thus making for precise bombing, even by night or in totally blind weather conditions. This technology, the invention of a German radio expert by the name of Dr Hans Plendl, adapted from the Lorenz blind-landing system that had existed since the early 1930s, was codenamed *Knickebein* (crooked leg).

Dr Jones was well informed on signals matters and one of the select few privy to the Ultra secret. He therefore knew that for the past two months or so the decryption teams at Bletchley Park, forty miles north of London, had been successfully intercepting and reading secret German military communications, of which the scrap handed to him by Blandy was clearly one. It seemed that this apparently innocuous piece of information had somehow escaped the notice of the decoders until someone with air knowledge had realised what it might refer to, and thence ensured that it was sent to Blandy and his team of experts at DDSigsY.

Initially, on the assumption that *Knickebein* might be some kind of enemy fifth column outfit based in the East Midlands, possibly operating a beacon to guide German bombers, a squad from the Air Staff had piled into vehicles and driven up the Great North Road to the map reference specified in the German signal. This had turned out to be near the small market town of Retford, in Nottinghamshire. No nest of enemy agents was found. Still puzzled, Blandy had nevertheless been canny enough to work out who might be able to clarify the mystery: Dr Jones.

The breakthrough confirmed Jones's suspicions. He had been pursuing investigations about the possible German use of radar beam technology to support night bombing ever since, in the early spring of 1940, he had heard part of a secret recording made of downed German pilots in conversation at the so-called 'Cockfosters Camp' interrogation centre for German POWs near Barnet in Hertfordshire. In the course of this, the Luftwaffe officer, who had no idea that the British were eavesdropping, had referred to something called the *X-Gerät*, or 'X-Apparatus'. This operated by 'pulses' he told his cell mate. In the context, it was obviously some kind of bombing aid. Further clues had come from documents found on a crashed bomber and through careful planting of questions to unwary Luftwaffe prisoners. It became clear that the 'pulses' referred to were short-wave radio signals. Jones was extremely interested in any more information regarding this potentially game-changing development.[3]

As it happened, later that same day Jones also had an appointment with the formidable Professor Lindemann at the Cabinet Offices in Whitehall. Born in Germany in 1886 of a German father, who had become a naturalised Englishman well before his son's birth, and an American mother, Frederick Alexander Lindemann had studied physics at Berlin University and the Sorbonne. Although a patriotic Englishman in every regard, he still spoke with a noticeable German accent. As well as becoming a leading international figure in the world of theoretical physics, professor at Oxford and chairman of the Clarendon Laboratory, he had also worked on aeronautical research during the First World War, developing a mathematical theory about the (usually fatal) problem of aircraft spin. Such was his dedication, Lindemann had learned to fly specifically in order to demonstrate the practical efficacy of his solution.

Lindemann had become friends with Winston Churchill in the 1920s after partnering Churchill's wife, Clementine, in a tennis tournament (Lindemann played well enough to have competed at Wimbledon), and had advanced in the course of the 1930s to become the maverick politician's scientific explainer and adviser. Churchill's 'wilderness years' came to an end in September 1939, when he was appointed First Lord of the Admiralty. He immediately appointed his friend 'the Prof' to an advisory role within the Admiralty, and after May 1940, when he became Prime Minister (and simultaneously Minister of Defence), within the Cabinet Office. Lindemann's years of influence as the great war leader's right-hand man in matters of science and technology had just begun when he and Jones met that day, but he already possessed great power and would accumulate ever more as the years passed, becoming a member of the House of Lords and Paymaster-General in the wartime government.

Lindemann had been Jones's tutor at Oxford some years earlier. Although, so Jones said, this was only their second official encounter, they were already on fairly familiar terms. The conversation was scheduled to involve a briefing by Jones about the state of radar development in Germany (many so-called 'experts' still believed that the Germans did not yet have it), and most of it was. Then the younger man mentioned the information he had just received from Blandy about *Knickebein*. Lindemann was sceptical. After all, the conventional wisdom was that short waves could not bend with the curvature of the earth, and so were unusable for any such purpose over the distances that would necessarily be involved. Jones produced calculations by a colleague which cast doubt on this, and then retired to consider his next move.

Now that he had the precious information from Blandy, Jones worked fast to join up the dots about *Knickebein*. The message mentioning it had been sent by a signals officer at the headquarters of

Fliegerkorps IV (Air Corps IV). Jones found out what kind of bomb-ers the *Fliegerkorps* had at its disposal, discovered there were two squadrons of Heinkel 111s. Next he phoned Squadron Leader Felkin, who was in charge of the 'Cockfosters Camp', told him what he had found out, and asked him to reinterrogate any Luftwaffe prisoners who fitted the bill.

Immediate interrogation seemed to draw a blank, but then another secret recording turned up a conversation in which the pilot of a recently downed Heinkel 111 betrayed some key information. The beam device, he told his cell mate, had been so cleverly placed that no matter how hard the British looked, they would never find it. This assertion caused great amusement among the Luftwaffe prison-ers. Clearly, Jones realised when he heard of this, the thing was right under their noses, so obvious as to be invisible.

A Heinkel 111 had, in fact, been shot down and recovered intact after a raid on shipping in the Firth of Forth on 16 October 1939 – the first Luftwaffe attack on British soil. Subsequently, the aircraft had been shipped to the Royal Aircraft Establishment at Farnborough, in Hampshire, where a technical team had taken it apart. Jones obtained a copy of the report. He quickly realised that the only thing aboard that might fit the bill was the receiver that made up part of the Lorenz blind-landing apparatus, a piece of routine equipment. Jones then rang up the radio expert who had overseen the examina-tion and asked if there was anything unusual about the on-board Lorenz receiver:

'No,' he replied – and then, 'But now you mention it, it is much more sensitive than they would ever need for a blind landing.' So that was it. I now knew the receiver, and the frequencies to which it could be tuned, and therefore on which the *Knickebein* beam must operate.[4]

On 13 June, Jones went in to see Lindemann again. He showed him the calculations proving that long-distance short-wave transmission was feasible, which Lindemann accepted. He also told him about his further investigations.

Without delay, Lindemann wrote a note to the Prime Minister, suggesting that 'the Germans have some type of radio device with which they hope to find their targets'. Churchill also reacted quickly, passing this on to Sir Archibald Sinclair, the Minister for Air, with the comment: 'This seems most intriguing and I hope you will have it thoroughly examined.'

The next day – the day, incidentally, that the Germans occupied Paris – Sinclair appointed a very senior officer, Air Marshal Joubert, to oversee research into the beam and how to counter it. By the next day after that, Jones, Lindemann, and Sir Hugh Dowding, C-in-C of Fighter Command, were among those at a meeting called in Joubert's office to decide on further action.

This amounts to an extraordinarily swift sequence of events – an illustration of how quickly and efficiently a wartime administration can react to, and begin to act on, truly crucial information. By the time of the big meeting on 16 June, Jones also had evidence from further covert recordings being done by Felkin's men. These proved that the Lorenz-based apparatus was indeed intended to aid accurate bombing, and that it worked by dint of intersecting radio beams, as Jones had suspected. Moreover, the pilot who had vouchsafed this fact was persuaded to provide drawings of the somewhat peculiar-shaped transmitting towers he had seen around the Luftwaffe Research Base at Rechlin, on the Baltic coast where *Knickebein* had been developed. Jones recognised this as what he had believed to be a Lorenz transmitter observed on the island of Sylt, off the North Sea coast of Germany. Felkin then supplied him with a note found in a German aircraft shot down in France which clearly gave the bearings of the Cleves transmitter and also another at Bredstedt near Husum, on the coast not far from the Danish border.

The immediate result was that RAF teams began work on several aspects of an anti-*Knickebein* strategy. First they would develop and install listening devices on existing radar towers, especially those on high ground, to locate and identify the German radio beams. Second, with the aid of Group Captain Blandy and his people at DDSigsY, a way of jamming these beams would be found.[5]

Britain still possessed no effective night-fighter force – on-board radar was still in development and would not become a factor in the struggle until early 1941. Consequently, during the summer and autumn of 1940 the Luftwaffe could overfly Britain in the hours of darkness with near-impunity. The few enemy bombers that had been shot down at night were lost due to chance encounters with patrolling RAF fighters.

The only consolation for the British so far had been that under conditions of darkness the enemy's bombers could not attack with any degree of precision. If, however, the Germans could indeed use these methods to bomb accurately at night, this would put them far ahead of the RAF, whose own bombers, navigating by traditional methods, had an extremely poor hit rate over Germany (though the British public were not told this). With the *Knickebein* beams in operation, the United Kingdom's cities and factories would lie completely exposed to concentrated and precise German night attacks, which, now that France had fallen, could not be long delayed.

Every British scientist and airman involved knew how vital this work on counter-measures could be, especially in the coming winter, when, with the long nights and deteriorating weather, the Luftwaffe's new guidance systems would come into their own, and perhaps even prove decisively important in the air war. So it proved, though not to the Germans' permanent advantage.

After some early setbacks, bureaucratic infighting – during which Jones had to rely heavily on Churchill's personal support – and renewed doubts about the very existence of the *Knickebein* system, on 21 June a specially equipped aircraft of the RAF's newly established 80 Wing picked up the Cleves beam over the Midlands. Its more northerly interceptor was also tracked. One beam was made up of Morse-style dashes, the other of dots. At the point of intersection, over the putative target, they merged into near-continuous sound, indicating that the destination had been reached. Jones and his colleagues had found what they were looking for.

Work began on measures to foil *Knickebein*. The German navigation beam technology was codenamed 'Headache' and, with typical schoolboy humour, the British counter-measures 'Aspirin'. The cat-and-mouse game that ensued would continue for some months and end in a British victory, but meanwhile the Luftwaffe was planning to use *Knickebein*, and the more sophisticated technologies that rapidly succeeded it, in their attacks on London and on British industrial targets. Chief among the latter were Birmingham, and Coventry.

R. V. Jones had pieced together sufficient information to identify *Knickebein* and to begin the so-called 'battle of the beams' with the aid of multiple sources, and three in particular: the enemy 'Enigma' signals messages being decrypted at Bletchley Park; human intelligence (in the form of interrogation reports and covert recording of German POWs' conversations); and close examination of captured enemy aircraft.

By the beginning of November 1940, *Knickebein*, which the British were in the end able to jam successfully – aided by the Germans' careless habit of setting up the beams well before they were actually required, giving the British ample time to locate them – had been succeeded by a more complex and precise system, the *X-Gerät* (X-Apparatus – also developed by Hans Plendl). Instead of using only two intersecting beams, the *X-Gerät* involved six Lorenz beams altogether, three pointing to the target, with three more intersecting them separately at set distances from the target to indicate stages of preparation for the bomb drop which would occur, over the target, when the directional met with the last intersecting beam.

The beams, each originating from individual transmitters, were codenamed after the names of German rivers: the main directional beam system called 'Weser', and the successive intersecting beams 'Rhine' (30 km short of the target), 'Oder' (10 km short of the target), and 'Elbe' (5 km before bomb drop). Further transmitters, as they were established, were called 'Isar' and 'Spree'. These were used ad hoc.

So far as the actual bombing aid part of the system went, a clock aboard the aircraft began going forward at 'Oder', then went into reverse at 'Elbe', which meant that by the time it got back to the start it was time to drop the bombs. The actual release was automatic, triggered by this final click on to zero. Because of the codenames of the transmitters, this was known by the British as the 'Rivers System', and this is how it was identified in many conversations and documents.

For a number of reasons, the *X-Gerät* was, initially at least, harder to counter than *Knickebein*. The earlier device had been based simply on a modified version of the Lorenz receiver, such as the British had become familiar with even before the war. It had, after all, been an internationally available blind-landing aid used by commercial aircraft as well as the military. The receiver for the *X-Gerät*, however, was a new, radically upgraded piece of equipment, operating at a higher radio frequency than *Knickebein* along much narrower and more precise beams. This meant that it had to be especially manufactured, and the aircraft substantially converted to carry it.

The fact that sophisticated new equipment was required led to a shortage, and consequently to a new method of use. Instead of fitting all the aircraft involved in a raid with on-board receivers, a relatively small pathfinder group of about a dozen, made up from the Luftwaffe's elite special operations unit, *Kampfgruppe* 100 (Battle Group 100), would be so equipped. Flying through the night ahead of the main pack of bombers, with the aid of this technology, K.Gr.100 would find the designated attack point with a high degree of accuracy – the *X-Gerät* could bring the pathfinder aircraft to within 100 metres of it, defying darkness or bad weather. There the pathfinders would drop flares and incendiaries, rendering the exact target area easily visible to the following unadapted bombers. These would then go on to drop their heavy loads of bombs and so wreak a horribly accurate work of destruction.

Unlike the original *Knickebein* transmitters, which had been constructed on German territory before the fall of France, those required for the new 'Rivers System' were all situated along the recently occupied coast of the Pas-de-Calais and the Cherbourg peninsula, only a short cross-Channel distance from the British mainland. It was later thought that the *X-Gerät* was used for the first time in an attack on a Spitfire factory in Birmingham on the night of 13/14 August ('Eagle Day').[6] However, Jones became properly aware of it in the second week of September, when decrypted

German radio messages, now collectively known as Ultra (from the specially created classification 'Ultra Secret') were found to refer to the *X-Gerät* quite specifically. Just as importantly, they mentioned it being specially fitted into an aircraft, proving that this was not simply a slightly modified version of *Knickebein* but, though related, to all intents a new device.

As it turned out, at least five transmitters had been constructed, and the equipment had already been tested in flights over England. On the main beam, they were operating at a higher frequency – around 73 MHz instead of 35 MHz – meaning that they had a longer reach and were more accurate, presenting even more of a danger than their predecessors. They were, however, also putting out a very fine beam which seemed to go beyond what the British had the capacity to cope with. Indeed, in October Jones reported:

> However incredible it may seem, it must be accepted that the Germans have a method of blind bombing which they expect to be at least accurate to the nearest 10 seconds of arc, or 25 feet at 100 miles . . .
>
> The accuracy of the *X-Gerät* system over London is expected to be in the order of 10–20 yards. A tentative method of operation is advanced involving a coarse and fine beam directed over the target, with one coarse and two fine cross beams. It is shown that this eliminates major bombing errors. The coarse beams are thought to be in the 65–75 MHz band, the fine beams on 10–50 cms [this latter a very short wavelength indeed, in fact almost immeasurable] . . .[7]

Locating these transmitters, and if possible putting them out of action, was one task that suggested itself. Another, perhaps more subtle and in the long term more beneficial one, was finding a way to interfere with the *X-Gerät* in such a way as to render it inoperative, or perhaps – even more usefully – inaccurate.

This latter proved very difficult, to Coventry's special disadvantage.

8

Korn

On Saturday, 9 November 1940, two things happened that would play a fateful role in the destruction of Coventry. First, a mysterious Luftwaffe signal was transmitted, picked up, and, over a period of between twenty-four and forty-eight hours,* decoded at Bletchley Park, using the Enigma decryption machine. It was then passed to the senior officials and commanders on the Ultra distribution list. Second, at 7:45 that same evening, a Heinkel III crashed in the London suburb of Bromley, demolishing two houses and killing all but one of its crew.

The secret message, intercepted by one of the 'Y' Service's listening stations and then decoded at Bletchley, emanated from the Senior Signals Officer of Fliegerkorps 1, headquartered at Beauvais, north of Paris, and had been sent at 14:00 on 9 November. The transcription and translation prepared by Hut 3 at Bletchley Park read (with comments):

MOONSHINE [sic] SONATA

W/T data of K.G. 100 for 'Moonlight Sonata':

---

* The date of the original document (see endnote 1) is mistyped as 11.10.40. Although the usual transcription time was twenty-four hours, whether this should have been 11.11.40 or 10.11.40 is not conclusively clear.

Frequency 4492 kcs., alternative 4730 kcs. K.G. 100: Ground Station's call-sign F4G; Hptm. ASCHENBRENNER's* aircraft, F4 GA; other aircraft use f4G with letters B, C, D, etc., added.

Aircraft, three-letter code LM4, with following 'Verfügungssignale'[†]:-

No. 9	KORN [sic].
No. 10	Weather at English coast.
No. 11	Weather over target.
No. 12	Bombing Conditions over the target.
No. 58	KNICKEBEIN Beam 3.
No. 59	KNICKEBEIN Beam 4.
No. 60	Beam interference.
No. 61	Beam very broad.
No. 62	Intersection of beams is over the target.
No. 63	Beam is to left of target.
No. 14	Beam is to right of target.
No. 15	Target Area 1.
No. 16	Target Area 2.
No. 17	Target Area 3.
No. 18	Target Area 4.

K.G.100 will give the tuning-signal at 1300 hours on day of operation, to be repeated at 1315 hours by Airfleet 3. Call sign D 3H.

In case the attack is not to take place on account of the weather report from K.G. 100, instructions to this effect will be issued:

By telephone via the Fliegerkorps (plural: but number of them unspecified).

By W/T: the main W/T station of the C-in-C., German Air Force, will send the code group 'MOND MOND' (i.e. MOON MOON) three times. Airfleets 2 and 3 will repeat the group three times.

---

* Hauptmann Kurt Aschenbrenner was the officer commanding K.Gr.100.
† *Verfügungssignale* = availability signals.

Call-signs:-

C-in-C., G.A.F.	–	MOR
Airfleet 2	–	ROS
Airfleet 3	–	BUR
K.G. 100	–	F4G

Five minutes after the signal 'MOND MOND' the KNICKEBEIN beacons will be shifted on to alternative targets: duration of shift over about twenty minutes. KNICKEBEIN will continue to operate during the shift over.

(Reliability (A) except for paragraph 3, which is (B). Source assumes that 'Moonlight Sonata' is a code name for a particular operation).[1]

Clearly a major raid, assisted by beam direction-finding technology, was to take place in the near future. The full moon was due in the middle of the month – hence, though not conclusively, the possible operation's codename 'Moonlight Sonata'. But for what, or where, was *KORN* (German for corn or grain) the codename? Jones thought it might be a descriptive name for the effect of jamming on radar systems.[2]

Some hours after this signal was sent, and intercepted by the British, came the second element in the 'Moonlight Sonata' jigsaw. As previously noted, at a quarter to eight that evening, a Heinkel III bomber was brought down by anti-aircraft fire in a south-eastern suburb of London.

The aircraft crashed into number 26, Johnson Street, Bromley, killing the woman of the house and the two German air crew who remained in the aircraft. It also injured several other residents, who for some time remained trapped beneath the wreckage. Another crew member had bailed out, but his parachute failed to open properly, and he died on impact with the roof of number 14, fifty yards or so along the road. The only survivor was the pilot, who had managed to ease open his roof hatch in time. He parachuted down safely on to a golf course, where he was quickly apprehended. A local police-man, Sergeant Grigg, later received the George Medal for removing several 'live' 50 kg bombs from the wreckage at number 26 so that the survivors could be reached by rescue parties, as did a local doctor who tended the wounded at the scene, despite great risk from the bombs that remained in the immediate vicinity.[3]

The fact that the German bombers had been having such an easy time of it on night missions, due to the general ineffectuality of both the British night-fighter force and anti-aircraft artillery, had led to a certain insouciance on the part of some Luftwaffe pilots. As the report from the Cockfosters interrogation centre noted after the survivor's first interrogation: 'The pilot, until his last flight, had held a very poor opinion of English A.A. fire, and always flew straight through it.' In this case, however, his aircraft, though flying at 13,000–16,000 feet, had suffered a direct hit. The impact shot away one wing (found in the area of the crash), causing the pilot to lose control of the aircraft, with fatal consequences for the rest of his crew as well as for at least one civilian on the ground.[4]

The survivor of the crash was twenty-year-old Leutnant Max Probst. According to a note on 12 November from Squadron Leader Felkin to the RAF's Director of Intelligence:

A pilot from 2/K.G. 1 from MONDIDIER shot down on the 9th inst. has told the following story to his roommate (a S.P. installed two days ago [if that isn't clear Group Captain Davidson will explain']). He believes that riots have broken out in London and that Buck-ingham Palace has been stormed and that 'Hermann'[†] thinks the psychological moment has come for a colossal raid to take place between the 15th and 20th of this month at the full moon and that Coventry and Birmingham will be the towns attacked. P/W[‡] stated he had recently made 2 to 3 attacks on London nightly but this attack will only entail one flight per night and that every bomber in the

* S.P. = A (German-speaking) stool-pigeon.
† Göring.
‡ Prisoner of war.

Luftwaffe will take part. He says that workmen's dwelling are being concentrated on methodically to undermine the working classes who are believed to be so near revolt. He thinks that every Knickebein route will be employed and that in future they will concentrate on 50 kg shrieking bombs.

As this came after S/L Humphrey's visit this afternoon when he mentioned that a gigantic raid under the code name of 'Moonlight Sonata' was in preparation, I thought it well to bring this information to your notice although on account of the source it should be treated with reserve, as he [i.e. Probst] is as yet untried.

I believe that S/L. Humphreys* has pretty definite information that the attack is to be against London and the Home Counties and he believes that it is in retaliation for Munich.† The objective should also be regarded as doubtful as probably his information is later.[5]

The nature of 'Moonlight Sonata' had rapidly become the subject of widespread speculation within British intelligence. The Germans' choice of codename for the operation referred to the famous Beethoven piano piece, the Sonata in C-sharp minor number 14. Like many Luftwaffe codenames, it was rather easily liable to interpretation. Moonlight was obviously the approaching time of the full moon in the middle of November. So the 'when' of the matter was clear enough. A sonata was arranged in three movements, but this aspect was a little harder to unpick. Could it be that it was one big attack in three waves or three separate big attacks? Pieces of paper flew back and forth, and no doubt many conversations and telephone

---

* Robert Humphreys was Senior Liaison Officer between Hut 3 at Bletchley Park (responsible for interpreting, translating and distributing decoded German army and Luftwaffe signals) and the RAF. An experienced intelligence officer and a fluent German speaker, he was a protégé of Wing Commander F. W. Winterbotham, head of the Air Section of MI6.

† On the night of 8/9 November 1940, the RAF had carried out a quite successful raid against Munich, one that Goebbels described as the city's 'baptism of fire'. That night, Hitler had been in Munich to address the Nazi faithful on the anniversary of his attempted putsch in 1923, and was not best pleased.

calls were devoted to the mystery. And that was before the discussion started about the 'where'.

The consensus was still that if there was going to be a 'gigantic' raid by the Luftwaffe, it would be directed against London and its environs. The Deputy Director of Intelligence at the Air Staff in London, Wing Commander G. W. P. 'Tubby' Grant, wrote a minute that same day summarising the current state of supposition about 'Moonlight Sonata'. Under possible 'Target Areas' in this regard, he noted the following:

Target Area I. It is uncertain where this area lies. It is possibly central London. There is, however, a possibility that it is in the Harwich–Ipswich district.

Target Area II. Greater London and within the circle Windsor – St. Albans – Epping – Gravesend – Westerham – a little south of Leatherhead – Windsor.

Target Area III. The Triangle bounded by lines connecting Farnborough Aerodrome – Reading – Maidenhead.

Target Area IV. The district Faversham – Rochester – Sheerness.[6]

There is no mention at this point of other possibilities as regards the likely target, and certainly no mention of the Midlands, let alone Coventry. Clearly, in the higher echelons of Air Intelligence, the garrulous Leutnant Probst was still reckoned to be either mistaken or lying. He had not, after all, specifically identified a codename for the projected Coventry and Birmingham raids. They might not be the 'big one' referred to as 'Moonlight Sonata'.

It is possible to see why Air Intelligence suspected that any truly striking demonstration of German strength would involve a massive attack on central London. The alternative supposition, that the entire might of the Luftwaffe's bomber force would be hurled, as a likely instance, against the Harwich–Ipswich area, came not from actual signals but from captured German Luftwaffe maps reckoned to refer to 'Moonlight Sonata'.[7] R. V. Jones recalls his scepticism about Grant's suggestion, despite its being the Air Staff's current favourite. It seemed to Jones much more likely that the map had to do with drop zones ahead of a putative German invasion.[8]

British intelligence was not, of course, aware of the discussions going on within the German Air Command Staff about the urgency of attacks on the aircraft industry. Nor was it aware of the more nebulous (but quite possibly additionally influential) suggestions from the Luftwaffe's Political Section, playing down the importance of London and advocating concentration of heavy bombing on the Midlands as the stronghold of 'true Englishness' and the backbone of British resistance.

It was nonetheless true that, when an update on the 'Moonlight Sonata' situation put together by the Air Staff was sent to the Prime Minister on 14 November, outlining the notion that attack would be aimed at targets in the south of England, Probst's assertions were mentioned. Until then, at least so far as the surviving paper trail is concerned, he had been dismissed as more or less unreliable. Now his predictions were being mentioned to no less a person than the Prime Minister. Moreover, in paragraph five the writer of the report, obviously a very senior staff officer, hedged his bet a little:

> We believe that the target areas will be those noted in paragraph 1 above, probably in the vicinity of London, but if further information indicates Coventry, Birmingham or elsewhere, we hope to get instructions out in time.[9]

There are further hints of reassessment. A scribbled minute from Air Commodore Archie Boyle, the Director of Intelligence at the Air Ministry, to the Director of Home Operations, slightly torn in one corner (hence author's query in the first sentence quoted) and dated 14 November but with no time indicated, may show more revisionist thinking going on:

> I think your [re?]interpretation of the 3 Phases of Moonlight Serenade [sic] is probably right and that will be an attack on <u>one</u> night in

3 waves. P/W states 500–800 aircraft but mentions 'the Industrial District' of England. I am trying to get more information.

By 14 November 1940, the Air Staff was therefore still tied up in some confusion as to where the blow promised under the deceptively romantic codename of 'Moonlight Sonata' was going to fall. What it had developed in the interim was a plan for all eventualities, to avenge and disrupt any German offensive action. This went under its own decidedly more prosaic codename: 'Cold Water'.

Ever since the first decoded Ultra signal had arrived over the teleprinter from Bletchley on 10 November, Air Intelligence and the Air Staff had known that if 'Moonlight Sonata' was going to happen, the key moment from the British defenders' point of view would be at 13:00 hours with the transmission of the approved code MOND MOND, meaning German reconnaissance aircraft over the target had checked the weather conditions and given the go-ahead. A scribbled marginal annotation (dated 14.11) to the note received by the Prime Minister, alongside an underlining of the words 'K.Gr.100', declared that 'This unit sent the approved code word at 13:00 exactly', though there is no other information supplied.

In fact, the order for the beginning of the 'Cold Water' counter-operation had already been issued ten hours earlier, at three in the morning of 14 November.[10] Since this operation was arranged in several and various stages, this was logical. It would basically involve first, from early in the morning, placing a continuous watch on German radio and signals activity, with heightened attention at 13:00 hours when, according to Ultra, the final go-ahead message was due. Second, as the daylight faded, British bombers would be sent over the Channel to attack the Luftwaffe airfields from which, it was expected, the enemy air fleet would be taking off for their night mission. Third, once the 'Rivers System' beam had been identified, the RAF's Radio Counter-Measures (RCM) force, 80 Signals Wing, would aid an energetic jamming effort.

Meanwhile, Whitley bombers subordinate to 80 Wing, from the experimental station at Boscombe Down in Wiltshire, equipped with tracking sets, would follow the beams back across the Channel and bomb the 'silent zones' that identified the locations of the German transmitting stations.[11] Fourth, the fighter force (including the few radar-equipped night fighters) and anti-aircraft artillery systems would be placed on intensified alert, awaiting confirmation of the target, if and when this became clear. Orders were to attack the expected waves of German bombers on their way to, and back from, their target, with some night fighters to be stationed on the return route in the vicinity of Fécamp Lighthouse, on the coast of Brittany. Here the German bombers were expected to reveal themselves by switching on their navigation lights in anticipation of landing. It was notably mentioned that the Air Staff had considered operating Blenheim night fighters with on-board radar in the area, but to have done so would have involved removing the AI (airborne interception – on-board radar) in case the aircraft were shot down over German-held territory and captured by the enemy along with their precious technology.[12]

Lastly, Bomber Command aircraft would attack as yet unspecified targets in Germany, thus providing a kind of instant retaliation as well as proof that, whatever havoc the Luftwaffe had wrought this night, the German Reich was every bit as vulnerable as the British home island.

The weight of anticipation attached to 'Moonlight Sonata' was considerable. R. V. Jones recalled that by early November it had become apparent that the 'Rivers System' stations on the northern French coast could set and reset their beams with such speed and skill that they could provide guidance for two succeeding attacks on the same night. So, based on precisely such switching, on 4 November, Birmingham and then Coventry were bombed; on 5 November Coventry and then Birmingham; on 8 November Liverpool (not at all effectively, as it happened) and Birmingham; and on 12 November Liverpool and Coventry, the latter an attack in which some damage was done to Coventry Cathedral. Incendiary bombs penetrated the roof of the medieval building, though on this occasion worse was prevented by the vigilance of volunteer firewatchers, who quickly summoned the Fire Brigade.[13]

In his memoirs, R. V. Jones recalled on Sunday, 10 November receiving Luftwaffe decrypts from Bletchley instructing K.Gr.100 to prepare for raids on targets 51, 52, and 53 and giving beam settings for these three. The target code numbers used by German planners were known to the British, so it was no problem to identify the intended targets. All were at industrial towns in the English Midlands: 51 indicated Wolverhampton, 52 Birmingham and 53 Coventry. Jones was, according to his recollection, surprised to see three in the same message. Were the German transmission teams to raise their game further and set beams for not just two but three targets in a single night? Also unusually, Jones recalled, the specifications were accurate only to the nearest minute (i.e. sixtieth of a degree) and not to the second (sixtieth of a minute), which meant, if this remained the only instruction, a considerable coarsening of the beam and thus less accuracy. This confirmed, in his recollection, that the beams were being followed only by the pathfinder aircraft, whose task was to scatter flares and incendiaries over a somewhat wider area of the target city, to make the bomb-dropping zone easily apparent to the following bombers. Unless the message Jones saw was different from the one still preserved in the archives, however, there is a problem with his exact account of this thought process. The coordinates listed in the preserved document were, in fact, precise to the second rather than just the minute.[14]

There was, as has been seen, a beam-guided raid on Coventry two days after Jones saw the message, on 12 November. Wolverhampton was not bombed that month and, though an important industrial town almost as large as Coventry, remained very lightly bombed in general throughout the conflict. When he saw the *KORN* codename mentioned in the German signal that alerted Allied intelligence to 'Moonlight Sonata', Jones thought, as we know, that it was not necessarily a target code but might refer to a technical problem that the Luftwaffe was having with their receivers.

There is other anecdotal, though otherwise unsubstantiated, evidence favouring the Midlands as the putative target for 'Moonlight

Sonata'. In a post-war book about her time at the Kingsdown 'Y' group station in north Kent, Aileen Clayton, née Morris, remembers her station commander travelling to London in the second week of November for a regular briefing at 'Y' HQ, where he was told about the big raid everyone was expecting. Group Captain Blandy asked him to have his teams, who normally concentrated on German aircraft radio messages, provide further backup by listening for the 'Moonlight Sonata' codes. She said that, according to her boss, a senior officer from the operational side was then called into the meeting. This officer told the man from Kingsdown that, so far as 'Moonlight Sonata' was concerned, they were all expecting a big raid on the Midlands.[15]

The confusion about 'Moonlight Sonata' was further added to by another, disastrous failure of British intelligence. This occurred on 5/6 November, when a Heinkel 111 of K.GR.100, having been involved in the second, later leg of the 'double raid' against Coventry and Birmingham that night, suffered a compass failure on its flight back to base and got lost. Because of this, it fell victim to a signals ruse that had been part of British counter-measures for some time. On the British side, transmitters had been set up that were able to masquerade as German beacons, by sending out identical signals. One such, at Templecombe in Dorset, mimicked the beacon at St Malo, in northern Brittany. The desperate German pilot had by now been flying aimlessly around for some time and was running low on fuel, so he proceeded to head for this. The aircraft crash-landed shortly before dawn on 6 November on what its pilot took to be a beach on the occupied French coast, around a hundred miles north of his home base at Vannes. It was, however, actually West Beach near Bridport, in Dorset.[16]

What followed was a farce with potentially tragic implications. An army coastal patrol approached the crash site and took charge of the aircraft. The observer – who as navigator/bomb-aimer would have been in charge of the *X-Gerät* – had been killed, but the other crew members were captured. The commander of the army unit left two other ranks on guard before leaving the site, with strict instructions (so Jones said) not to allow the navy, who would certainly arrive at the scene before long, to claim the aircraft – which at high tide was arguably on water rather than on land – as a prize. His words were apparently: 'I don't care if even an Admiral comes along. You are not to allow him near it!' A naval vessel duly appeared. And sure enough, the two hapless guards refused them access to the Heinkel. They stuck to their orders even when the rising tide started to swamp the aircraft and the representatives of the senior service offered to help drag it up above the high water line.

Any more or less intact German aircraft recovered on British soil had value, but this one was a special prize: the Heinkel carried a fully functioning *X-Gerät* on board, the first to fall into British hands. However, by the time the army–navy rivalry was dealt with and the aircraft, which had now spent time underwater, could be recovered for examination, some days had passed. As R. V. Jones, who naturally took a keen interest, observed, its radio gear was full of sand and the light alloy components had been subjected to corrosion.

Only after 'Moonlight Sonata' had already gone into operation would the RAF's technical teams at Farnborough manage to investigate the wreck properly and so begin to understand how the equipment actually worked.[17] What they eventually discovered might have profoundly affected Coventry's fate.

It would become apparent that, while Jones and his team had correctly guessed the layout of the beams, the modulation frequency to be used for jamming them and thus leading German aircraft astray had been measured wrongly. It had been noted as 1500 MHz, whereas in fact it was 2000 MHz. The assumption on the British side was that, even if this audio frequency was a bit out, it would not matter, because inside the aircraft it was so noisy that the operator would not realise that the jamming transmission was not a perfect match for the genuine X-beam tone. However, the *X-Gerät* was more sophisticated than that. A new on-board instrument was being used to decode the dots and dashes and display the results visually on a pointer in the pilot's cockpit, so it didn't matter how noisy the cabin might be. Even worse from the jammer's point of view, this decoder was fitted with a filter that excluded anything other than an exact match for the genuine frequency of 2000 MHz. Jamming of the normal (and hitherto successful) kind was now, therefore, ineffective.

The jammers were modified accordingly, though this came too late for the raid on Coventry. The modified jammers were able to successfully disrupt a raid on Birmingham on 19 November, but results remained patchy. *X-Gerät* would eventually be defeated, not by way of jamming, but by British radar specialists' creation of a 'false "Elbe"', which was set up to cross the 'Weser' guide beam only one kilometre after the preceding 'Oder' beam — much earlier than the expected five kilometres. Since the final stages of the bomb-release were automatic, the clock would reverse prematurely and drop the bombs kilometres short of the target. In turn, the difficulty with this was that often the false beam had to be set up very quickly, since the Germans – learning from their mistakes with *Knickebein* – now did not switch on the beams until the latest practicable moment, confronting the British signals teams with a race against time that they usually, but not quite always, managed to win.

The last round of the so-called 'battle of the beams' would be played out during 1941. From Enigma decrypts, Jones and his colleagues knew as early as autumn of 1940 that the Germans, aware that they were slowly losing the *X-Gerät* battle, were developing a new navigation aid called *Wotan*, otherwise known as the *Y-Gerät*. Deducing from the fact that this referred to a one-eyed god of Germanic mythology, British scientists realised that this must refer to a single-beam system.

Y-Gerät used a single narrow beam pointed over the target, transmitting a modulated radio signal. The system employed a new piece of equipment that received the signal from the beam and immediately retransmitted it back to the German ground station in occupied France. The ground station listened for the return signal and compared the phase of its modulation to the transmitted signal. This is an accurate way of measuring the transit time of the signal, and hence the distance to the aircraft. Coupled with the direction of the beam, the bomber's position could be established with considerable accuracy. The ground controllers could then give radio instructions to the pilot to correct his flight path where necessary. Setting up a fake distance establishing beam, as had ultimately been done with success in the case of the *X-Gerät*, would not help the British scientific team with this new challenge.

Aided by the foreknowledge provided by Enigma, the British were ready for this system from the outset. As it happened, moreover, the Germans had inadvertently picked their operating frequency for the *Wotan* system very unwisely. The device operated on 45 MHz, which happened to be the same operating frequency as the BBC's television transmitter at Alexandra Palace, in north London, which had been mothballed on the outbreak of war but could be reactivated for this occasion. Jones arranged for the return signal to be received from the aircraft and then sent to Alexandra Palace for retransmission. The combination of the two signals altered the phase shift – and thus the transit delay. At first, the signal was retransmitted on low power, not strong enough for the Germans to realise what was happening, but enough to spoil the accuracy of the system. Over subsequent nights, the transmitter power was gradually increased.

After a while, the air crew using *Wotan* began to accuse the people back at base of sending corrupted signals. In response, the ground station insisted that the aircraft must have loose connections. Like the proverbial frog placed in a saucepan where the heat is almost imperceptibly but steadily increased, Jones's victims did not realise that they were being boiled until it was too late. The increase in power was so gradual that the Germans did not realise anyone was interfering with their system. They began to believe that *Wotan* was suffering from inherent defects. As the power was increased to full strength the *Wotan* system started to suffer from massive feedback.

After 1941, the Luftwaffe gave up on electronic navigation systems. Had it changed the frequency on *Wotan*, or persisted with its research, it might have continued to enjoy an inestimable advantage in night bombing. Coventry might not have been their last great success.

So, the use of radar for aggressive purposes was abandoned. Like the British, Hitler's Germany began to transfer her research resources to defensive radar. Soon, of course, she would need it, as the British and the Americans began to bomb German cities and industries on a horrifically grand scale. At night. Without precise aiming aids.

With 'Moonlight Sonata' now given the highest priority by the Air Staff, all tracker stations were put on full alert. At Kingsdown, a particularly skilled wireless operator by the name of Corporal Allen had been instructed to listen on the expected frequency every afternoon. According to Aileen Clayton, on the afternoon of 14 November at 13:55,* he did indeed pick up the group MOND being sent out by aircraft of K.GR.100. Everyone involved was aware that, since early that morning, there had been preliminary activity on the beam frequencies. The conclusion was clear. The station commander checked with Cheadle, the radio tracking station in Staffordshire, but apparently they had not picked it up. He therefore immediately took the initiative and telephoned the Air Ministry in London to inform them.[18]

The raid was on. But exactly where was the target? Could it be identified? And how and when did those in charge of the air defence of the country find this out? Three-quarters of a century later, all this is a matter of continuing dispute and of conflicting evidence.

What we do know for certain is that late on the afternoon of Thursday, 14 November 1940 the Prime Minister, having that morning attended the funeral at Westminster Abbey of his predecessor, Neville Chamberlain, and then met with various officials and ministers,

---

* That is, 12:55 GMT, five minutes before the tuning signal was to be given according to the signals intercepted on 9 November. Normally, in November British time and GMT would have been the same. In early 1940, however, Britain had been put on permanent summer time, i.e. GMT + 1.

including his deputy, Clement Attlee, was on his way by car out of London. He planned to spend the night with old friends, Ronald Tree MP and his American wife, Nancy, a famous interior and garden designer, at Ditchley Park, in Oxfordshire. This secluded country house lay surrounded by tall trees and without visible access roads, while Chequers, the Prime Minister's usual country residence, had highly visible landmarks such as a large lake. It was considered by the security services as too easily identifiable from the air, especially on moonlit nights. Tree, like his guest a veteran opponent of appeasement, had recently offered Churchill the use of the house when the danger of accurate bombing was acute. The party had, however, not gone far when the Prime Minister ordered his driver to turn around and head back to Downing Street.

Less than forty-eight hours earlier, on the night of 12 November, while a relatively minor German raid on Coventry had seen the Cathedral struck by incendiaries, the Luftwaffe scored a direct hit on Sloane Square Tube station in Chelsea. The bomb destroyed most of the building and buried an underground train, killing 37 of its passengers and injuring twice as many again. On 13 November, the capital of the British Empire had been subjected to further bombing by seventy-three Heinkel 111s of K.G.26, while that same night sixty-three aircraft from K.G.55 had hit Birmingham.

Had Churchill reacted to a warning that London was definitely the object of the keenly awaited big raid known by the name 'Moonlight Sonata'? Was he, as seems later to have been claimed, determined to stay there and dare the enemy to do his worst? Or was precisely the opposite in fact the case? Did he now know for certain that the massed attack was actually intended for elsewhere, and so there was now no need to leave London?

Most crucially, did Churchill know from that moment that the overwhelming might of the German bomber force was to be directed during the night to come against the city and people of Coventry?

9

Finding the Beam

R. V. Jones is clear enough in his post-war writings and interviews that during the crucial afternoon of 14 November 1940, while he was on hand to aid counter-measures against 'Moonlight Sonata', he never saw information, whether in the form of Enigma decrypts or reports from 80 Wing's beam-tracing missions, that enabled him to identify Coventry as the night's target.

At about half past five in the afternoon of that late autumn day – just as night had begun to fall – Jones received a telephone call from Radlett in Hertfordshire, the headquarters of 80 Wing, the radio counter-measures specialists. Group Captain Edward Addison, its commander, wanted his help in deciding the frequency on which he should jam the beams which would guide the Luftwaffe's aircraft for the expected big raid. He was, Jones recounts, at this point 'fairly sure' that the target was 'somewhere in the Midlands'.[1] Could Jones help him further with target identification?

> I did not know. The Enigma had not [been] broken that night in time, although it had by the following morning . . . but that was too late. So I couldn't tell him where the target was.[2]

Even worse, so it seemed, after Addison then read out the list of radio frequencies that his aircraft had discerned during their investigatory flights, Jones realised his additional difficulty. From previous experience, he was certain that the information Addison had given him was wrong. Mistakes had been made in recording the frequencies. For all the noble work that 80 Wing did during this period, according to Jones this was a not infrequent occurrence, the result of equipment not properly adapted to the task.[3] Jones reluctantly made an educated guess at the probable frequencies to which Addison should set his jammers. He put the telephone down, unable to avoid some foreboding as to what was about to happen. But he was not, at this point, thinking specifically about Coventry.

R. V. Jones was nominally a low-ranking official at the Air Ministry (with the rank, and modest pay grade, of Scientific Officer), but as well as having a direct personal relationship with Lindemann, since his successes in the 'battle of the beams' he had access to Churchill, too. He was also closely connected with MI6, the Secret Intelligence Service. In fact, he worked out of its offices at 54 Broadway in St James's. His account of what happened on the afternoon and early evening of 14 November 1940 nevertheless seems to be contradicted by one of his most important superiors at MI6, Group Captain F. W. Winterbotham.

Winterbotham, a First World War veteran who had piloted aircraft on the Western Front with the Royal Flying Corps, was the long-serving head of Air Intelligence within MI6. He was also the man who, from the autumn of 1939, when Britain had first acquired the means to break the Enigma code, had set up and extended the all-important system of translation, transcription and distribution of the Ultra reports gleaned from these intercepts. A tall, handsome and clubbable man with, as the *Oxford Dictionary of National Biography* comments, 'a disciplined air', he was born in 1897, making him forty-three years old to Jones's twenty-eight.

The group captain's later accounts of what happened on the afternoon of 14 November 1940, as the British military and political elite waited for the big attack expected under the codename 'Moonlight Sonata', begin in all cases with phone information from Bletchley Park early that afternoon, at about two o'clock. Differences in further details – over some years of the telling – are nonetheless striking.

Although a great and loyal keeper of secrets all through the war and beyond, it was Winterbotham who, in fact, broke the post-war silence on the subject of Enigma and Ultra. Even his wife, whom he had started courting in 1942, had no inkling of his role, or of Ultra, until many years after the war.[4] For three decades after the Second World War, the world knew nothing of the code-breaking triumphs that had, it is now generally agreed, skewed the war in the Allies' favour. Many of the successes the British and American commanders enjoyed as the war went on, and most especially the victorious North African and Italian campaigns and the successful landings in Normandy, were crucially influenced by the knowledge of German movements and intentions that the Ultra information supplied.

Winterbotham was the man who set up and ran the confidential distribution system to the (very few) commanders and officials granted direct access to the Ultra information. He did all of this, by common consent, extremely well. It must have seemed, therefore, truly remarkable that it was he who revealed everything, in 1974, in a book titled *The Ultra Secret*. He had not been allowed access to documents while writing the book, and therefore relied on memory alone, with all the possibilities for error that this implies. Nonetheless, after much harrumphing from the powers that be, the book was finally allowed to be published, and turned out be a sensational bestseller, completely transforming the public's perception of how the war had been won. Victory had not been due exclusively to the genius of our commanders and the bravery of our fighting men, it was now clear. Instead, it had been won in great part due to the fact that we had, as the saying goes, been engaged in the ungentlemanly business of reading the Germans' mail. Most of the time, we knew what they were going to do before they did it.

In the matter of Coventry, however, Winterbotham lit a fuse that still, despite all attempts to extinguish it, occasionally seems to sputter into life. He insisted that Winston Churchill had indeed known that Coventry was the target some four hours or so before the big attack. Bletchley had somehow found the name of the target being sent, not as a code, but *en clair*, and the counter-measures, especially those involving Fighter Command, were duly put into operation. He – Winterbotham – had then informed the Prime Minister's office, and Churchill had decided not to prepare the defences of Coventry, or warn its population, because of the sanctity of Ultra, which might have been imperilled by any such obvious special measures. Had the Germans noticed these measures – they were capable of a level of eavesdropping themselves – it might have occurred to one of their finer minds that somehow, from somewhere, the enemy had been forewarned. This realisation might then lead the Germans to abandon Enigma as their code-producing machine, thus plunging the British political leadership and General Staff back into their ancient darkness so far as their knowledge of enemy intentions was concerned. Or so, Winterbotham wrote, Churchill and his intimates supposed.

There was a great deal of controversy about this, and many other aspects of Winterbotham's book. The group captain, who had retired at the end of the war, had not gone on to a splendid second career, unlike Jones. After three years working for the state-owned airline, the British Overseas Airways Corporation (BOAC, later British Airways) Winterbotham moved, still in his early fifties, with his third wife to the West Country to run a small farm. Here, in Devon, he stayed for more than forty years, amounting to most of the rest of his long life. He was not, and never became, rich.*

The great criticism of Winterbotham's book was that, being based on memory, it was inevitably inaccurate. Winterbotham, so his critics maintained, was also possessed of a considerable and continuing desire for recognition, which tended to place him, in his account, in a more central position to all these proceedings than many thought accurate or appropriate.

* This was true even after the successful publication of *The Ultra Secret* and several other books by Winterbotham. According to the *Oxford Dictionary of National Biography*, on his death in 1990 the sum he left, subject to probate, was only a little more than £20,000.

Ten years later, in 1984, he gave another account, as part of a lengthy (thirty-six reels) tape-recorded interview about his life, a sort of apologia, for the Imperial War Museum in London. This was rather less sensational, and differs in some regards:

We got . . . a signal which was telephoned down to me from Bletchley at 1.55 when I got back from lunch, giving instructions to the pathfinder squadron, which was stationed in Brittany, called *Kampfgruppe* – K.G. – 100 as to what course they would take and giving them where the beam was going to be laid, and the coordinates. Now, some people say that we didn't get that. But we did get it, but it was kept very secret by the Air Ministry. They didn't even give that to Dr Jones because he was in close touch with Downing Street and they didn't want Churchill to know anything about this until they were certain about it. I didn't even send over at that time the signal which had been telephoned down to me, which . . . was that the target for tonight is Coventry.[5]

As for the reason why Churchill turned his car around:

. . . . so he went off in the motor car believing the raid was going to be on London. But around three o'clock the Air Ministry had found the beam and I had sent my delayed message over to Downing Street. This was put in a case and a despatch rider was sent off after Churchill, which managed to pick up the car before he'd left London. He opened the envelope and read it and he remarked to his secretary that he was going back to Downing Street. The secretary of course did not see Ultra, and Churchill gave the excuse that he wasn't going to desert London. It was quite a good excuse.

Concerning what followed, Winterbotham was quite specific:

Now, the Air Staff had also informed Fighter Command, and that happened between three and four o'clock. I know somebody who was in the Filter Room at Fighter Command, and of course my wife was a plotter in the other room. Our chief sergeant was the present Lady Tweeddale, and the Tweeddale Watch – it wasn't then because she was Sergeant Dutton – went on duty at four o'clock that afternoon, and when she went on duty she was told to take her best plotters off the area of No. 11 Group, because that was the area they were normally on – that's where all the air raids came from, from the continent towards London – and to put the plotters on No. 10 Group, which covered the route from Brittany to Coventry, where the Pathfinder one would go.

Aileen Clayton, working at the Kingsdown listening station, where they were intercepting the Germans' preliminary radio conversations, especially those of the pathfinders belonging to K.Gr.100, backs Winterbotham's version.[6] David Irving, who interviewed Winterbotham for his book *Churchill's War* in the early 1980s, followed up the reference to Lady Tweeddale (then Sergeant Dutton) and she, too, so he says, confirmed the information.[7] The Director of Home Operations' post-event report on the raid, dated Sunday, 17 November, also specifically states that Coventry had been identified as the target by three o'clock and that orders had been issued to all the relevant Commands involved in the counter-strike known as Operation Cold Water – Fighter and Bomber, Coastal and Anti-Aircraft – shortly thereafter.

So, what of Jones's assessment? There is not necessarily reason to impute his integrity. If it was indeed correct, as Winterbotham maintained, that the Air Ministry, moving into operational mode and wanting to keep things quiet, had decided to leave Jones, as an intelligence man with connections to Downing Street, 'out of the loop', then certain things become plausible. The ministry's man Addison of 80 Wing, for example, when ringing the scientist to seek the benefit of his knowledge on jamming the beams – which clearly, by 5:30, had been identified – might have been deliberately vague about the expected target.

The explanation for Churchill's sudden return to London – that by this stage he knew that 'somewhere in the Midlands', quite possibly Coventry, but definitely not the capital, was the target for 'Moonlight Sonata' – seems on balance much more likely than the notion that he suddenly, impulsively, decided not to 'desert' London. The Prime Minister having previously decided to accept the advice of his security paladins and seek the safety of the country in the face of such a raid, exactly why would this have been so?

Winterbotham's later, less sensational view is more convincing if we resist the powerful lure of the anti-Churchill conspiracy theorists – who, like the Churchill worshippers, place the Prime Minister, for good or ill, at the centre of every wartime story – and simply treat the entire events of that afternoon as a series of reactions to an approaching German air attack on a major scale – worrying and problematic, but not inherently unusual after a summer of frequently heavy air raids. There is no evidence, in any case, that Churchill demanded special measures of any kind, even if he knew that Coventry was 'for it'. Indeed, as Winterbotham suggests in his later account, even if the great man did contact the Air Staff, he seems simply to have concurred with its decision to treat the raid on Coventry like any other.

With only two to three hours to go before the first German bombers arrived over the city, it would count, moreover, as a unique feat of organisation to have conducted an orderly evacuation of an entire population of a quarter of a million in good time (there is no record of such a thing ever happening in the history of air warfare). In this booming, bustling, sprawling city, men and women were at work, children arriving home from school or sitting down to tea. Imagine the panic-stricken reaction to the announcement of an impending air raid so menacing that everyone had to flee the city, immediately. The result would be chaos. Once the raid began, how could you then bring the firefighters and civil defence workers and ambulances into the city to deal with its consequences? The streets, and especially the main roads leading in and out of Coventry, would remain impassable, as civilians attempted to escape the impending catastrophe.

In short, if such a decision was indeed made, it cannot be dismissed as mere cold calculation. There would have been plenty of recent examples, in the minds of Churchill, his cabinet colleagues and commanders, of how the threat of destruction by the enemy, through bombing or through imminent massive aggression, had led to debilitating and ultimately self-defeating panic. The disastrous mass flight from Barcelona in January 1939. Warsaw in September, with fleeing columns of refugees clogging the roads, easy meat for the German Stukas. Even more recently, seared into any even half-aware English consciousness, the hasty, panic-stricken exodus from Paris before the French capital fell to the Wehrmacht, in June 1940. As one who was there wrote in her memoir of that terrible time:

> So many images, chaotic and incoherent, jolting and jostling for space in my head. Leaving Paris among so many thousands of others, on foot or by bicycle or in cars – cars that had to be abandoned almost immediately for lack of petrol or spare parts. Mothers carrying small children . . . One young woman, dropping with exhaustion, pushing a strapping baby squashed into a doll's pram that was far too small for it . . . Such a mass of people, laden down with the most unlikely looking parcels and packages – almost invariably including a washtub and a birdcage.[8]

There is a problem with Winterbotham's recollection of that afternoon, nevertheless. There is no physical evidence, traceable to those crucial hours, of the decrypted German signal, about which he was, so he said, informed by telephone shortly before two o'clock. Three and a half hours later, still well before British coastal observation units could spot K.Gr.100 heading from their base in southern Brittany over the Channel on a trajectory that would take them to Coventry, 80 Wing had certainly found the beam, and in Addison's words, 'somewhere in the Midlands' was most likely the target – not London. Apart from the untimed notes mentioned earlier, which give tantalising glimpses of the changing state of opinion at the Air Staff, we have no concrete evidence either way. According to David Irving, Winterbotham remained convinced that the specific Ultra information he recalls has been deliberately withheld by the authorities from inclusion among the records held at the National Archives in London, and is unlikely to be released in the foreseeable future.[9]

Various conspiracy theories apart, as we shall see, no branch of Britain's air defences would cover itself in glory during the coming hours. Instructions had indeed been issued to counter, so far as was possible, 'Moonlight Sonata'. The notion that these efforts were somehow deliberately limited in their scope, in order not to give the Germans any suspicion that British intelligence was reading their codes, mistakes the actual limits of those capabilities and the exigencies of the time. Had so many lives not been at stake, the inability of RAF Fighter Command and the anti-aircraft artillery network to successfully oppose, let alone deter, any major night attack on any of the island's cities – including London as well as the likes of Coventry – would be almost comical. This was especially the case given the government's propaganda assertions to the contrary.

The state of official knowledge during the preceding hours apart, any claim that Churchill, his ministers and commanders 'sacrificed' Coventry – the centre of the British aircraft industry – would have to be based, not just on their readiness to do so, but on the assumption that, had they so desired, they could have 'saved' the city. As the story will tell, this was, tragically and humiliatingly, not the case. Hence the basically generic nature of the counter-measures. The same weakness would be shown six weeks later, on 29 December, when the Luftwaffe devastated the City of London, again with virtual impunity – even though, as in this latter case we know for certain, the government and the Air Staff had clear foreknowledge of the attack. No matter the size of the expected raid, this was what Britain had to throw at it, and the painful fact was that, in late 1940, it was not much.

The particular cynicism of many Coventrians regarding the authorities' ability to protect them and their city had been noted in official circles even before the big raid. The events of 14/15 November would see that cynicism, where it existed, richly justified.

The first of a dozen or so specially adapted Heinkel 111s of K.Gr.100 took to the air in the November twilight at around half past five, British time. They were easily recognisable by their group code,

6N + BH, the painting of a Viking ship in sail on the nose of each aircraft – a memento of their successful role in the Norwegian campaign that spring – and by the prominent pair of extra aerials they carried atop their fuselages, to pick up the beam transmissions.

As was appropriate for the tasks they were called on to perform, the crews of K.Gr.100 were generally experienced, often older men, many with substantial pre-war flying experience.[10] One such, Horst Götz, later described his feelings that day:

> The Coventry raid had at that time no special significance for us in K.Gr.100. All we knew was, that night various bomber squadrons would be following us and that our planes were loaded only with incendiaries.
>
> I see from my log book that at 18:28* I was among the first planes to take off on this raid. However, shortly before the English coast my Heinkel developed engine trouble and I had to turn back. The weather was good and I got back all right.[11]

Their base at Vannes, on the south coast of Brittany, facing the Bay of Biscay, had been included in the target list for 'Cold Water'. However, it was specifically not a part of that plan to attack the aircraft on the ground before the raid could be launched. For now the Germans remained unmolested, on the ground as well as in the air.

The total distance to the target was about four hundred miles. Initially, the pathfinder group flew north over land towards the French Channel coast, lightly loaded with the target-marking flares and incendiaries, as mentioned by Horst Götz, and therefore able to fly at up to 230 mph. This kept them ahead of the first of the 400-strong, heavy-laden mass of bombers from Air Fleets 2 and 3 that would

---

* After the French surrender, German-occupied northern France, including K.Gr, 100's airfield, had been put on German summer time, which was British summer time + 2. It was therefore still 17:28 in England.

inflict the night's actual destruction. While crossing the Channel, the aircrafts picked up the coarse 'Weser' beam emanating from the coast of Normandy, near Cherbourg. This would guide them on the first, longest part of their flight, bringing them into British air space at a point between the Dorset town of Swanage and the Isle of Wight, a hundred and more miles south-west of London.

For a while they followed a course roughly north-east, over Wiltshire and the Vale of the White Horse, as so many times before when heading for London during the ceaseless Blitz of September and October. This time, however, there was a late change of direction. At a point near Chipping Norton in Oxfordshire, the aircraft's observers picked up the visual indicator of the first of the fine cross beams, 'Rhein', transmitting from Calais, that was set to guide them to Coventry itself. The *Geschwader* (equivalent to an RAF Wing) turned and set course due north across the Cotswolds for the final stretch of its approach to target 53, now just a little more than sixty miles distant.

The beam, meanwhile, remained intact, precise and fully functioning. As it happened, Jones had guessed right about the actual frequency of the signal, but not about its modulation frequency. Because of the delays in analysing the precious *X-Gerät* aboard the Heinkel that had crash-landed on the beach near Bridport a little more than a week earlier, the radio counter-measures operatives of 80 Wing still knew nothing of the equipment's true modulation frequency or of the filters that protected it from misleading transmissions. It was roughly at the same time as the Heinkel pathfinders took off from Vannes that, following Addison's telephone conversation with R. V. Jones, attempts were made to jam the pathfinders' reception. They failed. Even the brand-new 'Bromide' jamming transmitter that had begun functioning on 1 November near Kenilworth, just seven miles south-east of Coventry, had absolutely no effect.

The crews of the attacking aircraft were even more surprised and delighted that, despite the clear and moonlit conditions, they encountered no British fighters on their approach.

K.Gr.100 arrived over the city at 19:10, according to schedule, ready to commence what a British government report coolly referred to as 'the first example of a night attack of maximum intensity on a target of limited area'.[12]

The weather had remained clear, bright and cold. Down below the approaching German pathfinders, firewatchers stationed on the roof of the medieval cathedral could see a light frosting reflected white by the light of the moon.[13]

The Luftwaffe had started off with everything going its way, and that was more or less how the night, this long night for the people of Coventry, was going to continue.

10

Red Alert

The yellow message was received at 1905. The purple at 1908, and the red warning at 1910.* Action commenced quickly in brilliant moonlight, and the first fire was reported at 1914.[1]

Thus Chief Officer Cartwright, commander of the Coventry Fire Brigade, began his report on 'Moonlight Sonata'. The stages of alert would have been sent through to his headquarters from the civil defence command post situated beneath the Main Post Office, 500 yards away in Hertford Street. In terms of direct warning, FCO Cartwright had between fifteen and twenty minutes to ready his forces. Once the aircraft of K.Gr.100 had dropped their marker bombs and flares at the final intersection of the *X-Gerät* beams, the centre of the city began to burn.

The first bombs fell in the area around the Cathedral, slightly to the east of the ancient city centre and about a quarter of a mile north of the Armstrong Siddeley Works in Parkside. The Germans had code-numbered this factory as Target 53. Though some of the bombs contained additional explosive charges, they were all incendiaries.[2] This was an unusual pattern, proof that the Germans were using a revolutionary new system of marking targets in large night raids, just as Dr Jones had suspected some days earlier.

* Yellow = First Warning. Purple = Douse Lights. Red = Action.

Once the fires had been set – aided, five minutes after the raid began, by a conflagration in one of the city-centre gas mains – everything happened with astonishing speed. Within minutes, the following aircraft began to drop a more obviously lethal mix of high-explosive bombs, incendiaries and parachute-borne air mines, including delayed action bombs. The effect of this was to destroy almost all gas, electricity and water mains, as well as large parts of the telephone network and the central exchange that facilitated it. The city was now almost entirely cut off from the outside world.

Firefighters found themselves being forced, at an early stage, to fall back mainly on whatever few resources of standing water they could access: the Coventry Canal, the River Sherbourne, Swanswell Pool. As we know, due to pre-war failures, emergency storage facilities were inadequate. The ability of the fire service to respond quickly to requests for help came into serious question. The Coventry Fire Service was forced to call upon men and equipment, first from nearby services (officially designated as 'First Stage'), then second and third stage help from as far away as Aylesbury, in Buckinghamshire, more than sixty miles to the south and almost two-thirds of the way to London.[3] Chief Cartwright wrote afterwards in his report, at 19:40 that night:

> . . . all fires were being controlled, but at 19:59 it was felt that the attack was developing on a large scale and Second Stage . . . was operated. By now seventy-one calls had been received and all the local pumps were in action, and First Stage assistance was only just beginning to arrive. Thirty pumps from Third Stage and two turntable ladders were requested at 20:02, as it was now apparent that the raid was unusually heavy.

> The intensity of the bombardment increased and all reports indicated that the attack was of an unprecedented nature for a provincial town. Incendiary bombs, explosive incendiaries, oil bombs, H.E. of all calibres, parachute mines and flares were all being used. This 'all-type' bombardment continued throughout the night, whereas in previous raids incendiaries had been used only in the early stages, followed by High Explosives.

Sixteen minutes had elapsed since the first emergency call. Quickly the attack began to spread, as some of the Germans began to release their bombs outside the existing fires. The Fire Chief's account reported that 'in this first half-hour there were fires in six widely separated districts'.

Even the Fire Brigade headquarters, in its historic building in Hales Street, next to the centrally located Triumph Motorcycle Works, rapidly found itself confronted with fires in the roof space. Attempts to douse this led to water being sprayed all over the telephone switchboard, which 'caused the switchboard to become "alive", and by 20:00 all the lines . . . were out of order. The main lighting failed and the emergency lighting was badly affected.' Eventually, the situation caused the abandonment of the main control room. For most of the night, telephone communication remained either impossible or only intermittently enabled through ad hoc hook-ups to surviving parts of the telephone network. Messengers, many of them teenage boys on bicycles, had to be employed.

All over the city, at ARP posts, 'rendezvous' locations, hospitals and police stations, volunteers were reporting for duty. Fifteen-year-old Dennis Adler was a cadet in the St John Ambulance Brigade. As soon as the alarm was sounded, he reported for duty as a stretcher-bearer at the Gulson Road Hospital, just south of the city centre. Dennis found himself in the thick of things as casualties started to be brought in:

I could see by the number of casualties and the number of bombs raining down all the time that this was more than the smaller air raids we had had so far.

We carried on as well as we could during the night. We were kept very busy. But the thing is I was not in a position to do anything about dealing with their injuries. And of course the full time staff at the hospital were very busy. To be blunt, what happened was, quite a lot of the people died with their injuries untreated because there just wasn't the people there to deal with them because the numerous injuries they had had to be dealt with as and when.[4]

At sixteen, Alan Hartley was a messenger based at the ARP post operating out of the Three Spires, a pub in Grayswood Avenue, an Edwardian development of semi-detached housing west of the city centre:

> On the night of the Blitz, round about half past six, the sirens went. The head warden said it's only a purple warning. And a purple warning means aircraft in the vicinity. So you can lose yourselves for a while, but don't go too far from the post. And as I got to the top of Grayswood, over Radford, I saw a light in the sky, burning very brightly, and when I looked closely I could see it was a parachute flare. And then to the left, another one, and another one, until the whole city was ringed with parachute flares. And after the second or third one dropped, I realised this was going to be serious.
>
> We then heard the approaching aircraft coming in, the deep throb of the diesel engines of their bombers. So bombs started to fall, and they was dropping in a straight line, and it's most frightening to be in line of a load of bombs coming towards you. You don't know which way to run, or if it's worthwhile running, or when he's going to run out of bombs.[5]

Meanwhile, the German aircraft kept coming, and would do so all night, sometimes apparently alone, sometimes in waves. At one point early in the raid, observers on the ground counted forty in the sky,[6] but this was exceptional. Nonetheless, the bombers, with their characteristic threatening, arrhythmic drone – a torment printed indelibly on so many survivors' memories – seemed constantly present above the city from shortly after 7 p.m. until shortly before dawn on 15 November.

The pathfinder Heinkels of Kgr.100 had flown in along the sophisticated (and still unjammable) beams provided by the 'Rivers' transmitters. The following bombers were not equipped to receive and use the new system, but meanwhile the old, basic *Knickebein* beams – accessible via the Lorenz equipment installed in every bomber – were

also activated that night,[7] not for ultimate guidance or for automatic
bombing – the Germans had realised that the system was vulnerable
to British counter-measures – but in essence as a kind of fail-safe,
in case the aircraft got lost. Every German bomber involved in the
raid on Coventry had actual or potential use of radio-based guidance
systems, at a time when their British counterparts still habitually flew
by the stars.

The Luftwaffe command need not have worried, however. Conditions were said to have been so bright by the full moon that the
German air crew on their way to Coventry could read their maps
without lights. As the pilot of one Dornier 17 bomber of K.G.78,
attacking Coventry later that same night, put it:

> The raid took place in exceptionally good weather – we started at
> Abbeville directly on the coast and as we were flying over the Chan-
> nel we could clearly see Coventry burning. We had no need of radio
> aids . . . there was no defence. The flight had been routine, there was
> very little flak and no night fighters and when we reached the target
> there was a huge sea of flames. I have never seen such a concentra-
> tion of fire during a raid, not even on London. Usually in our target
> cities the area of fires was dispersed, but not this time. There was no
> chance of missing the target.[8]

Some did use *Knickebein*, all the same, often quite casually, and
apparently sometimes with success. The observer of a bomber belonging to *Lehrgeschwader* 1 and carrying only high-explosive bombs,
described to his unit historian how it was used for the final run to
Coventry that night:

> To the horizon everything is so strangely bright. It can't be the moon
> this time, because that has been way above us for a long time since.
> OK, let's see. 'Radio Operator?' – 'Yes?' – 'Switch on Knickebein!' 'Just
> a moment!' – Now we intend to use the signal beam, coming from
> far across the sea, to make the approach to the target. A little more

to the right, then we are right on course. The previously observed illumination ahead has now taken on a blood-red tint. The whole sky above it is lit up. Since it is exactly on our course, this has to be Coventry, already burning from the previous waves of attacks. In anticipation, the anti-aircraft fire is getting more insistent. Now we are over the burning town, at our great altitude visible down there like a blood-red speck the size of a five-mark piece. 'Boy oh boy, I've never seen anything like this,' said Hans, our pilot, who has already had the experience of sixty to seventy missions in this war. What must it look like down there? Far away we see a few flares swaying wearily back and forth. Their glimmer is as nothing against the powerful light of the moon and of the fires down below. No, those are no longer individual fires, this is one huge conflagration! – How ridiculous seems the blue-tinted shimmer of the decoy fires that Tommy has just lit to one side of the target, in an attempt to distract us. Now we are really close to the target. Pillars of smoke rise up towards us.

A short discussion with the crew. We intend to fly right over the burning town, then turn and fly back, with the moon behind us, to attack a huge building whose wide roof we can see gleaming below us. I check my bomb-release and aiming equipment. We make the turn and reverse our course. Getting to my knees, I am able to use the optical mechanism to release the bombs . . .⁹

There were indeed landmarks visible in the extraordinarily clear conditions. After the raid, Coventry legend had it that the Germans had oriented themselves by looking out for Coombe Pool, a large lake on a country estate east of the city that had long belonged to the Earls of Craven. The Sixth Earl had the place laid out by the famous eighteenth-century landscape architect Lancelot 'Capability' Brown, a man fond of large water features. However, the house, known as Coombe Abbey, had been sold off after the First World War, to a prosperous Coventry house builder by the name of John George Gray, who was still in residence in 1940. There was, in fact, truth to the legend. It was learned from a captured German airman, who took part in the Coventry raid – which doubtless destroyed at least some of the numerous homes Mr Gray had built earlier in the century – that crews on 14 November had been briefed to 'use a small lake north-east of Binley as a pin-point, from which Coventry was about one minute's flying time to the west'. Another was recorded referring to a 'large lake to the right of the target' (i.e. east of Coventry) which, along with a fork in the main northbound railway line, had enabled him to find the factory he had been told to aim for. In both cases, the description and location of the lake fitted Coombe Pool.[10]

Each crew involved in the raid had a specific target, in fact. Many certainly tried to find them, either by sight or by beam. Some, of course, were situated quite near the heart of town. Others were not. All the same, it was soon clear that, although bombing was scattered over a wide area, the damage diminished noticeably with the distance from the original aiming point. Most of the crucially important 'shadow factories' on the outskirts were unaffected. All in all, an extraordinary proportion of the bombs dropped fell in or near the city centre, with obvious consequences. It was hard to ignore the impression, correct or not, that this had been deliberate policy on the Luftwaffe's part.

Everyone still alive in Coventry who was there that day remembers the sounding of sirens a few minutes after seven that evening. Others had already left the city before dark, whether by coincidence or habit developed during the previous weeks of constant alarms and regular air attacks of varying severity. Their story would be different, but for the vast majority of ordinary Coventrians, unwilling or unable to leave their homes and factories to avoid the bombing, the long night began with more or less practised moves to places of safety.

There were, of course, initially no indications that the attack was special or unusual. After weeks of false alarms and relatively minor attacks, some civilians had become blasé:

. . . for some reason the sirens seemed to go off quite early in the evening. And because of that we went into a street shelter, which we didn't normally do, we normally went into the underground shelter in Primrose Hill Park. Looking back, I think my mum must have thought, oh, it's early in the evening, it's only going to be a short session. Which turned out to be a very, very long one.

Maybe people weren't taking it too seriously, but they started to come in almost as if they were coming off the street, you know. As it got worse, you could actually feel the road shaking, not really moving, but it was certainly shaking. Each time we had the lull, people started saying, oh, it'll soon be the All Clear, but it wasn't. Then the men who were on the street, in the Home Guard, kept coming and saying, oh, it's quite close, it's in the city centre.[11]

Not everyone had a shelter in the garden, and by no means everyone trusted the public shelters, especially the brick-built surface ones. Plenty of families did what they could in the house. Favourite refuges were improvised dens beneath a sturdy kitchen or living-room table or under the stairs. As one woman who was ten years old at the time of the raid recalled, 'We went under the stairs in our house . . . it was all made out, there were some cushions to sit on, and my brothers put up some shelves and we used to have little tins of sweets – Parkinson's Humbugs and acid drops and all sorts . . .'[12]

For most families, however, their procedure following the air raid warning had already become routine. As Stan Morris described the experience:

All our shoes and clothes went into a big bag, like a pillow case hanging on the bedroom doorknob. It was a case of, grab this bag, down to the shelter. To a child, it was more exciting than scary. And of course then the real bangs and whatever started. You just had to learn, every time you heard the crunch and things like that, the actual place it shook, you know, just like a jelly![13]

The Morrises' shelter was an Anderson, in their back garden. In many cases, the family would be sent to the shelter at the start of the evening, even before the alarm. The first raids, earlier in the autumn, had terrified Beryl Brown's family so much that her father installed two bunks in their shelter – one for her brothers, the other for her parents and her, who had to share – 'so we could sleep some time anyway, before the raid started or after the raid's finished'.

Some suburban families shared a shelter with neighbours:

At the time of the great Blitz, the council had provided us with an Anderson shelter in the rear garden, which we had to share with the Rose family that lived next door to us. Inside the shelter we had a bunk bed.

I was on the top at the time of the big raid. We just got in the shelter as soon as the sirens went. It was a very frightening time for all concerned. I could sense amongst the adults the panic when the raid started. I wasn't particularly fearful myself because I didn't appreciate what it meant, but certainly my godparents, my mother and my grandmother were all in a state of panic. The noise of the planes was overwhelming. It was a monotonous drone . . . you know, err-uh-err-u-err . . . wave after wave came over, dropping their bombs, and their incendiaries of course.[14]

Doubly terrifying was the plight of three young, even more recent, immigrants who, extraordinarily, had been born and spent most of their childhoods in the same country as the Luftwaffe pilots now bombing the city. Bertha and Inge Engelhard, then seventeen and ten respectively, along with their thirteen-year-old brother, Theo, had been spirited out of Munich just before the war, beneficiaries of the great rescue project for Jewish children in Nazi Germany, the famous *Kindertransport*. As part of this scheme, one of the few generous practical gestures extended towards Germany's imperilled Jewish population by the outside world, almost 10,000 Jewish children from Germany, Austria, and, after its absorption into the Nazi sphere, Czechoslovakia, were allowed to come – without their parents – to Great Britain.

Since it was a condition of the British parliament's approval for the scheme that the young refugees not become a 'burden' on the taxpayer, it was financed by Jewish charities. Many of the *Kinder* were allocated foster parents among the British Jewish community. Some were not,

and the Engelhard children were among these. They ended up with
Bill and Vera, a Coventry couple, and, though they were grateful to
have got out of Nazi Germany, it was not a happy arrangement.

The fostering couple turned out to be very interested in the pay-
ments they got from the sponsoring charity, to the exclusion of many,
if not most, other considerations. The children were also expected
to work in the home, especially Bertha, who acted more or less as an
unpaid maid. 'Uncle' Bill, it further turned out, was dangerous if left
alone with the Engelhard girls – initially with the elder, Bertha, and
later with Inge as she grew into adolescence. As for school, although
the children made friends, they could nonetheless find themselves
being bullied as 'Jews' one moment, and as 'Nazis', the next, by fellow
pupils with a limited recognition of political realities.[15]

In fact, neither the Engelhard children nor their foster family should
have been in Coventry on the night of the big attack. Although he
had built a shelter in the garden, Bill, who seems to have earned a
good living from repairing bomb-damaged buildings, had decided,
after the first German night attacks earlier that autumn, to find a
refuge outside the city. He had managed to rent a room in a cottage
in a rural village outside the city limits, where they could sleep safely
through the dangerous hours. Initially, they had all piled into his car
before nightfall every evening and driven out there. As Bertha, the
oldest, recalled:

Of course it didn't take the people there long to cotton on to the fact
that we weren't English, by the way we spoke, and they said, who are
these children? Oh well, they are from Germany, they are Jewish children. Well, the word Jewish didn't mean anything to them, they were
very sort of uneducated, quite ignorant people, and to them we were
the Germans. We don't want any b***** Germans in the house, you
can come but you leave those kids behind, we don't want them.

So what do they do? They are in a terrible quandary. A beautiful
shelter had been dug in the neighbourhood, we were on the outskirts
of Coventry . . . there was nothing to stop us from staying home.
We were begging, let us stay home and you go! We don't mind. In

fact, we would have been ever so happy down in the shelter with the other residents. But of course they were ashamed. How can you blame them? How can they? So what do they do? They couldn't let us stay in the shelter, they were ashamed of the neighbours. So they had the brainwave of sending us to their mum's, on the Holyhead Road, right in the thick of the Blitz.[16]

Bill and Vera, and their own young daughter, continued to leave for the country every night before the alarm sirens went. Every evening, instead of accompanying them, the Engelhard children would walk two miles into the city on the Holyhead Road.* Fortunately, Vera's mother, Queenie, who ran two boarding houses with large cellars that were used as shelters, was altogether more kind to the children than her daughter had been. Queenie, as it happened, had another teenage German Jewish girl from the *Kindertransport*, Elsie Pape (from Nuremburg), living with her and working as a maid. Elsie, who was the same age as Bertha, became her friend. Terrifying as the experience of bombing remained, when the Engelhard children were with Queenie and Elsie, at least they felt looked after.

At the factories, too, both in the city centre and the suburbs, the workforce also took to the shelters. Most of the larger works had spacious, purpose-built shelters available in or near their premises by the time the big attack occurred, though usually a small number of men volunteered to stay upstairs in the factory to watch for fires and other disasters, ready to try to tackle them before they got out of control. Len Dacombe, then twenty-three and working at Coventry Climax Engines' factory in Widdrington Road (known as the Godiva Works), about a mile north of the centre, was just such a fire-watching volunteer:

We had several strings of bombs across, fairly early on. One hit a machine and knocked it over, and another one hit a sprinkler stop-valve system, and I could see the factory's getting flooded, and so I

* The busy main road (now the A4114) leading north-west out of the city centre of Coventry, linking up with the A45 trunk road to Birmingham.

managed to find a wheel to turn it off. Later on, we had another string
of bombs right across the factory. I had a little brick shelter in the
middle of the machine shop and this string of bombs, it had seven,
I could hear these seven coming down. And one crashed through the
concrete about ten, fifteen feet away and I felt it tunnelling underneath the concrete, going underneath me, and I thought, this is the
end. But it didn't go off. It was a delayed action bomb. The rest all
exploded, so very, very fortunate.[17]

It was at this time, fairly early in the raid, that a schoolboy who
lived between Coventry and Birmingham had the chance to examine
the situation above the city from a place of relative safety. His mother
was working nights in a munitions factory, his stepfather, a storeman
with the local council, was on duty ensuring that supplies of sand,
ballast and sandbags could be sent where needed. Donald Thompson,
thirteen years old, ventured out of the shelter in the family's garden,
where he had been told to spend the night, and stared out at the sky
over Coventry:

I was absolutely fascinated – if that's the right word – to be standing
outside the shelter literally watching the German aircraft circling
above the city with their navigation lights on, if you please, so
that they wouldn't collide with each other before they started their
bombing run . . .[18]

Young Donald was most certainly not the only observer, whether
fascinated, terrified or both, who, as the Germans appeared to bomb
Coventry with insouciant impunity, was asking, from outside or inside
a shelter, a crucial question, spoken or unspoken.
Where was the RAF?

11

Executive Cold Water

The formal order – 'Executive Cold Water' – had gone out from the Air Ministry at 16:15, addressed to Bomber, Fighter and Coastal Commands, plus 80 Wing.[1] It was the signal for upgraded defensive operations and a series of pre-arranged retaliatory measures.

A minute from earlier that day, signed by Air Commodore Stevenson, Director of Home Operations at the Ministry, had contained a later handwritten note with updates on the situation regarding intercepted German communications and the RAF's reaction:

> The 13:00 hours signal was made today and acknowledged by HQ, Air Fleet 3:
>
> C.A.S.* decided to go with 'Cold Water', and I spoke to Commands and issued instructions . . . at 16:15 hours.[2]

As the codename implied, the grand idea was for a cold douche that would, so the Air Staff hoped, make the Germans realise that they could not act without consequences. It would also coincidentally help counteract any negative effects that a major attack such as 'Moonlight Sonata' might have, should it succeed, on popular morale.

The original 'Cold Water' memo had been submitted by the Director of Home Operations on 12 November 1940 when, so he wrote,

* C.A.S. = Chief of Air Staff.

the information (from Ultra and other sources) that they had was 'good enough to prepare a plan':

> In all probability, we should get further information from the same sources which should indicate at short notice the night on which Moonlight Sonata and our counter-plan 'Cold Water' should take place.

The actual detailed and apparently comprehensive aspects of this plan have been described in chapter eight. So, what actually happened once the target was identified and the order had gone out? It might be thought that, given K.G.100's key role in setting up the target for the main bomber fleet, its base at Vannes would have been bombed as early as possible. Indeed, the order had specifically stated: 'This attack, if not carried out at dusk, should be carried out as early in the night as possible.'³ This would be the responsibility of bombers from Coastal Command.

The RAF report on the attack on Vannes gave no time, simply stating (under the rubric, 'Coastal Command's Effort'):

> No. 59 Squadron dropped 32 bombs on Vannes aerodrome plus 6 incendiaries. One large fire and several small ones seen. Bursts were seen on runways and also in dispersal areas.

At any rate, it is clear that the pathfinder aircraft were by this time long gone, and Coventry was under accurate and concentrated attack due in great part to K.G.100's efforts. According to a German post-war account, based on war diaries and personal accounts, the attack on Vannes did not, in fact, take place until well after midnight, and the details were somewhat different:

> During that same night, the aerodrome at Vannes-Meucon was attacked between 00:50 and 07:50 by British bombers, which dropped around 20 high explosive and numerous incendiary bombs. This attack led to the destruction of a barracks building, while three aircraft were slightly and one seriously damaged.⁴

No explanation is available as to why this was the case, totally against the original intention of the plan. It's hard to see the silence on this matter as implying anything other than a bureaucratic cover-up.

Another account described a solitary British attack on an aerodrome as twenty aircraft from KG2* prepared to take off for the first of two trips to Coventry planned for that night:

We are standing by our aircraft, on the runway and ready to take off, when a 'Tommy' appears. It is almost full moon, with a cloudless sky. The 'Tommy' is flying at around 800 metres [2,600 ft], he can be recognised as a 'stranger' quite clearly from the sound of his engines.

We are standing by our 'crates', each loaded with twenty bombs, when suddenly there's the howling and whistling of sirens. Three flares light up.

Now everyone rushes for cover or lies flat on the ground. Already the first bombs are whooshing down. I go like the blazes for an open shelter trench, don't see the wires stretched at the entrance and fall headlong – but into full cover. The aerodrome flak hammers away for dear life.

Then, for a short while, there is peace. 'Tommy' has hit nothing. All the same, we can't yet think of taking off. So we withdraw to the edge of the airfield, into a sunken lane. We hear the Englishman coming back. Our light flak opens fire, with around six guns. It is a glorious drama, with the tracer bullets whizzing cross-cross around the aerodrome. The entire event causes general hilarity.

For a long time, even after the shooting has stopped, the fragments of anti-aircraft shells come whining down from the sky, clattering harmlessly down to earth. 'Tommy' repeats his attack, with admirable boldness, another five or six times. Once I can't resist, and I peep over

---

* According to the operational list, that would be one of two airfields in the neighbourhood of Cambrai, inland near the Belgian border, or (less likely) one at Boissy-Saint-Léger, south-east of Paris.

the top of the sunken lane. In fact, on the other side of aerodrome, two bombs have fallen, and they create glowing fountains of fire.

The bogus aerodrome that has been created next door supplies the much-needed distraction. 'Tommy' dumps his entire 'offering' on the festively lit 'night aerodrome'. 'Fires' show him that he has bombed successfully. In fact, these are heaps of hay, soaked with used engine oil.

Finally, we take off . . . [5]

There was clearly some inconvenience caused to the Luftwaffe units queuing up to take off for Coventry. Once they got into the air, there was virtually no problem for them, except missing a beam – but in that case, the clear, moonlit night made it easy for them to find the target by other means.

A great deal of Bomber Command, meanwhile, was committed to attacking the Reich, and especially – so it had been decided – Berlin, which always seemed favoured by the RAF planners when it came to showing the British capacity for striking back. According to the official report, twelve Wellington bombers were recorded as having attacked the 'Schlesiger station' (sic – the *Schlesischer Bahnhof*, now known as the *Ostbahnhof*) in the Reich capital. 'Incendiaries were seen to burst in and around the station and marshalling yards, with 12 explosions alongside a train. 3 large explosions caused red fires which in turn caused green explosions. 3 fires on the S.W. edge of the target were seen for 20 minutes by circling aircraft.'[6] Eight Whitleys also attacked the 'Pulitzstraße' (sic – actually Putlitzstraße) marshalling yard in Moabit, a working-class suburb in the west of Berlin. 'Many large and small fires started. Explosions seen in target area.'

Another group of bombers raided the aerodrome at Schiphol in the Netherlands, now an important Luftwaffe base. There was also a small raid against Hamburg, and some isolated 'disturbance attacks' on the Luftwaffe model against the Ruhr and the synthetic oil plants at Gelsenkirchen and Leuna, but the Berlin raid was the 'headliner'.

Stevenson had written two days earlier of the necessity for a 'big bang': '. . . we should remember that the best way of turning cold water on an operation of this kind from the point of John Citizen is to hit back at a similarly important area in Germany as hard as we can'. He had requested that special whistles be fitted to the bombs to create the most marked effect on enemy morale.[7]

However, as things turned out, and as so often at this stage in the war, this was by no means Bomber Command's finest hour. Of the eighty-two bombers that took off from British airfields that night for the great retaliatory raid, fifty were supposed to attack Berlin, but of these only half reported reaching the city. Ten aircraft were lost, the highest number during any single night so far in the war.[8] The next day, the Air Ministry communiqué referred mainly to a 'Successful Attack on a Railway Station'.[9]

In other retaliatory operations, while the attack on Coventry was already at its height, two of 80 Wing's specially equipped 'radio bombers' did manage to fly 'down the beams' and attack some of the German transmitters on the Cherbourg peninsula that were perceived as helping the Luftwaffe's bombers on their way to Coventry. Too late, of course, to stop K.G.100's pathfinder activities, which were the key to the lethal accuracy of the raid that followed. And, as we know, attempts at jamming the 'Rivers' beams were wholly unsuccessful on this night. One transmitter was seriously damaged, nevertheless, and another shut down, while the raid was still proceeding, meaning that some of the main bomber force that attempted to use *Knickebein* for their return from Coventry to their bases could not do so.[10] The beam station that shut down was thought to have switched off its signal in order to prevent the RAF from finding the 'silent zone' directly above it that indicated the presence of a transmitter complex.[11]

The next day, Squadron Leader S. O. Bufton, commander of the 'radio bombers' unit, put in for another six Whitley or Wellington aircraft, protesting that he could not do his job effectively with only two. As his superior reported, writing on Bufton's behalf directly to the newly appointed Deputy Chief of the Air Staff (Air Vice-Marshal Arthur Harris):

> He points out that with only two aircraft operating he may succeed in putting a station out of operation for a time (as he did last night) or a lucky shot may score a direct hit. But he cannot hope, with this small effort, for destructive effect. [12]

Bufton's small victory against the danger presented by the German beams was one of the few positive aspects of the night's operations, so far as the RAF was concerned. A curious discovery is that, vital as these beams were to the success of the Luftwaffe's night bombing, some German air crew, at least, were afflicted by a strange belief. They worried that, if the British could track the guidance signals, then the RAF's night fighters would be lurking along the beams, ready to destroy any German bombers following them to or from their targets. In consequence, such air crew tended to use traditional navigation methods whenever weather and visibility permitted. [13]

The Germans were surprised that, given the perfect conditions, hordes of British fighters were not waiting for them as they approached the target that night. A conversation secretly recorded at the POW. Interrogation centre clearly expressed this (participants in conversation identified only by numbers in original):

> A 659: Did you see any night fighters?
>   A 653: No, none.
>   A 659: We had two. I saw tracers whizz past my cockpit.
>   A 653: One crew is supposed to have seen sixteen in formation. They flew past pretty close.
>   A 659: We flew at 4,500 [metres = around 15,000 ft] over Coventry. I was surprised we saw no night fighters there. From above they could have seen us wonderfully clearly, because everything was illuminated below. [14]

The truth was, in fact, that the Germans' fears were utterly unnecessary. Although the British night-fighter pilots knew the enemy bombers were there, and were, on occasion, informed by observers watching from the ground that they were present in huge quantities, they still could not find them.

John Cunningham, a British night-fighter pilot who patrolled the air over England all through that autumn and winter, including the night of 14/15 November, recalled ruefully of the German bombers:

They were certainly very seldom if ever intercepted, certainly in the main mass of the raids, so that I remember being surprised that sometimes the gunners didn't fire back, or didn't fire at us. I remember one or two of us thinking, perhaps they're so confident, they're not even looking out. They may even be playing cards or something. But not concerned. Because the night fighters, as far as they were concerned, were very ineffective – well, totally ineffective . . .[15]

As for the night when Coventry was bombed:

I remember seeing the enormous glow in the sky. We were flying from Middle Wallop,* and from Middle Wallop generally southwards to the Channel, and one could see this glow in the Midlands. I didn't know exactly where, and that was a very long distance away. Before taking off, on one of those nights, on the ground at Middle Wallop, I was not only able to hear but to see, on some occasions, a few trails. They weren't very high, those German aircraft then, about ten or fifteen thousand feet was the sort of average height they were coming in, but in November on some occasions propeller aeroplanes would leave trails. And being on the ground looking up, of course . . . [but] going off in the Beaufighter you neither hear anything nor do you see – when you're flying at that height you can't see – these trails, and feeling not really impotent but thinking, oh God, if only this radar will work.

It was not incompetence that caused Cunningham's frustration. He was a brave and highly skilled airman. The problem was, indeed, that in November 1940 on-board radar, by and large, did not work.

* Near Stockbridge, in Hampshire.

Within a few months, with the introduction of improved equipment and aircraft, and a new ground control system (GCI) it would be a different story. Cunningham himself would achieve his first 'kill' roughly a week after the Coventry raid, and, soon nicknamed 'Cats-Eyes Cunningham' by the British press, would become a recipient of the DFC and Britain's most celebrated night-fighter pilot.[16] But that was much later in the winter.

Meanwhile, fighters without radar had virtually zero chance of success. One pilot, based at a small airfield near Northolt, just outside London, described his experience in even gloomier terms. Having heard there was something 'going on', he returned to the airfield and met up with a fellow pilot there:

I mean, I didn't know at that time, it was the night of the Coventry thing. And he said, I'm taking off now, you take off three quarters of an hour's time, and we'll see what we do after that. Well, we didn't have a flare path, we had nothing except one Glim lamp at the end of the runway. It was a moonlit night, I mean it wasn't pitch-black or anything like that. And I duly went off. The air was full of bombers. It just shows what I think everybody knows. Without a radar it's like looking for a needle in a haystack. I was being told from the ground that there were bombers here there and everywhere. They would pick one and I would go for it, but I never saw it. And eventually I went all the way down to the south coast, with a bomber allegedly off my starboard wing tip. From the ground. I never saw it. And then it was time to come home.[17]

The next day, a demand would go out from the highest Air Ministry quarters to Fighter Command, asking for explanations of why, with well over a hundred fighters patrolling the approaches to Coventry, so few contacts had been made with German bombers, and why none of the intruders had been shot down:

C.A.S. would appreciate detailed information as to reasons for com-
paratively few interceptions made on night of 14/15th Nov. in spite

of fine weather, moonlight, and considerable fighter effort exerted. Details of A.I. performance particularly requested.[18]

The answers would make excruciating reading.

And then there were the final elements: the barrage balloons and the anti-aircraft artillery. Eight extra balloons were, in fact, launched into the air above Coventry on the day of the raid, reinforcing the fifty-six already active around the city.[19] Their main effect was to keep the enemy aircraft, wary of getting caught in the dangerous jungle of hawsers that kept the balloons aloft, as high as possible, so as to make aiming more difficult. The evidence seems to be that on the night of 14/15 November this more or less worked. However, given the other meteorological and technical advantages enjoyed by the German attackers on that occasion, this did not seem to affect the accuracy of their bombing to any serious extent.

Like the Fire Brigade, the dozen anti-aircraft batteries of 95 Heavy AA Regiment in and around Coventry suffered serious practical problems due to the intensity of the bombing. Attached to the 34th (South Midlands) Brigade of the Royal Artillery, 4th Anti-Aircraft Division, they were technically part of the army. However, like all AA units at that time, they were in practice subordinate to and in direct receipt of instructions from Fighter Command. In this case, orders were issued by 12th Fighter Group, based in the East Midlands at Hucknall in Nottinghamshire. The AA had been further reinforced on 12 November with a dozen light Bofors anti-aircraft guns, in response to the calls for improvements in the city's defences that had gone out at the beginning of the month.[20]

Regimental HQ was quartered in Rosehill, a fine old mansion in St Nicholas Street, less than a mile north of the city centre. In the early Victorian era, the house had been home to the wealthy Bray family, whose thriving ribbon-making business had supported a range of philanthropic and artistic endeavours and a lively social circle that included the Nuneaton-born novelist George Eliot (Mary

Ann Evans), author of *Middlemarch*, who during the 1840s lived in nearby Foleshill with her father. A hundred years later, bombs were dropping around the grounds, and all except those directly involved in directing the defence took to the shelter. The main problem was loss of communication during the early part of the night between HQ and the batteries. According to the regimental War Diary, 7,290 rounds (i.e. shells) were fired during the course of the night, in 128 barrages. A 620-lb delayed-action bomb landed in the grounds (it is not recorded if it went off).[21]

The serious difficulties with the telephone lines, which began at around 19:40, forty minutes after the 'Take Post' message had been received from RAF Hucknall, included frequent complete loss of contact and unexplained interference from the BBC Radio (service not specified). Attempts to get help from the faults department at the Post Office, then responsible for the public telephone system, proved fruitless – as the report commented drily, 'the staff having presumably retired to a place of greater safety'. The local electricity mains was shattered by a bomb impact, but at HQ an emergency generator quickly came into action, restoring lighting and the operation of essential equipment.[22]

By the small hours, contact had been restored with almost all the batteries, whether by direct phone line or by radio. Any injuries were slight. Coventry's gunners certainly made every effort. At the height of the attack, they had even managed to transport mobile guns into the centre of the city and start firing up at the German raiders from Broadgate, the main shopping street, and Pool Meadow – the latter the largest open space left in the city centre, used for fairs and parades.[23] All the same, according to a later account by the CO of the Coventry batteries, Colonel Lawrence of the Royal Artillery, he was called to the telephone at around 10:30 p.m., to find himself addressing an extremely irate Prime Minister. Churchill demanded to know who he was and what he was doing about the Germans who were devastating the city. 'With bombs dropping all round my Gun Operations Room,' Lawrence told Norman Longmate many years later, 'I assured him that all were doing their best.'[24]

As for the point of the night's work, three downed enemy aircraft were claimed in the regimental War Diary. Whether there was much truth in this seems very doubtful. The claim had gone down to two by the time the Brigade's War Diary was written up.[25]

In fact, the only German aircraft officially considered to have been shot down that night actually crashed, killing its crew, near the East Midlands town of Loughborough (almost forty miles from Coventry) at 10 p.m. The Dornier 17, supposedly following a *Knickebein* beam, had been supposed to bomb Coventry at around half past nine, but it never got there. According to RAF Intelligence estimates, when lost the aircraft had gone twenty-five miles off course. There is no indication of whether this was due to 'bending' of the *Knickebein* beam or some other interference by British radio counter-measures units, but it can be said for certain that local batteries around Loughborough and not the Coventry AA were responsible.[26]

It was always hard to avoid the impression that, at least at this stage in the air war, the chief function of anti-aircraft guns was to hearten those under attack, to provide some proof that they were not entirely helpless and defenceless; that somewhere, perhaps nearby, someone was striking back against the cruel and relentless threat from the sky.[27]

Of course it was frightening, but there was great excitement too, and I used to go out, if I could get out of the house, and listen to the shrapnel and the shelling, the anti-aircraft fire and the bombs, which would come down like rain on the roof tiles. You could hear that clattering away.[28]

The din they made, explosions often all but indistinguishable from the detonation of bombs, was nonetheless also frightening and unsettling. The air raid victim was grateful for the guns but unnerved by them, too.

The raids were so loud. The anti-aircraft guns, really, made it louder than anything. They were all round. There must have been hundreds around Coventry. Along the railway line they were going off all night, trying to get these German bombers down, and the searchlights were criss-crossing the sky. It was a moonlight night. Everything was clear. Sometimes they got a bomber in it and you could see it, the black dot of the bomber, and the guns tried to get it. That was awe-inspiring.[29]

It must have felt as if there were 'hundreds' of guns around Coventry, as nine-year-old John Huthwaite supposed, and perhaps that too was a comfort, for all the horrific noise. There was, of course, also physical danger from the guns, especially those dispersed among the city streets.

There was also a very large naval gun at the end of our road, at the pub. And when that fired, it lifted you off the ground. Literally, lifted you off the ground. Incredible.[30]

The guns fired their shells thousands of feet in the air, aiming for the enemy bombers. Then, of course, obeying the law of gravity, the shells had to fall to earth, by which time they were shattered to shrapnel and the metal of their casings was often on fire. As one eyewitness, then a teenage ARP messenger running errands through the mayhem, remembered:

I got on my bike, and I went down the Allesley Old Road towards town. All the searchlights were swinging round the skies, and cross-ing. The anti-aircraft guns were exploding. The bombs were falling in the city centre, and towards where I was cycling a great big red glow where the centre of the city was already burning. This shrapnel, big shards of red hot shrapnel were coming down, hitting the roofs, and bouncing on the road in front of me as I cycled towards the town.[31]

This happened after midnight. 'Cold Water' was now all but over. The Luftwaffe's punishment of Coventry continued unabated, however, and would do so almost until dawn.

12

'A seething mass of flame'

Almost every street in Coventry, deep out into the suburbs, would suffer more or less badly that night from the bombing, but it was the centre that underwent near-destruction. With the advent of the first waves of the main bomber force, high-explosive bombs began raining down on to the largely medieval streets, devastating old buildings, further opening up roof spaces – many of them, given their age, wood-framed structures – to the danger of rapid-spreading fires from the great quantities of incendiary bombs that continued to be dropped. This was, of course, all part of the plan.

At Gulson Street Municipal Hospital, on the southern edge of the densely populated historic area, casualties were beginning to pour in. As a mere volunteer stretcher-bearer, young Dennis Adler felt helpless as he watched those who had suffered horrible injuries, and those already beyond hope, being brought in from the surrounding streets:

A lady was brought in a stretcher carrying a baby but both of them were dead. They had been killed by blast. There was no injuries. No damage on them at all. It was just a matter of moving her into an area where we already had a number of people who had died, unfortunately.[1]

Much closer to the centre, and so to the developing inferno, was the hundred-year-old Coventry and Warwickshire Hospital, in Swanswell Terrace, up from Pool Meadow. The staff had been sitting down to their evening meal when the sirens sounded and preparations for possible casualties had to begin. It was not the first time Coventry had been bombed, of course, but within a quite short time it was clear that this attack was something different and infinitely more serious.

Dr George Forrest was a young house physician who had only been in his job two weeks and whose knowledge of the layout of the hospital and the whereabouts of all the necessary equipment was still rather sketchy. On his way to his assigned post, he was passing one of the wards when the sister in charge grabbed him and said: 'There's an incendiary bomb in here.'

It had come in through the glass conservatory. So there was a St John's Ambulance man there and I got the stirrup pump and worked the stirrup and he hosed the incendiary bomb down. And that almost put it out so he then took a pail of sand and put it on the top and the damn thing exploded and he got badly cut, I remember that. I had to deal with him before I got to my own official post. The air raid was ushered in by a kind of *whoosh* and these are the incendiary bombs coming down by the gross. And the house governor, that's the administrative head, was up on the roof watching to see whether they were landing. And Winter was patrolling the grounds because there was nothing, nobody had come in at that time, just the incendiaries you see, just the fires, and Winter shouted, 'There's a fire in the laundry'. By this time guns were firing and distant bombs and lights in the sky and patients all sat out under the beds and the rest of it and the house governor shouted from the top, 'Be quiet Mr Winter, you'll waken the patients'.[2]

The 'Winter' mentioned in Dr Forrest's account was Harry Winter, another doctor at the hospital. 'We put the patients on stretchers and blankets along the main corridor,' Dr Winter wrote later. 'Then the casualties started to come in, so fast that we didn't have time for detailed examinations. All we could do was divide them into resuscitation cases and those requiring immediate surgery. I suppose I did about 15 operations throughout the night.'

Like so many others who had crucial tasks to perform in Coventry that night, Dr Forrest fell back on training and routine as a way of pushing fear into the background:

There's a tendency when the chips are down that you tend to follow your routine and just keep on doing it till something stops you and that's the way we were I think. I don't think many of us had any real thoughts along these – I mean every time the bombers came you thought to yourself, is this my lucky or unlucky day or time, but it wasn't, I don't think there was any, there was no panic in the place at all.

Soon the electricity supply had gone, the water had gone, windows had been blown in by explosions in the vicinity of the hospital. Operations became impossible because of lack of light and power. Though the structure of the hospital was still intact, the staff were reduced to parking patients in the corridor on stretchers and doing what they could with the dressings and basic painkillers they had to hand.

We became very expert at diving below beds when the bombs were coming. And they used to come in sticks of four; one, two, three, four. After the fourth one you breathed easily for a few minutes till the next plane came along and then four came again. You could hear them, obviously could hear them wherever they were landing in the town or round about. So you just, you could hear them coming nearer, which wasn't very nice at all.

The hospital dealt with hundreds of casualties that night, up to four or five hundred. Especially in the early period of the raid, the fire service was put under huge stress, dealing with the combination of incendiary and high-explosive bombs that was already threatening to destroy the entire city centre.

Twenty-six firefighters, many of them volunteers, died, and thirty-four were seriously injured during the course of the night.[3] An entire team of firefighters from Stoke-on-Trent, who had answered Coventry's call for help, were killed by a high-explosive bomb while trying to lay surface pipes from the Swanswell Pool, one of the few remaining sources of usable water once the mains had been put out of action.[4] Dr Forrest added: 'I used to hate to see the stretchers coming in . . . with men wearing long black boots. They were the auxiliary fire service and they took an awful beating that night, an awful lot of casualties. They were the ones I remember best.'

By nine o'clock that night, more than two hundred fires were registered as requiring Fire Brigade attention. Others were dealt with on an ad hoc basis by emergency services on the spot. After the telephones broke down, many more were not registered at all.

With almost no mains water available, the Fire Brigade was forced to lay hoses to the River Sherbourne, which fortunately was in full flow that night, and proved a reliable, if limited, source of water to fight the fires, and also, initially, to the canal basin, which abutted the city centre at Leicester Row. There was also some supply from Swanswell Pool, just a block away from the Coventry and Warwick Hospital, as well as swimming pools, static tanks and reservoirs – including those belonging to factories, which, as the Chief Fire Officer's report tartly pointed out, ' in some cases . . . had only been installed after much persuasion'.[5]

All the same, as the night wore on the water situation deteriorated dramatically. The most painful further loss to the Brigade's hope of getting on top of the fires was that of the Coventry Canal, which before the war had been earmarked as the crucial reserve of water in a serious fire emergency.[6] A storm water culvert that ran under the canal was blown apart by a German bomb, leading the water from the canal to drain away. This suddenly and very effectively eliminated the canal as a firefighting resource in the city centre, though its waters could apparently still be used for putting out fires in the factories and residential areas that lined its banks further out in the suburbs.[7]

There was a slight veil drawn over the city centre water supply situation in Chief Cartwright's otherwise exemplary report. Others would be more frank about the real situation, in private, when the time came. What remains absolutely clear is that the greatest, most dramatic and symbolic loss to the city that night – its historic cathedral – occurred in great part because the fires that began to rage within its structure could not be limited, let alone extinguished. They could not be put out simply because there was insufficient water available for the Fire Brigade to do so.

Coventry Cathedral was no less well loved because it had not been a cathedral for long. Coventry had become a bishopric, the town a cathedral city, and the nearly 600-year-old parish Church of St Michael a cathedral, only in 1918.

In the Middle Ages, Coventry had in fact been the seat of the Bishop of Lichfield and Coventry. He resided in Coventry, but at the time of the dissolution of the monasteries the city and its Cathedral – which was historically a Benedictine minster – were demoted by Henry VIII. The treasures were sold off, and the monastery Cathedral church itself demolished on the orders of the King's chief henchman, Sir Thomas Cromwell. It was the only cathedral in England to suffer such a fate.[8] The 400 years it took for Coventry to get back its own bishop and Cathedral is less remarkable if it is remembered that the great city of Birmingham, with more than half a million inhabitants at the time, was only granted the status of an independent bishopric in 1904. Like Coventry a decade and a half later, it had been hived off from the powerful bishopric of Worcester, a clear indication of how long it could take for the Church of England to take account of historical details such as the Industrial Revolution.

Well before it had cathedral status formally granted, St Michael's was a great and rich church – one of the largest parish churches in England – crammed with architectural and religious treasures. In 1900 it was made a Collegiate Church, lending it a status somewhere between a parish church and a cathedral, governed by a college of canons, under the authority of a Dean, but with no bishop as its figurehead.

Unlike most cathedrals in England, St Michael's also retained its status as a parish church, with its own vicar. Beyond parish duties, he also became the Dean, or senior priest, of the Cathedral, with the title of Provost. In 1940, the office of Provost had been exercised for seven years by the fifty-six-year-old Very Reverend Richard Howard. He was present at the Cathedral on the night of 14/15 November, played a prominent role in the gallant but eventually doomed attempt to save it and its contents, and within days of the bombing wrote a vivid eyewitness account of the church's destruction.

Howard describes, in his account, how he and his staff, religious and lay people, did their best to protect the Cathedral from the threat of bombing. There had been several intense raids on Coventry in the late summer and autumn, and they were under no illusion that the Cathedral was safe from attack. At one point, there had been suggestions that the word *KIRCHE* (German for church) should be painted in huge letters on the largely flat roof of the Cathedral – wooden in construction and supported by wooden beams, covered with an outer layer of lead – but this idea was rejected, as was the possibility of covering it with a thick layer of turf to stifle any incendiary bomb that might land there (the latter decision one that Howard later regretted).

Firefighting equipment, including buckets of water and sand, was stored at key points in the building, both down at ground level and immediately beneath the roof space. Fire-watching rotas were set up, though since many able-bodied men were already committed to defending factories and other buildings vital to the war effort, the so-called 'Cathedral Guard' was often understrength. There were supposed to be four on duty every night, but Provost Howard recounts that he and his spouse often found themselves alone on the roof, keeping watch over the Cathedral during the dangerous hours of darkness.[9]

It was clear that the chief threat to the Cathedral, with its wooden roof and interior furnishings, would come from incendiary bombs. On the night of 14 October, exactly a month before the big raid, an incendiary penetrated the lead outer layer of the roof and set a fire in the ancient carved oak ceiling beneath. It was in a place that could not be reached with the stirrup pump and sand buckets that were the only fire-fighting resources immediately to hand. A thousand pounds[*] worth of damage had been inflicted before the Fire Brigade arrived with their hoses and ladders and managed to bring the fire under control. Ladders, axes and crowbars (to force access, where necessary, to the narrow roof space) were duly purchased and stored at the Cathedral. The most precious examples of medieval stained glass had been removed to a place of safety outside the city, and there were plans well advanced to do the same for the precious carved woodwork that was a superb feature of the interior.

Then came 'Moonlight Sonata'. Howard described the scene:

On the night of November 14th the Cathedral roof was slippery and shone white under our feet, for there was frost, and the bright light of the full moon was reflected on the lead.

The guard for that night consisted of Mr Forbes [a stonemason who had recently been hired as a full-time caretaker], aged sixty-five, myself, fifty-six, and two young men in their early twenties. Shortly after we had assembled at seven o'clock, the sirens sounded; and in little more than five minutes we heard the raiders overhead.[10]

The watchers on the Cathedral could see and hear the bombs falling closer and closer until, at eight o'clock, the first incendiaries hit the Cathedral. One fell on the roof of the chancel towards the east end, another burst right through to land on the floor of the church between wooden pews, near the nave, while a third impacted on the roof of the south aisle above the organ. The watchers called from the roof down to the main police station, which lay just across the cobbled street, on the corner of Bayley Lane and St Mary's Street, and alerted them to call the Fire Brigade.

* Around £60,000 in modern values.

The watchers neutralised the bombs on the chancel roof and in pews by smothering them with sand. The bomb above the organ was much more difficult to deal with. It had come in through the lead roof and set the oak ceiling on fire. The roof space was proving to be a deadly nestling place for incendiaries. The watchers hacked a hole in the lead and poured sand in, but the fire had spread out of reach. It took a long time to pump enough water into the space to finally put it out. More incendiaries hit the building. These, too, were put out, but soon the watchers were exhausted and running out of supplies of sand and water. Then came a new shower of incendiaries, four of them striking the roof of a corner of the Cathedral known as the 'Children's Chapel'. A large fire started to blaze in the ceiling. The four of them fought it for a while, until their supplies and their strength gave out and they were forced to retreat.

Still the Fire Brigade had not come. Of course, given the scale of the bombing, Coventry's firemen were totally overwhelmed. The entire city centre was by now a mass of fires, threatening many key factories and public buildings. Roads and streets were blocked, littered with bomb craters. One of the watchers tried to get more water from the only source inside the Cathedral, a tap in a corner of one of the chapels, but was overcome by smoke and had to be rescued by the others.

Finally, Provost Howard and his helpers decided to save what portable treasures they could. The altar cross, candlesticks and the standard candlesticks were rescued from the Smith's Chapel, though it was impossible now to retrieve the fine carved wooden cross from the Children's Chapel, with its sculpted figure of a child kneeling before it. Valuable ornaments and vessels from the sanctuary and the vestries were taken out next, plus precious candlesticks from the high altar, and some medieval silver items and a wooden crucifix. These were all taken across the cobbled lane to the relative safety of the police station. Then all they could do was wrap themselves in blankets in the shelter of the south porch, and wait. For Provost Howard, this time of inactivity, at the mercy of yet more falling bombs, was the worst of all.

At half past nine, the Fire Brigade arrived. Not the Coventry serv-ice, but a team from the Birmingham suburb of Solihull, fifteen miles to the west. They unravelled an extensive set of hoses and raised their ladders. Soon powerful jets of water were playing on the two most dangerously affected parts of the Cathedral: over the blazing roof up top and among the burning pews below.

A few minutes passed, during which the watchers must have permitted themselves to hope that the ancient building might still be saved. Then the mains gave out. The firemen from Birmingham fought gallantly to find another working hydrant, scored two brief successes, but in both cases pressure was low and water soon non-existent. A few more things could be saved, but by shortly after 10:30 the end of the struggle had come. As they prepared to evacuate the Cathedral, Provost Howard was forced to watch the exquisitely carved oak screens and carved misericords (also known as mercy seats) in the Lady Chapel, being consumed by the flames. They had been scheduled for removal to a place of safety and would have been saved had the raid been delayed for just a few more days.

'The firemen now left the Cathedral for the last time,' Howard wrote within days of the church's destruction. 'Nothing more could be done.'

A few more precious objects were found and salvaged before the last firefighters abandoned their task.

> It was now eleven. From then until 1:30 a.m. I was in the porch of the police station in St Mary's Street, along with a dozen of the Solihull Auxiliary Fire Service men. Here we could watch the gradual and terrible destruction of the Cathedral. High explosives were falling continually, some very near; but in the porch we were comparatively sheltered. I had the companionship of the firemen, who, like all watchers of the scene, were filled with horror.[11]

Even the stone pillars in the interior of the Cathedral eventually weakened and collapsed, brought down by the fall of the roofs, which dissolved the finely balanced stresses on the pillars that upheld the heavy masonry above them. As the Provost pointed out, there was, moreover, another thing that the modern guardians of the church had forgotten to take into account. Fifty years earlier, in 1890, hoping to bring modern engineering to the support of medieval craft, late Victorian contractors had laid steel girders to reinforce the massive wooden beams that underpinned the ornate oak ceiling of the building. Now, with the intense heat of the fire, far from acting as a stabilising force, these girders became so twisted that they helped to collapse the walls in on themselves, so destroying the Cathedral to a degree that no one would have thought possible.

> The whole interior was a seething mass of flame and piled-up blazing beams and timbers, interpenetrated and surmounted with dense bronze-coloured smoke. Through this could be seen the concentrated blaze caused by the burning of the organ, famous for its long history back to the time when Handel played on it.

When it became clear that there was no water available to combat the blaze, everyone had expected to lose the interior furnishings and any treasures that could not be moved; in fact, by morning the entire Cathedral would be reduced to a jagged shell, all its interior walls destroyed and only the outermost, red sandstone structure partly intact. The crypt beneath the Cathedral, which had been in use as an air raid shelter earlier in the night but was evacuated for safety's sake when the fire got out of control, remained almost entirely undamaged.

The tall tower of the spire that adjoined the Cathedral remained whole, blackened on the Cathedral side but unharmed. Its clock continued to strike the hour, right through the night. It brought hope to many in the city, but also the illusory belief that the Cathedral had somehow miraculously survived. Only the light of morning would make the terrible truth visible.

Elsewhere, in the heart of the city, the fire struck (or in a few cases failed to strike) God and Mammon without discrimination.

In Spon Street, on the western edge of the city centre, a teenage girl whose parents kept the Rising Sun pub vividly remembered the blood-red reflections in the windows of neighbourhood buildings as the sun set on the cold evening of 14 November. 'As if they were on fire', but the actual fire was still to come:

> We opened the public house at six o'clock, like you used to have to. Policemen knocked the door if you weren't open. And the sirens went off. And of course the bombs started falling. So we went down the cellar.
>
> We just sat there. It got so you listened to the planes coming over and you thought, well, is that one of ours or one of theirs. You could tell by the sound of the engines. There was noise all around. But we worked on the proposition that if you heard it, it had passed over you. It hadn't hit you. Then all of a sudden we heard a mighty crash, because a bomb dropped on Dr Sowen's house at the bottom of Holyhead Road, and Mr Vincent Wyles' butcher's shop, which was the other side of where Fairfax House is now. Missed us, missed the toy shop, and went on a row of cottages in the bottom of the Stretch Yard.* So we were lucky.[12]

Holy Trinity, one of Coventry's famous 'Three Spires' (St Michael's Cathedral and Christ Church were the others), which had dominated the city centre's skyline for centuries, was also the only one of the churches to remain mostly intact. Its vicar, the Reverend Dr Graham Clitheroe, unfashionably convinced that fire rather than gas would be the main danger in case of a major attack, had assiduously collected firefighting equipment and recruited a protection team long before the big raid on the city centre. His resourcefulness paid off when the bombers came.[13]

'Strangely persistent this raid tonight, Kenneth,' Dr Clitheroe recalled observing to his fellow priest, the Reverend Thornton, during

---

* A medieval courtyard behind Spon Street, accessible through an alleyway, so named because it was formerly used to stretch yarn.

the first phase of the attack. Holy Trinity, like the Cathedral, was also a very large and beautiful parish church. It contained, among other things, an early sixteenth-century 'Doom Painting' representing the Last Judgement – one of the few examples of this once common form of medieval church art to escape the puritan iconoclastic destruction of the Reformation. Somehow, apparently by a combination of good organisation and gut determination, Clitheroe and his team managed to save the structure, bar damage to the stained glass in the East and West Windows. They spent the entire night extinguishing fires throughout the building and even pushing bombs off the roof to stop them penetrating through into the church itself.

The saviours of Holy Trinity had to make a choice. The Cathedral was only a couple of hundred yards to the east, along Priory Row, and they could see it burning as they fought to protect their own church, but they felt that they could not leave their own particular piece of Coventry's religious heritage in order to help save another – which might be beyond recovery anyway. The same went for Coventry City Library (also known as the Gulson Library), just across the street. This building housed a conventional lending library founded by the wealthy Quaker silk manufacturer John Gulson but also contained many rare and historic books and papers. At one point, Clitheroe and his companions did consider aiding the fight to save it, but then a new fire broke out in the church, and by the time they had dealt with that, the fire in the Library was out of control and the building doomed.[14]

Broadgate, including the spot where the IRA bomb had been detonated fifteen months earlier, was also mostly destroyed, along with the surrounding business and commercial district. The steel-framed structure of the recently built Owen Owen department store, opened in 1937 on the corner of Trinity and Burges Streets, stood intact, but the roof was blown off and the building within the reinforced walls reduced to a shell. Despite a near-direct hit, the public air raid shelter beneath the store withstood the bombing, and there were no fatal casualties, though at least one auxiliary fireman was lost fighting the blaze.[15]

Another central shopping street, the ancient thoroughfare known for at least six hundred years as Jordan Well, ran west–east for a hundred yards or so from the Council House (Town Hall) to link up with Gosford Street. It was devastated by high-explosive bombs. Among its glories had been the Gaumont cinema, a resplendent Art Deco palace of entertainment built in 1931 in yet another tribute to Coventrian leisure time purchasing power. Because of its location, it was known as 'The Well' to the city's youth, who habituated the cheap ninepenny seats close up against the screen ('straight to the front – and keep your feet off the organ!' as the cinema manager put it).[16] The Gaumont was hit by a high-explosive bomb on the night of 14 November and five people died in or just outside it. Three of the male victims were eighteen, the other thirty-eight, and the solitary female victim was seventeen. Nearby flats and a shelter were also hit and another six killed, including two parents and their adult son, a seventy-one-year-old widow, a sixteen-year-old volunteer police messenger, and a twenty-six-year-old Special Constable, born in Ireland, who was killed outside the shelter while attempting to rescue victims trapped inside.[17] This made eleven deaths in one quite short stretch of street.

From the near-exhaustive lists of the dead drawn up since the war by local researchers, it is possible to plot much of the worst of the inner-city destruction and place it in human terms. Fatalities tended to cluster in individual shelters, when these suffered direct hits, as was the case in Jordan Well. Multiple members of families were often killed. The cellar of the West End Club, a public house in Spon Street, was blown apart, killing at least eight of the customers and local residents sheltering there. Their ages ranged from eight to sixty-nine, including Welsh-born Anne Audrey, wife of the pub's landlord, Bill Roberts, and her small daughter, Audrey Patricia. Mr Roberts, a civil defence volunteer, was away on duty.[18] In the equally historic street of Bull's Yard, a narrow thoroughfare running into the main north–south artery of Hertford Street, three to four hundred yards south of the West End Social Club, a high-explosive bomb fell on to a surface shelter and killed ten civilians. The casualties came entirely from two families: Clara Beatrice Ball, aged thirty-seven, and five of her children – the oldest twelve years old and the youngest three; and Ernest David (forty-four) and Rose May Roberts (forty-eight) – apparently no relations to the victims in the West End Club – and their children Ernest Eric (thirteen) and Leslie Arthur (eleven).

At the Armstrong Siddeley Works in Parkside, meanwhile, a direct hit on one of the factory's shelters caused sixteen deaths, with the youngest victim seventeen and the oldest sixty-one, including a twenty-eight-year-old works nurse, Irish-born Mary Ann Graham, née McCann. Four of those who died there were related – in this case, a Mr and Mrs Collett and their two teenage sons. At companies such as Armstrong Siddeley, children tended to follow their parents on to the factory floor.[19] According to the recollections of a teenage employee, the bomb had hit the shelter serving the office area:

> I made my way to my shelter, which was in my lane.* I was there for quite a number of hours until I think it must have been the early hours of the morning, when the security officer came round to tell us there must have been a direct hit in the shelter by the office, and would anyone go down to see if they could help out.
>
> And I remember going through part of the factory, and parts of the factory were on fire, and then I came to where the bomb had hit this shelter, and there was a huge heap of rubble that had collapsed on top of the shelter. And everywhere I could see in front of me was on fire into the centre of the town. There's nothing I could have done to help anybody. I was completely by myself and there was still bombing going on.[20]

Meanwhile, however, a worker who spent the night in one of the factory's other shelters later recalled that 'we didn't really know what was going on – we couldn't hear a lot down there you know – we didn't realise that the bombing was so much'.[21] The matter of personal

---

* That is, the row or aisle in the factory where he worked at his machine.

survival, and even the way in which the bombing was experienced by those who lived through it, remained a matter of chance.

The Fire Brigade had lost three experienced professional officers and several of its auxiliary firemen in the earlier part of the evening. Its work was now even more drastically hindered by the fact that, in the absence of working telephone lines, communications between units was possible only through messengers. In many cases, according to one who carried out messenger duties that night, the debris blocking the streets made it impossible to travel by bike, so these had to be abandoned and missions continued out on foot, effectively slowing down communications.[22]

So intense had the growing conflagration become that the service was forced to stop tackling individual fires in the city centre. From now on, the men concentrated on preventing their spread to other densely populated inner districts. This was the grim situation at shortly after eleven that night, a little less than four hours after the first bombs had fallen on the city:

By now the position was critical, but, having regard to the assistance on the way, did not appear to be beyond control . . . thereafter we had many difficulties with which to contend. Outside assistance was held up by road blockages at considerable distances from the Central Fire Station, and had to be marshalled and diverted. This presented almost insuperable difficulties. All available messengers and spare men were engaged on piloting and guiding out-of-town crews, but now road blockages were so frequent that traversable routes could only be found by actual trial. Even so it was impossible for the great majority of crews to report to our stations. In the circumstances, of course, guides were instructed to take them straight to fires. In addition, many out-of-town crews found fires and got to work on their own initiative. The messenger system was used to the full extent, but it will be realised that we had a tremendous task in attempting to pilot every assisting crew or convoy via innumerable diversions. The whole time there was a feeling of uncertainty regarding the safe arrival of messengers – not until each one returned to report could any satisfaction be felt.

The fires in the centre of the City eventually combined to make a single incident, and owing to the congested nature of the property there was no alternative but to concentrate on preventing the spread of fire. In spite of attacks upon pump crews working from static supplies (which probably reflected the moonlight and fire glare) and repeated destruction of relay lines, the spread of fire was checked with a large measure of success.[23]

Already, the attack on Coventry had started to resemble something that was, as yet, still new but which later in the war would become horribly familiar, not just to British but also German civilians: air warfare without restraints or limits. The firefighting services available were barely adequate for this scale of technologically sophisticated destruction.

The direction of operations called for strategy and resource for which there were few previous standards to act as guidance. Fatigued and under continual bombardment, they worked incessantly without relief or refreshment. Time out of number, fires were extinguished and buildings practically saved, only for the buildings to be partly or wholly destroyed by fire or H.E. [high-explosive bombs] due to renewed attacks under the eyes of the crews making up equipment.

The mayhem in the city's centre amounted to an even more novel and more frightening phenomenon, which was unleashed when the burning of whole buildings and streets in a heavily built and populated area became so widespread and so intense, and began to reach such a high temperature, that it would demand a new name to express the awesome power of its destructiveness: firestorm.

13

Death in the Suburbs

The 14 November mass raid on Coventry remains notorious for the destruction wrought in the centre of the city, where K.Gr.100 had set the target fires during the early evening. During the long night, its lethal consequences nonetheless spread out well into the suburbs, where many of the factories were, and where many of the people who worked in them, and their families, also had their homes.

In forensic analyses of bombing raids in the Second World War, the question most keenly pursued – by both sides – generally has to do with the extent to which the attack under investigation could be regarded as aimed at military or military-industrial sites, or whether it was, in fact, a 'pure' terror operation. The nature of aerial bombing was (and remains) such that the question keeps cropping up. The answer, in most cases of mass bombardment, is most likely that both elements are, in fact, present. The choice of the centre of Coventry as the target-marking area was visual (once identified, attacking aircraft could spread their attacks by compass points) and practical (a heavy early concentration of bombing there affected central utilities and also civil defence command and control). It was, however, also deliberately psychologically wounding, introducing a strong element of terror – especially as the city centre was internationally known for its historic and architectural significance.

So far as can be seen, most German air crew did actually have
assigned targets, many of them industrial and many in the suburbs,
but POW interrogations also suggest that the infliction of damage on civilian areas and their populations was factored into the
account. 'It is known,' claimed a report signed by Squadron Leader
Felkin, head of the interrogation centre, shortly after the Coventry
raid, 'that . . . on the night of November 14/15 K.Gr.100 were to
bomb the centre of the city. *Lehrgeschwader* 1 were to concentrate
on Workmen's dwellings and another *Geschwader* was to single out
the residential districts.'[1]

Whether the division of labour within the Luftwaffe that night
could be so easily sorted seems unlikely. There were, for one thing –
and contrary to some popular legends – several quite major industrial works in or close to the city centre. The Triumph Motorcycle
Works, originally founded and built up by a German immigrant,
Siegfried Bettmann, extended either side of Priory Street, a couple
of hundred yards north of the Cathedral. By the time of the raid,
it was making 300 motorcycles a week for the military. The factory was 'completely burnt out' on the night of 14/15 November
1940.[2] Lea-Francis, roughly the same distance to the south of the
Cathedral, in Much Park Street, and a few blocks to the north in
Ford Street, had switched, on the outbreak of war, from producing sporty automobiles to making trucks for the military. Not
very far from Ford Street was the Singer car factory. Charlesworth
Bodies, also in Much Park Street, had produced chassis for luxury
cars in peacetime and now made air frames. GEC had a cable and
wire factory that stretched between Whitefriars Lane and Gosford
Street. It was destroyed by fire.[3] To the south of Lea-Francis, in
Parkside, was the Maudsley Motors factory, making utility vehicles,
parts for tanks and aircraft components. Further along Parkside,
the very extensive Armstrong Siddeley Works was still producing
some cars (this would eventually come to a stop in 1941) but by
now mainly aero engines. It had already been badly damaged by

the Luftwaffe on 27 October, and bombed again three days later, though to less effect. On the corner of Spon Street and spreading down Crow Lane, what had until recently been the Rudge Motor-cycle Works, but then taken over by the electrical and recording giant EMI, was now making components for radar developed by its parent company. All of these inner-city factories were produc-ing vehicles, equipment and parts almost exclusively for the war effort, and all counted as being situated in approximately the same area as 'historic' Coventry. Many were very badly hit by the concentrated bombing in the area.

As for the outer districts of the city, this was where the majority (though, as we have seen, certainly not all) of the more important factories were situated, including the shadow factories in which the government and its sometimes reluctant allies in local manufactur-ing had invested so much money and materials. From here led the near-straight line of the Foleshill Road, heading north-north-east from the city centre for three miles or so to what, in the early nineteenth century, had been a ribbon-making village. Foleshill was now one of Coventry's chief industrial suburbs. There were many large factories, including Courtaulds, Coventry Climax Engines, Jaguar (at that time still known, curiously, as SS Cars), and the Riley motor company.

The Foleshill area, although at its furthest extent a considerable distance from the centre of the city, seemed to draw German bombers like a magnet. This was because the Luftwaffe knew what was there, and the factories themselves were fairly easy to find. The road itself was highly visible from the air. Also snaking down from the north at Foleshill to the basin that adjoined the historic centre, the Coven-try Canal likewise reflected the moonlight beautifully, exposing the factories that clustered beside it, or in the land between it and the Foleshill Road.

Of the something over 300 dead from that night whose last, fatal situation is recorded, 108 perished within the area that can be viewed as historic central Coventry (defined as within the postal district CV1 and no more than a couple of hundred yards outside the modern ring road – addresses still in CV1 but farther out are not counted). However, eighty-three were also killed within the modern postcode CV6 (roughly speaking, the extensive mixed residential and industrial suburbs to the north-east of the city). Seventeen civilians died there together at the so-called Foleshill Union* Shelter. Seven more were lost when another direct hit destroyed the nearby ARP post in Lythall's Lane, including four adults as well as three teenage boys who had just reported for messenger duties. Among the young victims was sixteen-year-old Gordon Edwards, a keen Boy Scout who had already been recognised for his bravery during one of the October raids.[4] Both locations lay three and a half miles from the centre of Coventry.

Closer in towards the city – about a mile from the centre – between Widdrington Road, the Canal, and then Foleshill Road to the east, was the old Riley car factory. After the sale of the main Riley company to the Nuffield Group in 1938, this had been taken over by the engine makers Coventry Climax. Hitherto manufacturers mainly of engines for light motor cars, during the Depression of the 1930s, when the car industry underwent a serious contraction, they had diversified into pumps (especially the 'Godiva', after which the Widdrington Road/Aldbourne Road factory was named) and diesel engines for marine use. Climax developed military applications and by 1940 was producing multi-fuel engines, mostly for tanks. Len Dacombe was a charge hand at the works (and a Special Constable), twenty-three years old on the night of the attack. The other workers had gone down into the factory shelter, but Len had volunteered as a fire watcher.

* The Foleshill Union was the result of the joining together of a number of rural parishes during the early nineteenth century, setting up, in effect, an unofficial rural district before such became established under local government reforms later in the century. It was well known for a very large workhouse, near which lay the large public shelter where so many residents died.

The other side of the canal was an ARP store, where they kept a lot of the equipment. And these were absolutely burning to a frazzle, you know.

About one o'clock in the morning, I was walking along the aisles in the factory, and there was a Mr Freeman with me. A parachute mine landed in the canal and blew it to smithereens. The blast caught him first. Luckily it blew him straight down a gangway onto a wall, and he only took me in the air. He crashed into the wall and I followed him. We picked ourselves up. A bit bruised but not hurt. But it blew all the wall down onto the machines and it blew the roof off. And tons of clay from the canal crashed through onto the machinery. It actually did more damage than the bombs, really.[5]

The damage to the Aldbourne Road works was serious. Len Dacombe was right about the destructive power of the parachute mine in the canal. According to a government report, 'the general test shop is wrecked and definitely beyond repair, being situated on the banks of the canal, where a high explosive bomb was dropped, causing a land slide from under the foundations of this shop'. The damage caused to machinery and structure by the mud and water was far greater than that directly inflicted by enemy bombs.[6*]

Half a mile to the north-east, in the suburb of Radford, another high-explosive parachute mine hit the modest church of St Nicholas, a Victorian mock-medieval construction of local red sandstone that had been consecrated in 1874, in what was then a rapidly growing area, as a 'chapel of ease' (i.e. subordinate church) of Holy Trinity. Shortly

---

* The government considered this factory vital to the war effort, as this same government report made clear. In fact, it was quickly rebuilt ninety miles to the west, at a new – presumably less vulnerable – location in Oswestry, Shropshire. Many of the company's existing Coventry employees, including Len Dacombe, were transferred there in early 1941.

after the turn of the new century, it was granted independent parish church status, its domain being carved out of Holy Trinity's.

Holy Trinity and St Nicholas retained their association until 1940. The energetic Reverend Dr Clitheroe had been air raid warden for the area of Radford surrounding the church, until, with raids on the city centre increasing, he felt compelled to resign to concentrate on protecting Holy Trinity. On the night Holy Trinity was saved, however, St Nicholas was instantly destroyed by the powerful bomb, literally reduced to a pile of stones. The vicar of the parish, though he survived, was blinded by the explosion, but four young volunteer fire watchers from the locality were killed outright. The eldest, twenty-two-year-old Alexander McArthur, worked at the Alfred Herbert Machine Tool factory. Nineteen-year-old Alan Hiscocks was an accountant's clerk. Bernard Harbourne, an employee of the Coventry Co-operative Society, died on the eve of his sixteenth birthday. All three were altar servers at the church. The youngest of the dead, still at school and a member of the Boy Scouts, was thirteen-year-old Douglas Hill.[7]

Tragic as this destruction might have been, there is no evidence that the Luftwaffe was deliberately aiming at the small and relatively undistinguished church of St Nicholas. Radford was full of factories and workshops as well as residential developments.

Around a third of a mile eastwards, on the junction of Sandy Lane and Lydgate Road, lay a large manufacturing plant belonging to the Coventry-based firm that had been founded in 1895 as the Great Horseless Carriage Company, but after acquiring British rights to Gottlieb Daimler's patents, had taken the German inventor's name and become, as Daimler Ltd, an internationally known motor marque. This factory, which in the First World War had produced engines for the early tanks as well as shell casings and aircraft parts, had once again been converted to military use. It, too, was bombed during the night of 14/15 November 1940, set on fire, and in part very seriously damaged, with some workshops near-demolished and others, though not necessarily rendered useless, suffering from widespread roof damage, letting in water on the machinery and thus rust and general deterioration.[8] Fortunately for the war effort, much of Daimler's production had been transferred to the shadow factory on the far outskirts of Coventry, which was not bombed that night.

A mile or so away, along the Holyhead Road (in fact, the main road to Birmingham), about a mile to the west of the city centre, lay the old Alvis factory (Luftwaffe target number L73 14[9]). Built in 1919 when the firm was founded, it was very badly bombed that night. A middling-sized producer of powerful luxury and sports cars, with a reputation for good management and engineering excellence, Alvis was by 1940 also involved in producing aero engines and spare parts. These new products were, however, manufactured at a new works, built nearby in 1935, also off the Holyhead Road but a short distance away, to the south of the railway line. After a brief suspension following the outbreak of war, the old factory continued to produce pre-war cars, alongside armoured cars for the military and bomb-carrying trolleys for the RAF. This work ceased abruptly on the night of 14/15 November. The initial official report, submitted to London three days later, detailed some of the very worst devastation visited upon any Coventry factory as a result of the raid:

Offices and Machine Shop completely razed to the ground. Land Mine [i.e. parachute mine] and High Explosives in centre of Machine Shop

Offices damaged by incendiary bombs

Machines lying in the open

Grinders, Capstans, Lathes, Splint Grinders, Gear Hobbers Fellows and Maxicuts, Milling Machines and large Automatics badly damaged with fire and rust; many can be salved but approximately 25% are completely beyond repair.

Fitting Shop in the rear where armoured cars and bomb carrying trailers were being assembled completely demolished but many of the component parts can be saved.

Raw material such, Forgings, Gear Blanks, Tools, Gauges, Reamers, etc. are lying on the floors and much of this can be saved.

Impossible to continue operation on the present site. Factory site will have to be completely cleared before rebuilding can be commenced.[10]

An account by Eric Bird, the government's leading bomb damage expert, was based on interviews with employees and works firefighters, and, though surrounded with cool, dour technical prose similar to that of the official report, tells a surprisingly vivid story:

The Alvis works . . . were inspected in some detail and we went round with the Chief Works' Fireman. This group of buildings is divided into two by a high railway embankment. On one side is the original works and on the other a factory erected in recent years. The Fireman told me that the old works had first been attacked with a few incendiary bombs, and while his men were dealing with these, 2 or 3 H.E. bombs had fallen, causing casualties among the firemen. Shortly after the water supply failed, he started pumping from the adjacent river and his reserve water pond. He was laying hose over the railway line from the new works when he saw a parachute mine descend on to the old works. He lay down in the steel troughing of the railway bridge and, though within 150 ft. of the explosion, he was uninjured. He said that when he got up 'the old works had gone'.[11]

The newer Holyhead Road factory, despite its proximity, was only lightly damaged. One relatively small high-explosive bomb and an incendiary caused some minor problems that were reckoned unlikely to hinder rapid resumption of production. The loss of the mains electricity supply was considered a much more serious impediment. Ironically, this factory, which was also larger than the original one, produced aero engines and parts, much higher priority targets for the Luftwaffe than the vehicles and bomb trolleys assembled at the old Alvis Works. Dr John Joseph Parkes, then a senior executive at Alvis, and from 1946 Managing Director, believed that the Germans' maps were, contrary to beliefs about infallible Teutonic efficiency, not fully up-to-date, so that they were actually unaware of the existence of the new factory.[12]

In neither case were the factory's bomb shelters hit, even though the old factory was all but destroyed above ground. The purpose-built shelters provided by major manufacturers for their workforces were usually among the most secure, although nothing was guaranteed. The Armstrong Siddeley Works in Parkside, by contrast, suffered minimal damage above ground, but a chance direct hit on one of the company's shelters caused many casualties. Fate decided.

At some point, probably around the same time the Alvis drama was being played out, the two *Kindertransport* girls, Inge and Bertha, were also gaining some experience of the role of chance in the matter of survival. It was happening just a bit further down that same Holyhead Road, on the outskirts of the old city.

That night, as usual, their foster parents, Bill and Vera, and their daughter had driven out to the safety of their rented country accommodation, where the girls' German background was considered unacceptable. This left Inge, Bertha and their brother Theo with Vera's mother, Queenie, who managed some boarding houses at the city end of the Holyhead Road. Queenie, by the girls' account a rough-edged but decent woman, had another German refugee girl, Elsie Pape, staying with her. All of them were together in one of the houses when, still in the early stages of the raid, this building was hit and set on fire. With the house threatening to collapse (it would eventually burn down), everyone fled as best they could. Ten-year-old Inge, separated from her teenage siblings, was scooped up on the street by one of the young women boarders and hustled into a shelter. Bertha and Elsie ended up in the cellar of another of Queenie's boarding houses, further along the street. Bertha described their further adventures that night:

Well, there were so many people crammed into the cellar and it was the middle of the night, large cellars, and well, people have to go to the toilet. Elsie and I were shy, we didn't do what the others did, just go into the corner and do what you had to do, we had to go up into the bathroom. So we waited for a lull in the bombing and went up to the bathroom. We went there together and, force of habit, we locked the door, which wasn't necessary. And then there was a god-almighty crash and the bathroom, which was next to the toilet had had it, a direct hit. And we were frantically trying to open the door . . . so there was a bit of staircase left. And we ran down the steps and went to the cellar. Well, they never thought they would see us again. They knew we had had a direct hit. It was just inches away.[13]

Young Inge survived in the shelter along the road, after spending a night anxious not only for the safety of herself and her companions, but also the family members from whom she had become separated. Having fled Germany and the anti-Semitic hatred that would soon enough lead to the mass extermination of almost all the country's remaining Jews, all three children – and Elsie – now narrowly escaped suffering the same fate at the hands of the German Luftwaffe.

The raid would, in the end, last almost eleven hours. Some accounts claim that the attack was continuous, but most eyewitnesses recall occasional lulls. Bertha and Elsie had used the opportunity of an apparent pause in the bombing to go up into the house and visit the bathroom. Others tried to put the kettle on, check on pets or family treasures, fetch a drink, or just find any excuse to escape the cramped, dark and damp discomfort of the shelter. As Gladys Cook, a newly married woman of twenty-three, recalled the situation that night:

It was packed, just like sardines. You couldn't move. You could hardly shut the door. All you could hear was bombs dropping. Everyone was scared to death. They were all screaming, it was, oh, I can see it now. Awful. My husband, he wanted a drink. I said, oh please, don't go out. He said, I won't be long, and he dashed in the house. He brought a bottle of Port and he was giving all the people a drink because they were all so thirsty. And I was terrified.[14]

Her husband could offer the excuse that he had been forced to head for the shelter just as he got back from work, and so had forgone his supper. Whatever the case, there was clearly an element of macho male behaviour at work. Another survivor, then an eight-year-old, later recalled wryly:

This particular night, we'd had this lull, and my dad, who liked his pint, had said to the man next door, who had been in our shelter, come on, Sam, I've got a bottle down the house. We'll go and have a drink. So we all got out of the shelter, went down to the house. He opens the bottle pours two glasses – one for him, and one for Sam Williams, the next door neighbour – they're sitting down. We were in the front room while this was going on, and all of a sudden there was such a tremendous explosion, which had been a landmine about probably five hundred yards at the back of the garden.

All the glass from the back window – they were sat in the back kitchen – all came in on the pair of them. We were in the front. And they never had a scratch. Dad must have been pulling slivers of glass out of his turn-ups and his pockets for six months after.[15]

Sometimes this kind of insouciance could have fatal consequences. A Mr Burrows, in his early thirties, was reportedly 'chatting with a neighbour over the garden fence' at his home in Heathfield Road, two miles west of the city centre, with the raid in full swing above them, when fatally injured by an exploding bomb.[16]

Being up in the house, or out in the open, during a major air raid carried obvious risks. It is true, all the same, that many of the fatal casualties, and the seriously injured, were in shelters, sometimes quite deep shelters such as the one at Armstrong Siddeley. Of course, when this happened, a lot of people would die together. Whether a bomb fell nearer or farther from the refuge, whether the blast was direct or oblique, and above all, whether the bomb hit the shelter or house directly, were the key factors. Chance always played its role, and that role was often a pitiless one.

Everyone was aware of the part of luck. Did a German bomb 'have your name on it'? 'You could hear the bombs going down and you just ducked and held your ears and just waited, waited to see whether you were going to be hit or not,' one woman remembered of her reactions as a twelve-year-old in the Blitz. The family's house was very close to the huge Alfred Herbert Machine Tool factory, which covered 22 acres at Edgwick, alongside the Coventry Canal two miles north of Broadgate, as well as to the Morris factory, and everyone knew the area was a likely target.[17]

Slightly further out from Edgwick, in the district of Holbrooks (near the Foleshill Gas Works, also a major target), the Huwson family and their neighbours, who were also young Brian's godparents, took to the Anderson shelter in their garden. There they sat in terror as the aircraft droned overhead and the bombs fell. Their neighbours at the back, the Worthingtons, were also crammed into the home-built shelter at the bottom of their garden. Sometime after the raid had begun, there was an enormous explosion. The Worthingtons' shelter, a bare 30 feet from the Huwsons', had been hit. Brian Huwson described what happened next:

When this bomb dropped, our shelter shook. I was thrown in the air and hit the roof of the shelter and went back down onto the bunk. We'd got a huge privet hedge between us and them. That would have helped save us from the blast. Our shelter saved our lives.

And when the earth and all stopped falling, my godfather got out of our shelter. You knew, you know, someone was going to be badly hurt from that. He scrambled his way across to the Worthington shelter. There was one girl had survived. Unfortunately, she'd had her legs blown off across the thighs. And he picked her up, but the girl died in his arms. Um, a very sad time. He had to go back into the house and clean himself up. Such as, whatever he could do in the circumstances. All the windows blown in and the doors blown off in the house. His clothes went in the dust bin and he got himself dressed again and went back in the shelter and stayed the rest of the night.[18]

Similar tragic scenes played out across Coventry's sprawling suburbs. South-west of the city, right on the edge of the urban area and
until recently wholly rural in character (it had been incorporated
into the city just a decade before), Beanfield Avenue was part of
a 1930s development of middle-class, semi-detached houses of the
kind found all over England. The area was named after the main
local road, Green Lane. Though entirely residential, Green Lane lay
around a mile from the Standard Motor Company's large factory
at Canley, and the Luftwaffe certainly knew where the Standard
Works were. On the evening of 14 November, fifteen-year-old Sheila
Ward's father had been in the city centre when the raid began, and
helped out with extinguishing incendiaries. Then, realising that the
raid was spreading into the suburbs, he decided to bicycle home to
be with his family.

> He arrived at the top of Beanfield Avenue, where I lived, to be told
> by the air raid warden that there was a time bomb in the middle of
> the road at the top. So he got off his bicycle and crept past it.
>
> And he'd only been in the house about half an hour when every-
> thing started flying around. Glass shattered, and there was a great
> big flash. All I can remember is my father leaning over us, standing
> in the entrance just by the stairs saying, don't worry, it's all over now.
> And that was a land mine which demolished at least six houses. It
> killed eight people, because a lot of the people who had been where
> the time bomb was had been moved to number 28, which was abso-
> lutely flattened.
>
> We were all taken out of the houses by the air raid wardens after-
> wards, because apparently the gas was burning in the gas pipes in
> the hole made by the land mine, and they thought the whole avenue
> could blow up.[19]

The damage was indeed great, and the situation in this normally
peaceful suburban street as dramatic as it was unexpected, but Sheila
Ward's memory may have exaggerated it. The actual number of dead

seems to have been three – tragic enough – including a retired railwayman, Mr Rutter, at number 29, a thirty-nine-year-old man, Richard
Newall, seemingly at number 28, and, at the same address, a four-
year-old boy, David McMurdie. The child was badly injured when
recovered from the shattered building but died just after Christmas
in hospital.

Across the road at number 30, Beanfield Avenue, Gwendoline
Ryland, a student teacher aged nineteen who had returned earlier
that evening from her classes at Birmingham University, found herself
at home with her mother, her elder sister, Christine (Chris) and their
cat, Figaro, when the big parachute mine hit. Their father, a lieutenant
in the Territorial Army commanding an anti-aircraft battery, was on
duty with his men in the city.

'Get under the stairs', my mother shouted. We were on our way,
making sure our mother was with us, when Chris suddenly called,
'Where's the cat?' and ran into the dining room where we had left
'Figaro' in front of the fire. She managed to grab him but at that
moment the house began to collapse around us. The dining room
door came off its hinges and fell against the sideboard – Chris and
Figaro were safe in the gap underneath the door as our home began
to disintegrate and tumble down. Mum and I had made it to the
cupboard under the stairs when I suddenly said, 'Mum, my face'. I
put my hands up to my face and my fingers just went straight into
flesh. At the same time I could see my mother had tiny cuts all over
her face – we had been hit by flying glass.[20]

Eventually her mother and sister (the latter still carrying the cat)
managed to help her to the nearest first aid station, which initially
seemed near-deserted. Two ARP wardens appeared but could do little
but make Gwendoline comfortable, explaining that in this semi-rural
location casualties had not been expected. Eventually they found a
car to take her into Gulson Road hospital, in the former workhouse

near the city centre. It was a strange journey into the Coventry firestorm.

> We went down Kenilworth Road – there were bombs dropping seemingly all around us. By now it was bright moonlight and we could see clearly. I knew my Dad was manning the guns in the Memorial Park which were firing away. We went past the station and Greyfriars Green and up Hertford Street. There seemed to be bombs raining down everywhere – it was a miracle we weren't hit. As we got to the city centre we could see up the narrow lanes by the cathedral and there were flames shooting out of the cathedral's upper windows. The Council House seemed to be alright but behind you could see the cathedral and many other buildings on fire and burning fiercely.

Once she had arrived at the casualty department, to her distress a nurse had to cut off the dress she had been wearing ('my first proper grown-up one') so that they could access her injuries. The staff gave her what treatment they could, working by the glow of candles. By this time there was no power and no lights, and operations were not possible. Despite the lacerations in her face and a wound in her chest, it was decided that Gwendoline's injuries were not life-threatening, and so the terrified young woman was left in a bed on one of the wards while the staff turned to more urgent cases. She lay there with the raid still raging all around her. 'You couldn't even try to get sleep,' she said, 'because they had started to bomb a factory just opposite the hospital and there were anti-aircraft guns banging away near at hand.'

The parachute mines were not only the deadliest, if they went off, but also the most indiscriminate. Unlike the conventional high-explosive bombs, which could be dropped on a pretty straight trajectory, with high potential accuracy, the parachutes floated down, buffeted by the wind. They might land anywhere. In fact, they might not land at all. An eyewitness who was a small boy at the time recalled seeing one suspended from a tree on Max Road, a residential street in Radford. Its harness was caught up in the branches, representing a dangerous challenge to the bomb disposal team that would have to get it down and make it harmless.[21] There were yet other perils associated with what was essentially a terror weapon. Another survivor reported how the inexperience of civilians faced with such devices could cost them their lives:

At the top of Woodside Avenue, along what is now the A45, the Kenpas Highway, a . . . I suppose it was a land mine . . . floated down and exploded at the top of the other side of Woodside Avenue. People rushed towards it, thinking it was an airman coming from a German plane, seeing the parachute. But then they were sadly killed because when they got close to it, it exploded.[22]

14

The Long Night Ending

Alan Hartley finally arrived in the city centre, on his bicycle, between one and two in the morning. The head warden of his ARP post had been badly injured, and the unit had had its telephone line cut, not as a result of enemy action but because of clumsy shooting by a mobile anti-aircraft gun in the vicinity. Sometime after midnight, the sixteen-year-old civil defence messenger mounted his bike and set off on the risky two and a half mile ride into town to summon an ambulance. At his destination, young Alan took in the scene there with a mixture of wonder and terror.

Right ahead of me was a huge crater, where a huge bomb must have dropped at the bottom of Smithford Street. And in this huge crater I could see the River Sherbourne, glinting in the flames. And when I got to the other side of the crater, I couldn't ride the bike because of all the rubble and the glass and the cables and everything lying in the road in Smithford Street. To my right-hand side, suddenly, the roof of the arcade collapsed. That was a glass arcade. Further up, Marks and Spencer's was burning on one side, Woolworths was burning on the other, and then I got into Broadgate, off into High Street, and as I just got to the Council House, on the right hand side an incendiary had landed in a shop, and a fireman stood there with a tiny, tiny trickle of water coming out of his hose pipe, because all the mains had gone.[1]

The situation was desperate. In the interim, however, the outside powers that be, despite the lack of reliable communications, had started to move their people in on the city. Sometime after midnight, a representative of the regional government, Captain le Grand, having driven from Birmingham without lights, arrived at a pre-arranged 'rendezvous-post' set up on a roundabout at Allesley, where the bypass built just before the war met the main road coming out of the city towards Birmingham.[2] He took as his headquarters a pub, which seemed to be the only place in the area with a working telephone, and began to build his forces and make plans for the aftermath of the still-active catastrophe.[3]

Le Grand's main job was to direct the outside help that would be needed to support the local civil defence teams struggling to save what could be saved in the stricken city. For this, he needed to liaise with the 'Controller' of Coventry (*ex officio* Chief Constable Hector of the city police). Telephone contact was briefly established with the Control Centre, in the basement of the main police station – adjoining the rear of the Council House – but after a short while the line went dead. As a consequence, le Grand decided he should travel into the city to consult with those in charge there, and get a picture of what was required in terms of outside help. 'I have never forgotten that drive into Coventry,' he wrote more than twenty years later in a letter to the Lord Mayor of Coventry:

It was as dark as pitch except for the glare from burning buildings, and I lost my way due to the many diversions I had to make caused by bomb craters. But I knew the situation of the Control-centre and eventually found it . . . Enemy bombs were falling around it (I do not think it was actually hit) but the calm atmosphere within the Centre, with all the different CD [civil defence] officials 'carrying-on' made me then, as it has many times since when thinking of it, very proud of my countrymen. It was a shattering experience, in more ways than one, to visit the Controller and watch him and his officials at work under these most difficult conditions. The room

Historic Butcher Row, in 1933 admiringly compared by the writer J. B. Priestley with medieval Nuremburg, but demolished by Coventry Council four years later.

The scene in Broadgate after the IRA bomb, August 1939.

German aerial reconnaissance photograph of Coventry dated October 1940 with factories marked and numbered.

A Luftwaffe navigator map reading by moonlight.

A beam transmitter, probably X-Gerät.

Heinkel III bomber with X-Gerät reception masts.

Coventry immediately after the raid.

Anderson Shelters provided a basic refuge in suburban back gardens.

Blasted houses in outer suburban Beanfield Avenue.

Broadgate and the shell of the Owen Owen department store.

Soldiers march into the ruins of Coventry to help with clearance and 'keep order'.

The ruins of Coventry Cathedral, immediately after the November raid.

The young driver of the car was killed by the bomb impact.

Firefighters at work in Coventry city centre, 16 November 1940.

Rescue parties search the rubble.

With basic utilities damaged or destroyed, the grave danger for the population was of diseases such as typhoid.

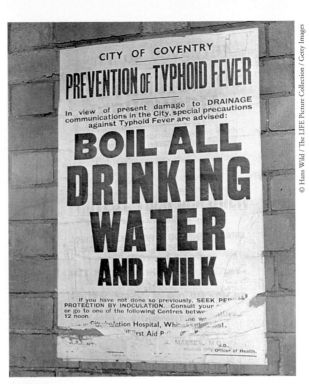

King George VI (*left, in uniform*) tours the ruins with Coventry Mayor Jack Moseley (*to his left*). Following them are Home Secretary Herbert Morrison (*back, second from left*) and Chief Constable Hector (*back, third from left*).

After the raid on 10 April 1941, children search the ruins of their school for books.

Temporary shops in the city centre, many built of wood and corrugated asbestos. The last were demolished in 1974.

A 'Food Flying Squad' mobile canteen in Coventry after the April 1941 raids. Administered by the Ministry of Food, these canteens were funded by donations from the USA.

20 November 1940. 172 victims of 'Moonlight Sonata' are buried at London Road cemetery.

Winston Churchill visits Coventry Cathedral, autumn 1941.

Coventry's rebuilt city centre, 1962.

The new Coventry Cathedral, 1962, with the ruins of the old Cathedral (*far left*).

was in semi-darkness and every time a bomb fell the whole room seemed to reel from the concussion of the enormous explosion of the bombs the enemy was dropping. But no one appeared to turn a hair . . .[4]

Once he got back to his rendezvous-post, Captain le Grand began receiving the reinforcements that were coming in from other parts of the Midlands. The neighbouring Fire Brigades had already gone into the city to help, but at the rendezvous-post there were now a growing number of rescue teams, ambulances, extra police and military and the like. These teams could realistically only be sent into the city once the All Clear finally sounded. They still had quite a wait until that occurred.

Many of the German bombers based in France, refuelled and rearmed, were still coming over the city for the second time that night. A report by a Luftwaffe crew who carried out their second attack in the small hours said that 'already at the English coast, the gigantic pillar of smoke was visible, showing us the way'.[5]

By a quarter to two in the morning of what had now become 15 November, perhaps following le Grand's dash into the centre of Coventry, the Home Office in London received the most ominously detailed, though still very approximate, report on the state of the city that it had yet been sent by Home Security's team in Birmingham:

Coventry has suffered and is still suffering severe damage from H.E. Land mines and fires, many fires are still raging and already a number of shops, commercial premises and the Cathedral have been gutted. The streets are littered with debris and casualties are likely to be high. Several police officers are known to have been killed and it is estimated that at least 200 additional police will be required to be drafted into the city.

The following cannot be vouched for as regards the severity of damage sustained, owing to breakdown in communications. So far as can be ascertained at present the following factories and other establishments have been damaged by H.E. and/or I.B.

Thos. Smith stampings Ribble Road; Sterling Metals Ltd, Northey Road, FOLESHILL; Pattison and Hobourn Ltd; British Pressed Panels Ltd, Humber Ltd: Renold and Coventry Chain Ltd: Clarke Cluley and Co: Transformer Station, Sandy Lane: The Royal Naval Stores at STONEY STANTON and O'Briens Works: R.A.F. Stores Sandy Lane: Courtaulds Ltd. Foleshill Road: Co-op Warehouse Lockhurst Lane: Bushills Cow Lane: Stevengraph Cox Street: A.T. Aircraft Works Priory Street: Morris Bodies Ltd. Quinton Road: Home Office Store Paynes Lane: Lloyds Bank: G.P.O.: Isolation Hospital: Two First Aid Posts: Two Churches: Public Baths: One Hotel: Two clubs: One school: Four public shelters: Five cinemas: Central Police Station: A.R.P. Stores Greyfriars Lane: and numerous retail shops, gas, water, electricity and telephone services badly damaged. Damage to house property considerable.

Unexploded parachute mines are reported at:-

Stoney Stanton Road: Nuneaton Road: Graveswood [probably error for Grayswood] Avenue: Crecy Road: Middlemarch Road: Woodside Avenue:* Holyhead Road: Sherbourne Crescent: Ro' Oak Road: Haynes Lane BEDWORTH.

Land Mines at Washbrook Lane ALLESLEY resulted in extensive damage to several houses, casualties slight, most of the roads in Coventry are blocked.

Raid still in progress.[6]

Just over half an hour later, Birmingham reported that those police reserves would be reporting to Coventry at daybreak or soon after, equipped with blankets and rations. The Chief Constable of neighbouring Staffordshire had been warned to have 100 men

* This may have been the mine that would kill several unsuspecting civilians when they mistook it for a German airman who had 'bailed out' of his stricken bomber.

available at short notice. The Chief Constable of Warwickshire, the rural area surrounding Coventry, was asked to have men 'picketing' all roads out of the city to prevent unauthorised groups and individuals from gaining access to the city centre and adding to the mayhem. At the Controller, Coventry's request, 200 troops would be going in 'for morale and control purposes' at daybreak, and 50 sappers from the Royal Engineers, with explosives, would be arriving 'as soon as possible'.[7]

Arrangements were already beginning to be made for dealing with the aftermath, the damage and the rescue and recovery process. Meanwhile, however, the raid dragged on and on. At 3:30 a.m., a more terse but dramatic message came out of Birmingham:

Attack continues in intensity not only in the city but in the suburbs. Damage to house property very extensive, hardly any street has avoided some damage. 200 fires reported. Very large fires reported and impossible to get them under control as there is notwater [sic]. In many cases fires not being attended to. Casualties will number many hundreds including a number of the Civil Defence Services, Police and Fire. Owing to telephones being out of order it is impossible to get information of Key Points and factories but it is very extensive.

Hundreds of people have had to be evacuated owing to the presence of unexploded land mines.[8]

A little over eight hours had now passed since the first incendiaries had been dropped on the city centre. The attack on Coventry was now by far the longest-lasting enemy bombing raid yet experienced in the British Isles.

Meanwhile, outside reinforcements in the form of police, civil defence workers, rescue parties and military personnel were starting to arrive in numbers. All had to be asked to wait and were directed to dispersed parking places, so that they would not all be grouped together in case of an enemy air attack. Le Grand admitted ruefully that he had a hard time keeping control of the mass of vehicles and people soon gathered at the roundabout: 'My greatest difficulty was in holding them in the Rendezvous until they were asked for – they all wanted to tear into the city on their own and get to work and give a hand.'[9]

In the case of rescue parties, which had often been transported quite long distances crouched on their equipment in open-topped lorries, in miserable weather, le Grand noted that these men were so affected by the cold that they would have been 'useless' had they been required to start work immediately. The wiser authorities, he noted, had sent their rescue parties along in closed cars that followed the trucks carrying their equipment. A mobile canteen operated by the Women's Voluntary Service fortunately stopped by for a while, offering reviving hot drinks and snacks as the reinforcements waited for dawn.[10]

As the night wound down, the raid continued. Some fancied it was easing off, but for now the bombs kept coming. Len Dacombe, at the Coventry Climax Godiva Works, was still above ground, fire watching in the small hours. He and a colleague narrowly avoided being among the Luftwaffe's last victims that night.

> There was a bit of a lull at three o'clock in the morning. And the fireman and myself, we had a look at all the damage. We were out in the yard where we could see some tracer bullets going up in the sky. They were going up in threes, probably trying to locate the aircraft up there. We heard a string of bombs coming down, and we dashed into an air raid shelter at the side of the canal. And one bomb actually came through the side of the canal into the air raid shelter, into the base at the bottom of the stair. And that one never exploded as well. And that fireman and I was in there with them.[11]

The last German aircraft came over Coventry about an hour and a half before dawn on 15 November 1940. By all accounts, many anti-aircraft batteries had long since ceased to fire at the intruders, having run out of ammunition. There was still little sign of RAF night fighters either. The raid ended, in other words, when the Luftwaffe decided to stop coming, and not before.

It seems that the last stick of enemy bombs fell on Shortley Road, in the suburb of Whitley, south-east of the city centre, at 5:30 a.m., though another source gives the time as twenty minutes earlier.[12] The location was near London Road cemetery, Whitley Common, and lay a little over half a mile from Coventry's Isolation Hospital, where several children had been killed earlier in the night.

The All Clear ('Raiders Passed') was confirmed at 6:16 a.m. This signalled the official end of the attack, and remains the time usually given for this, although it could be guessed that anyone within hearing distance of the surface had probably realised by now that the Germans had gone. However, since most of the city was now without electricity, the sirens that would normally have sounded were out of operation. In many, if not most, cases, local air raid wardens and policemen went from shelter to shelter and street to street letting the huddled and sleep-starved masses know that 'It's all over!' Whichever way they got the good news, it was a signal for the people of Coventry to begin cautiously emerging from the public and factory shelters, from their half-sunk Anderson shelters and their cellars, from under their stairs or kitchen tables, and to venture up into the pre-dawn streets. The moon had reached fullness around three hours earlier, but as it set and daylight started to creep into the sky, between 7 and 8 a.m., they could see ever more clearly what the enemy had done to their homes, and to their city.

In the worst case, the sight that greeted those who emerged from Anderson shelters into their back gardens could be a truly shocking one. Ten-year-old Roma Buckley had spent the night in just such a shelter with her mother, uncle and aunt and neighbours. At some point, there had been a loud explosion and the whole shelter shook. Her mother had thrown herself on top of her. The relatives had been hit by slivers of metal: her aunt spent the night with her face covered in blood. Then came the morning, and their worst fears were confirmed.

I remember coming out and thinking, oh my God, how the hell did we survive it? There was not any earth on it [the shelter roof] it had taken the lot off. The front was all twisted. There were big holes from all the shrapnel – you could get your hand and arm in. It was absolutely full of holes where it had come through. When we went to see the house – what was left of it – the first bomb I think must have hit the staircases where they came together, bringing our house down, and the house that was being prepared for somebody else. We just couldn't get in anything. The doors were all off and it was in a terrible state. So from then on we had to find somewhere else to live. We'd got nowhere to live.[13]

The boy whose father had shared a beer with his neighbour in the middle of the night and survived a near-direct hit to tell the tale, also ventured into their house after the All Clear was sounded. The top half of the front door had been blown off.

In the morning, as I opened this door to go up the stairs, there was about two foot of clods of earth in the stairwell as you'd call it. We went upstairs. All the windows were in upstairs and all the ceilings were down, where all these great big clods of earth from the landmine had all come in through the roof, through the ceiling, and was all on the bed. And all the broken glass was on the bed as well.[14]

Fifteen-year-old Sheila Ward and her parents had been evacuated from their house in Beanfield Avenue while the raid was still in progress, because a parachute mine had broken all the mains pipes, bringing the danger of a gas explosion. Having spent the rest of the night in a surface shelter at the top of the avenue, they also returned to their house to find only desolation.

> The glass was everywhere, scrunching under foot. All shattered. No windows. Of course, the ceilings came down in the house as well. And of course that takes forever to clear up. My mother was very upset to discover that our canary was dead in the bottom of the cage. That was the first job – bury the canary in the garden. And we'd got no gas, water or electricity. Got no roof. I mean, the water comes straight through. Of course it rained immediately afterwards.[15]

The weather was indeed miserable. 'We all came out of the shelter, and it was a very cold, damp November morning,' as one survivor recalled. 'The streets were running with water. There were ambulances, buses, people just walking about. They didn't know where they were going or what they were doing. People absolutely shell-shocked really.'[16]

Some houses were completely intact, though many had lost at least some windows. Even the centre of the city administration, the Council House, was said to have lost just about every one of its dozens of windows in the course of the night, and this sense of being cast open to the elements was everywhere in Coventry, right to its outermost rim.

What to do? The raid appeared to be over, but there was no guarantee that the Luftwaffe would not reappear, perhaps to machine-gun survivors. After they got back into their house in the morning of 15 November young Reg Kimber remembers that he and his exhausted parents lay down in the upstairs bedroom, ignoring the fact that the ceiling was half blown in.

> We lay there, and a plane went over. And my mother said, ooh, they're back, they're back! And I remember my dad saying that classic phrase: It's OK, it's one of ours! And I can remember the sound of the engine of that plane to this day. It must have been a Spitfire or a Hurricane.[17]

There were many who survived the raid, saw the devastation, but somehow convinced themselves that the best response was to behave as normal. Two teenagers insisted on getting dressed in their uniforms and following their school routine.

My brother and my cousin, who went to Bablake,* set off for school and, I don't know, they just went. I certainly didn't set off for school. I remember them coming back some time later. They said they had got into town. They told us about fires burning. There was a butcher's shop, and they told us about these animal carcasses all over the road.[18]

A teenage secretary at Bushell's, a printing firm in the city centre, made a similar decision. She even packed some sandwiches for her lunch.

I couldn't cycle to work all the way because of the damage. By Queen's Road there was this cycle shop and a lovely dress shop that I used to like to look at, and that was all piled in the road, so I thought, how am I going to get round this. Then I saw two men who worked at Bushell's and I could see them over the road, so I followed them. Then I saw Bushell's and it's been burnt completely down.[19]

Meanwhile, the Engelhard children had survived the destruction of Queenie's boarding house on the edge of the city centre. Once the All Clear sounded, they began a trek back out to the outer suburban home of their foster parents, Bill and Vera, who themselves had spent the night in their rented country cottage. 'We walked over the burning debris,' as Bertha put it, and set off up the Holyhead Road. When they finally reached the house, their foster parents had returned, and soon something quite dramatic

* A historic school, thought to have been founded in the early sixteenth century as a charitable institution for poor boys. Since the 1920s it had been a 'Direct Grant' selective grammar school, situated just north-east of the historic city centre.

became apparent. Bill and Vera had decided, after the big Blitz of the previous night, that they wanted to leave Coventry permanently for somewhere safer.[20]

The urge to move out of the devastated city, whether temporarily or for good, was strong. Who could be sure that the Germans would not be back during the coming night of the fullest moon, when its light would once more shine treacherously brightly all the way through from dusk to dawn?

'Everybody was leaving the city the day after,' recalled one witness who had been twelve at the time – though, actually, that 'everyone' did not, as she admits, include her own family. Her father insisted they had to stay because he had to make sure that his mother, who lived in another part of the city, was all right. He and his daughter, she recounts, walked from their suburban home towards the heart of the city. On the way they saw a corner house that had had its entire front wall blown off. Firemen were in an upstairs bedroom, which was open to the elements, trying to coax an elderly lady to come with them. Still confined to her bed in the far corner of the room, she kept demanding for them to shut the door, because it was so cold. They realised that she was deaf, had heard nothing of the night's bombing, and understood nothing of their entreaties to her to leave the collapsed building.[21]

Other desperate Coventrians, fleeing the city, had already reached the small market town of Bedworth about eight miles north of the centre, shortly after the raid ended. At 7:20 that same morning, the Warwickshire police informed the Regional Office that two busloads of refugees from Coventry had arrived in Bedworth and been given succour at the Feeding and Shelter station there.[22] Over the border in Northamptonshire, to the east and south-east of Coventry and only ten miles distant at its nearest point, police headquarters told Birmingham that 'the Public Assistance Officer* . . . is opening eleven

---

* A local official (previously known as a 'Relieving Officer'), whose job under the still-extant but soon-to-be-defunct nineteenth-century Poor Law was to scrutinise requests for public aid or public healthcare and direct qualified applicants to the appropriate institutions.

feeding stations to accommodate homeless persons from Coventry. The numbers to be dealt with are not yet known, and they are expected to arrive during the course of the day.'[23]

Some frightened people fled immediately but, in fact, much of the exodus from Coventry seems to have been more of a gradual, though insistent, drift, throughout that chill, drizzly Friday. Winifred Dales, who had returned to her parents' city-centre pub the previous evening and seen the windows blood-red in the setting sun as a kind of premonition of fires to come, safely emerged with them from the pub cellar when the All Clear sounded. They emerged into rubble-strewn streets and the smell of burning. Then her parents, when ten o'clock came and they were obliged by law to open up, duly did so. 'And everybody came into the pub,' she remembered. 'I think they wanted to see who was there, you know. And someone got on the piano. It was just like a party. I just think it was, everyone was so pleased to be alive, and they were just so relieved.'[24] Soon afterwards, however, there was a conference among the extended family. The plan changed, and it, too, involved Bedworth:

> Then my uncle, who used to go round the family to see if they were all right, he came. And then the aunts came. And we walked to Bedworth. Up along the Foleshill Road. Just like you see refugees on the continent, that's what it was like, people walking out of Coventry. Some walked to Meriden, some walked to Kenilworth. We walked to Bedworth, because the aunts knew someone in Bedworth.

Those who lived in small towns and villages outside Coventry found themselves acting as a reception centre for relatives who had decided to abandon the city. One witness who lived as a child in Nuneaton, a smaller but still sizeable industrial town three miles or so north of Bedworth, recalled his uncle Jack arriving on his bike at their house after the raid. His uncle, who worked at the Three Spires cycle factory in Priory Street, had witnessed the night's horrors and seen the works almost entirely destroyed. 'He broke down. Couldn't believe it, he said.' At Kenilworth, another smaller town to the south-west of Coventry, ten-year-old Doris Dawson saw more streams of refugees leaving the city for unknown destinations:

> We went out in the front garden, saw these single Midland Red buses . . . it was just a convoy, one after the other. And they had stretchers across the seats to bring people from Coventry. And then there were people walking with packs of stuff on their backs, carrier bags, just as you would see in a film of refugees leaving a place from fear. Yes, you could feel the fear, it was unbelievable. Don't know where they went or what happened to them.[25]

To the small-town folk who were receiving them, the demoralised city people must have seemed oddly pathetic. Unsurprising that this was so. Unsurprising also that all the refugees felt was relief, especially if, like Brian Kelsey (later a Lord Mayor of post-war Coventry), you had been evacuated from your house in the small hours due to a massive, unexploded land mine nearby. He and his family also took the road from their house in the outer suburb of Exhall to Bedworth and beyond, looking for shelter at his grand-mother's house:

> Most people were walking fairly silently. There wasn't much talking that I remember. People – adults – were probably quite frightened. There were the fires. The debris from the fires was falling on you. We actually got quite dirty. I always remember at my grandmother's realis-ing how grubby I was after the night, and I suppose we all were.
> Well, we first walked to Bedworth. And then we had to walk to Bulkington* with my dad. Three miles. Quite a long way when you're eight and a half years old. We went to my grandmother's, actually.

---

* A large village south-east of Nuneaton, between six and seven miles from Coventry.

The smell of fried bread and bacon, after spending several hours in a cold, damp air raid shelter, was absolute heaven. It was delicious.[26]

There was already a hint of defiance in the attitude of some, even as they tramped on to the roads leading out of Coventry. It expressed itself in small but powerful and very characteristic ways. One family headed off towards Wolverhampton, forty miles or so away, where they had relatives they could stay with. The mother of the girl who recounted the story many years later had firm ideas about her priorities:

We trotted off. Over the rubble, the craters in the roads. We had a lift in an army van, which they weren't supposed to do, but on that morning nobody cared. And we had various lifts until we got to Birmingham. My father said, Sally, I don't know what you've got in this bag, but it is heavy. And she said, well, Hitler had my windows, and he's had my three-piece suite, he's not going to have my Christmas puddings that I saved all those coupons for to get the fruit! So we didn't carry any paper or anything, we took to Wolverhampton three Christmas puddings. That's all we took! [27]

It was, at least in the short term, a happy end to a night of fear and danger. For others, the new day did not dawn so hopefully. In fact, for many it did not dawn at all. There had already been mention, among the mass of phone calls, teleprinter messages and hand-delivered notes flying, often still haphazardly, between the beleaguered city and the regional government, of deaths in the high hundreds. Already fire teams and volunteers were moving into the ruins and the rubble, looking for those still alive and those who could only be recovered in order to give them a decent burial. A young Red Cross volunteer, also from a small Warwickshire town within Coventry's orbit, was among those admitted to Coventry in the dawn twilight:

The phone rung about half past five in the morning. Commandant told me to go to Coventry station, on the old back roads there to

Coventry. To see a town like it was – I'd been through it a couple of days before – to see it then, it was a disgrace. I never seen a place like it. Now when we got there to the station it was straight round to Gulson Road. They said you'll be operating from here. You'll be following the ambulance, the ambulance will be there to pick the injured up, and you'll be there to pick the rest.

We went to Corporation Street first. I couldn't tell you whether it was in a hospital or a nursing home and they was all burnt on the bed and we had to shovel them up and put them in paper bags, big sack bags. And put the names if they knew who it was and that.[28]

The immediate ordeal was over. The even more terrible task, that of managing the aftermath, had begun.

15

The Martyred City

'Refugees from the first big night Blitz on the provinces streamed from Coventry,' wrote a journalist in the London *Daily Mirror*, beginning his front-page report from the city. 'Pathetic streams of refugees, men, women and children were trekking to the safety of the countryside when darkness fell last night,' he continued. 'Every road out of the city, which had a bomb rained on it at the rate of one a minute, was filled with the same tragic procession.'

'Thousands Stay' was the headline to the next section of the article, but even that was qualified in the text. These 'thousands', the report added, had remained in their homes 'in the hope of saving more of their treasured belongings'. It was a measure of the frankness still permitted to the British press, despite a plethora of wartime controls, that the left-leaning *Mirror* could write these unheroic truths. However, there was another measure being expressed here and in the other British newspapers, and it also had to do with the magnitude of what had happened to Coventry on the night of 14/15 November 1940. For the first time, the British government had decided to abandon its general rule of not allowing the BBC or the press to name specific cities that had been bombed.

The decision to identify the city that had been the Luftwaffe's most recent victim was not an immediate one. In the BBC's 9 a.m. radio bulletin, the newsreader told listeners that 'Last night's enemy air attacks were mainly directed against the Midlands, where a very heavy attack was made on one town in particular. Many fires were caused and considerable damage done. This was stated this morning in an official communiqué which added that full reports are not yet available, but that it is feared the casualties were heavy.'[1] The same tack was taken at lunchtime, at least initially. On the 1 p.m. news the reader led with the 'Cold Water' RAF raids on Berlin before issuing a similar statement about the German raid against 'the Midlands'. Then, in mid-broadcast, a piece of paper was handed to the newsreader, Bruce Belfrage. On it was written a revised official communiqué, which he proceeded to read:

> The city of Coventry was heavily attacked last night; the scale of the bombing being comparable with the largest night attacks on London. The enemy was heavily engaged by intensive anti-aircraft fire, which kept them at a great height and hindered accurate bombing of industrial targets, but the city itself suffered very seriously. Preliminary reports indicate that the number of casualties may be of the order of a thousand.
>
> The attack was begun by the scattering of incendiary bombs over a wide area. Fires broke out at many points and an indiscriminate bombing of the whole city followed. It is feared that extensive damage was done and many buildings destroyed, including the Cathedral.
>
> The people of Coventry bore their ordeal with great courage. It is known that at least two enemy aircraft were shot down during the attack.[2]

There is no record of exactly who took the decision to release this information to the public – and thereby to the world – but it was not the War Cabinet. This inner circle of senior ministers, including the Prime Minister, had met at 11:45 on the morning of Friday, 15 November, in the underground office complex known as the Cabinet War Rooms. Herbert Morrison, the Labour Home Secretary and *ex officio* Minister of Home Security, was absent from the meeting. Within hours of the All Clear, Morrison, who was already in Birmingham on a routine visit, proceeded to a tour of inspection in Coventry, along with the Minister of Aircraft Production, the powerful press baron Lord

Beaverbrook, and, trailing at the rear somewhat in political terms, Ernest Brown, the Minister of Health. If any proof were needed of the importance of the city to the British war effort, this immediate visit by two heavyweight ministers was it.

Significantly, censored press reports only mentioned Morrison's presence, most likely because admitting that Beaverbrook was also there would have given away to the Germans even more than they already knew about the central role played by Coventry in British aircraft production. At the War Cabinet, meanwhile, ministers were given a fairly accurate run-down of what had happened overnight, though with the proviso that, since communications with Coventry were still poor, this could only present a partial picture.[3]

From Morrison's statement to the next meeting of the War Cabinet, which took place on Monday, 18 November, it would appear that some unease was expressed by ministers about 'the degree of publicity' given to the Coventry raid in the press and the BBC the previous Friday. Morrison admitted that in his absence a joint Home Security–Air Ministry communiqué had been issued by unnamed 'high officers of the ministry'. He took, so he said, 'full responsibility' for this. 'There was advantage,' he added, according to the minutes, 'in stating the number of casualties in a heavy raid, as otherwise rumours of exaggerated casualties passed into currency.'[4]

The decision to permit the naming of Coventry allowed British newspapers and broadcasters to cite comments in the German press that could, with some justice, be described as 'gloating'. This freedom was vital to the task of discrediting the enemy's motives, which was already under way. In the *Daily Express* (part of the newspaper empire controlled by Beaverbrook, the Minister of Aircraft Production), the precise headline was, 'Berlin Gloats'. It quoted a German radio broadcast's description of the raid:

The raids by 500 German bombers on Coventry at one stroke destroyed the skyscraper of illusions built up by Churchill.

When 500 bombers appear over London, that means a lot, but imagine 500 bombers over a town of 170,000 people. Each plane dropped a ton of bombs on Coventry.

German thoroughness used to be a byword abroad. It is true we do not like half measures, particularly when we are taking revenge.

For British blockade, German blockade. For Munich, Coventry.[5]

The London-based dailies carried reports about the Coventry raid only in their Saturday editions (available from late on Friday evening), but Coventry's local daily newspaper, the *Midland Daily Telegraph*, carried a surprisingly comprehensive report on the raid in its later editions on 15 November. The account included references to Herbert Morrison's visit and the minister's remarks praising the reaction of the local civil services and the regional government and its director, Lord Dudley.

The promptness of the *Midland Daily Telegraph*'s response – indeed, the fact that it appeared at all – was the more remarkable considering that its Hertford Street offices and printing presses, in the centre of Coventry, had been heavily bombed the previous night. The edition was actually printed in Birmingham at the presses of the *Birmingham Gazette*. Significantly, like some of the nationals, the paper led (in terms of size of headline) the front page with the 'Cold Water' attack on the German capital, which was lauded as 'Berlin's heaviest raid of the war'. The Coventry attack appeared beneath this. And in a box beside that, the headline 'Coventry Pays for Munich – Nazi Radio' with a summary similar to the *Express*'s.

How many actual Coventrians were reading these reports is open to speculation. Many had left, either permanently or (much more frequently) temporarily. Later estimates supplied to the Home Office would reckon that 50,000–70,000 would be regularly out of the city at nights from this time on until the serious bombing ceased,[6] though most were 'commuting' back to their usual work places. Others, like Bill and Vera and their *Kindertransport* charges, would leave altogether, in their case for the small Yorkshire textile town of Delph.

The people of Coventry were reacting instinctively to the 'hot' war, the war of parachute mines and incendiaries, probably unaware of the war of words that was already beginning on the radio and in the press. In its Saturday edition on 16 November, the London *Times* had headed its leader article, about Coventry, with the powerful phrase: 'A Martyred City'.[7] This description, often accompanied by poignant images of the devastated Cathedral, was to be the view of Coventry that gained currency all over the world – and especially in the United States – from this day on. The next morning, above a front-page article by its star columnist, Godfrey Winn, who had visited Coventry the previous day, the loudly patriotic *Sunday Express* carried a huge headline, said to represent the words of a young airman whom its reporter had encountered outside the ruins of Coventry Cathedral: 'Please God you will avenge what was done to us that night'.[8]

German triumphalism was all very well (and, at least in part, justi-fied), but in both the shorter and the longer run martyrdom would trump it. In terms of consequences in blood and steel, however, revenge would exceed the power of both.

In the case of the unexploded bombs in the city (estimated as amounting to more than four hundred[9]), this was the responsibility of bomb-disposal squads from No. 9 Company, the Royal Engineers, based in Birmingham, who came into the city after the All Clear. Under their commander, Captain Biggs, they worked systematically over the next few days, dealing with what was an unexpectedly high volume of UXBs. This meant that large numbers of Coventrians had to be evacuated from their homes during the course of the night, and also after the raid had finished. They would not be allowed back until the specialist disposal teams had exploded the bombs or made them harmless, and sometimes the wait was a long one. Meanwhile, regular units from the Royal Engineers mainly worked on blowing up dangerously damaged buildings, and on clearing a way through blocked streets.

We have a more detailed account of another, more specialist, bomb-disposal unit that arrived a little later that same day. Lieutenant

John Miller and his team of Royal Navy anti-mine experts arrived
in Coventry at around 2:30 p.m. on Friday, 15 November. Captain
Biggs's people would deal with the regular bombs. The naval experts'
job would be to tackle the unexploded German land and parachute
mines that had been reported from all over the city (which were basically, in design, the same as naval mines). Miller's unit was actually
attached to the Admiralty's Department of Torpedoes and Mines,
which was among those government departments that had been kept
informed through the night of the German raid's progress. Along
with other aid teams, they were ready to go in as soon as practicable
after the All Clear.

   Miller's report to the Admiralty painted a bleak picture of the city
early on the first afternoon after the attack:

> The centre of the Town, which includes the Main Police Station and
> A.R.P. Report Centre, was much ruined, and the ruins were still in
> flames. Our eyes smarted and ran in the heavy smoke; it was clear
> that there was going to be grave difficulty in the mere finding of our
> mines; most of the streets, in a wide ring round the centre of the
> City, were blocked with craters or falling buildings; the telephone
> system was out of action, and it was obvious that communication,
> both within Coventry itself, and with the outside world, would be
> next to impracticable.
>
>   By the time we found the local Control, it was too late to do
> more than have a list made out of the mines so far reported, secure
> a map of the town, fix up a programme, and retire for the night in
> Leamington Spa to establish our headquarters.[10]

   Finding accommodation for the officers was almost impossible,
because Leamington was full of evacuees from Coventry. In the end,
pressure had to be applied by both the Admiralty and the Ministry
of Home Security. Following threats to evict evacuees from their
rooms at a local hotel, the naval officers – Miller and his two sub-
lieutenants, Woolley and Cummins – were found lodgings with 'well-
to-do residents in the town'. The situation of the drivers and naval

ratings, meanwhile, was a bizarre expression of the British military's
class system at its most crass – almost risible if one could forget that
many of these men would be risking their lives in the morning on the
perilous task of disarming up to nineteen unexploded thousand-kilo
high-explosive mines.

> The Army Authorities undertook to put up the Drivers and ratings.
> Unfortunately, we discovered next day that they had shoved the men
> into some sort of room in the Grandstand on Warwick race-course,
> with wire mattresses, but no fire, one blanket only and no black-out,
> so that the fellows could not even strike a match to sling their ham-
> mocks by. Rather than that, they went into another room and slept
> on a concrete floor. We were informed that no food was provided
> that night, and though breakfast of a sort was forthcoming in the
> morning, they had to eat it with their fingers, as no utensils were
> available. We made such a row about this that the next night, and
> the rest of the time, the men were accommodated in billets similar
> to our own . . .

It was true that the situation in Coventry itself remained, in many
places, pretty chaotic. Lieutenant Miller's more jaundiced impression
should be kept in mind, whatever soothing pronouncements the
authorities might make, including the Chief Constable's claim in a
telephone message to the Home Office, just four and a half hours
after the All Clear on 15 November, that 'the situation arising from
last night's raid is in hand and all services working smoothly'.[11]
   Another outside presence in Coventry on that day was one whose
view of the aftermath was even more critical, and therefore less welcome to the authorities. In the latter part of the summer, the quasi-
governmental Mass Observation Unit had been commissioned by
the Post Office Savings Bank to carry out a survey on the Coventry
workforce's attitude towards savings. A group of its reporters, led by
the twenty-nine-year-old journalist and anthropologist Tom Harrisson, who was one of the co-founders of Mass Observation, were in

nearby Birmingham on the night of 'Moonlight Sonata', completing work on this project. On the afternoon of 15 November, they drove over from Birmingham and, despite the large numbers of police road blocks aimed at preventing unauthorised visitors, managed to sneak into Coventry.

Harrisson's team, which had been reporting on the Blitz since it began in September, and were accustomed to its horrors, seem nevertheless to have been genuinely shocked by the quite drastic effect that the bombing had on the local population in Coventry. As their report stated:

> There were more open signs of hysteria, terror, neurosis, observed than during the whole of the previous two months together in all areas. Women were seen to cry, to scream, to tremble all over, to faint in the street, to attack a fireman, and so on
>
> The overwhelmingly dominant feeling on Friday was the feeling of utter *helplessness* . . .[12]

Moreover, for the population 'from the Town Clerk down', the attack seems, according to Harrisson's experience, to have come as a complete surprise. The senior city officials 'faced dawn as pulverised as anyone else', as Harrisson put it, with all the cool objectivity of the natural scientist (his anthropological experience included research among the head-hunters of Borneo).[13]

The Labour Mayor, J. A. (Jack) Moseley, a railwayman, had spent the night in an Anderson shelter. When he and his wife emerged, they had found their house severely damaged, after which Moseley made his weary way to the Council House. Fire Chief Cartwright, still unwashed and unshaven after an entire night without rest, fell asleep while the meeting with the government ministers was in progress. Huddled in the draughty Council House, whose windows had all been blown out during the night, the visiting ministers were initially assailed with bitter complaints from the local officials about the inadequacy of the fighter and anti-aircraft defences. There was also, it seems, much criticism of the Fire Brigade. Sir Frederick Delve, who had driven up from London, recalled his irritation at the attitudes he discovered around the table in these bleak surroundings:

> And to my surprise – I was younger then, and . . . . trying to think of a nice word . . . resentful of things and critical of what was happening with people . . . and to my surprise instead of thinking of the things that needed to be done they were criticising the fire brigade and the poor showing they had done and all that kind of thing. And I quickly told them that it doesn't matter how good a fire brigade is – it could be the best in the world – if they've got no water they're like an army . . . you've got the guns but if you've got no ammunition you can't defend yourself. And you can't extinguish fires without water. And since they hadn't provided water, any emergency water, when the mains supply was damaged they couldn't do a thing.[14]

Morrison was reportedly offered a restorative glass of neat whisky by the Mayor, a gesture that apparently served mostly to underline the fact that, in the absence of mains water, it was the only liquid refreshment available. None of this helped shape an auspicious start to the urgent task ahead.

The minister, for his part, was not convinced of the council's ability to manage the situation on its own. Even more drastically unimpressed was his cabinet colleague, Lord Beaverbrook, who that evening rang Lord Dudley and demanded that he, as Regional Commissioner in Birmingham, take full control of the city administration. Dudley, perhaps knowing his Midlands politics, refused. Instead, a National Emergency Committee was set up at the Council House involving service chiefs and a stiffening of representatives from the Regional Government, operating alongside and, where necessary, putting some backbone into the weaker brethren among the council officials. They managed, somehow, to work together.[15]

'Coventry is finished' and 'Coventry is dead' were, according to the Mass Observation reporters in Coventry at that time, 'key phrases'.

Almost everyone expected a second attack during the coming night. After all, London had been bombed on dozens of nights in a row, and Liverpool had been brought almost to a state of collapse by attacks over several nights earlier in November. Rumours quickly began to spread, as in other bombed cities on both sides of the conflict (Germany was no different). Coffins of air raid victims had supposedly been seen dripping with blood. A German bomber had crashed into a Co-op store. A man had been shot for signalling to the German raiders with a lamp, to guide them to their target – apparently a common rumour in Coventry after the attack. This was a legend that would be repeated in almost identical form in German cities throughout the war. One spectacularly bizarre story confirmed what would become a familiar trope of 'warning':

Woman: 'There was a swastika in the sky before the raid – not long before the bombs began to drop. To warn fifth-columnists to clear out.'

Man: 'How do you mean, there was a swastika in the sky?'

Woman: 'Made in smoke. I've seen aeroplanes make question marks myself.'[16]

Another Mass Observation reporter described the situation at dusk, shortly before the Germans could be expected to return, if such was their intention:

On Friday (15th) evening, there were several signs of suppressed panic as darkness approached. In two cases people were seen fighting to get on to cars, which they thought would take them out into the country, though, in fact, as the drivers insisted, the cars were going just up the road to the garage. If there had been another attack, the effects in terms of human behaviour would have been much more striking and terrible.[17]

Those survivors who had not already left took to the shelters, such as they were. Harrisson described one: 'Mainly occupied by elderly folk, it had no bunks; no sanitation; candlelight. The stench was overpowering.'[18]

In fact, contrary to the widespread fear, the night of Friday, 15 November turned out to be a quiet one for Coventry. A few German aircraft were seen, a handful of bombs were dropped, but no damage was done. Many were not even aware of this small incursion. The Luftwaffe had returned to bombing London, not especially effectively, though causing damage in the ritzier parts of the West End.

As Harrisson remarked, once Coventrians had passed something approximating to a quiet night, 'the dread passed'. This did not necessarily reduce the urge to absent themselves from the city, at least for a time. The continuing exodus was not necessarily a sign of continuing panic. After all, many houses were damaged, with windows blown out and roofs stove in, and basic utilities, such as electricity, gas and water, were for the most part inoperative. It must have seemed tempting just to pay a visit to friends or family, where such existed, in undamaged areas outside the city, if only to take a bath or get a hot meal, as well as an undisturbed night's sleep. At nine o'clock on Saturday morning, the Mass Observation report recorded:

> Coventry people were looking calmer and more purposeful. The central area was thronged with sightseers. The roads leading from the city were equally thronged, however, with pedestrians carrying suitcases, carrier-bags, and bundles, and motors filled at the back with bedding.

Saturday, 16 November was, then, about movement, sometimes from the city and sometimes within it. Many suburbanites and their families decided to go the opposite way to the 'trekkers' (as the refugees became known) and get a measure for themselves of what had happened in other districts of the city, especially the centre. This happened despite the presence of military units dynamiting buildings, and the bomb disposal squads, the road clearing gangs, the firemen struggling to douse the last of the smoking ruins and the rescue parties

digging away in the rubble. These journeys were part quest for reas-
surance about family, workplace and friends, part a kind of gentle,
bewildered disaster tourism – to which they were perhaps entitled,
since this was their city that had suffered. Certainly, towards the end
of the weekend, the police were reporting that they 'were having great
difficulty with sight-seers at the principle scenes of damage'. Saturday's
urge for mobility, following a precious night without bombs, could
nonetheless be counted as the first, faint sign that the city was coming, however slowly and sluggishly, back to life.

Already on Friday, much of the centre – an area about a mile in
radius – had been cordoned off to motor traffic, mostly so that the
Royal Engineers could concentrate on blowing up dangerous ruins.
After breakfast on Saturday, Lieutenant Miller's anti-mine unit set off
from Leamington and after their ten-mile drive arrived at the edge
of Coventry's innermost restricted zone, 'We found the situation, if
possible, even worse than it had been on the Friday afternoon,' he
reported, continuing:

> We forced our way through the cordon – our drivers, incidentally,
> showing considerable courage.
>
> No telephones were in operation. We had secured two A.A. scouts*
> as despatch riders, but in the conditions it was clearly impossible, at
> that particular time, to ask them to risk taking any messages. Until
> the late afternoon we were, therefore, cut off from communication
> with our own office at Leamington and with London.
>
> One peculiarity was that the City was littered with unexploded
> bombs. Sub-Lieutenant Woolley . . . observed an unexploded bomb
> buried within ten yards of his first mine, and reported to the centre.
> I interpreted his message as an appeal for consultation and drove out
> at once to the spot, only to find the job completed. Woolley explained

---

* Uniformed patrolmen of the Automobile Association, whose motorcycle and
sidecar combinations were a familiar sight on British roads until the late 1960s,
speeding to the aid of distressed AA members.

that he had merely wished the Royal Engineers to know that the bomb existed and would require their attention in due course.

The naval team managed to disarm nine unexploded mines during the course of Saturday. Cummins, Miller's other sub-lieutenant, narrowly avoided serious injury or worse when he accidentally activated the fuse of one mine. There was, fortunately, time for him to reach and to dive into an underground shelter some fifty yards distant and for the sailor assisting him to get far enough away that he escaped the explosion with 'a shock and a couple of abrasions'.

The army bomb-disposal crews, commanded by Captain Biggs, had many more bombs to deal with, and there always existed the possibility of the booby-trapped or the delayed action device. Only one crew proved to be unlucky, leaving total fatal casualties among the bravest of the engineers at three during the aftermath of the big raid on Coventry. They were killed, along with an employee of the Humber company, while attempting to defuse a bomb at the Humber Motor Works, a short distance south-east of the city centre.[19]

It was ironic that the greatest toll among bomb-disposal experts had occurred a little over three weeks earlier. On 18 October, a unit of seven men of Biggs's No. 9 Bomb Disposal Company, under Second Lieutenant Alexander 'Sandy' Campbell, had all perished while transporting an unexploded 550-lb bomb (dropped during the 14 October raid on Coventry city centre) to Whitley Common, a large green space to the south-east of the urban area. They had managed to detonate another, similar, German bomb safely on the common the previous day, the device (excavated with great effort from beneath the Triumph Works) having been loaded on to a truck and driven the mile and a half to Whitley. Throughout the journey, Lieutenant Campbell lay next to it listening for any change in the tempo of the bomb's ticking that might indicate it was about to go off. They followed the same procedure on 18 October, removing a 'UXB' from E. Laxon & Co., a wholesale grocer in Chapel Street, in the city centre. This apparently had a 'tricky' fuse that had been somehow shaved off on impact – as Campbell apparently told a fellow officer before attempting its removal. They got the bomb all the way to Whitley Common, and were attempting to lower it into the pit that they had already dug there to make such detonations safe (known, it seems, as the 'bomb cemetery'), when it exploded.

The Whitley Common tragedy remains famous as an example of doomed heroism. There is still speculation as to whether an officious policeman or an overlong traffic light delayed the truck sufficiently that the bomb's timer ran out and set off its high-explosive pay-load.[20] Curiously, and in stark contrast, the three bomb-disposal men – colleagues of the late Second Lieutenant Campbell and his team – and one civilian, who were all killed while trying to defuse a bomb at the Humber plant after 'Moonlight Sonata', scarcely fea-ture either in Coventry folk memory or in many popular accounts of the raid.

As early as the morning of 15 November, hundreds of soldiers had been drafted into Coventry, in response to the Chief Constable's urgent requests in the small hours, while the raid was still continu-ing. Six hundred had arrived by the time the Home Security office in Birmingham sent in its report at 9:15, three hours after the All Clear.[21] A hundred and forty of the troops were used to help enforce the cordon placed around the city centre (mentioned by the naval mine expert Lieutenant Miller with some irritation), while the rest began to help with clearance and rescue work. It was also clear that they were there to help 'keep order' if that became necessary. A member of one local family, bombed out of their home on the Foleshill Road and beginning its trek to stay with relatives in Nuneaton, described walking through the city centre on the Friday:

We walked across to Swanswell. Swanswell was nearly empty, because all the fire hoses were in it and they'd been drawing water from it like, you know. And then walked up Trinity Street into Broadgate. Owen Owens, that'd been the new store, it was just a smoking ruin. The whole of Broadgate smelled of burning. There were a lot of soldiers marching about, clearing the roads. And some soldiers with rifles, to stop looting, I suppose, like, you know. We walked towards the station. It was all completely smashed up, you know, walking over rubble and everything like.[22]

By Saturday morning, the number of soldiers, who seem to have included units from the Czech army in exile (based at nearby Wellesbourne), had almost doubled to 1,130. The number deployed in Coventry would eventually reach 1,800. Signals units helped to start restoring communications, initially providing emergency wireless links to replace wrecked telephone lines. Engineers began laying temporary water pipes and repairing shattered sewage systems. Army field kitchens had also been established, since it was clear that the majority of the population, in the absence of gas, mains water and often (though less frequently) electricity, had no means of cooking food. WVS canteens were also brought in from other parts of the Midlands.[23]

Despite (or perhaps in part because of) the dazed and resentful mood of the population, the problem of 'order' (or 'control' as it was usually referred to) did not prove to be a serious one. Apart from the troops, an extra two hundred police had quickly been brought in from neighbouring county forces, including Worcestershire (fifty) and Shropshire (fifty) as well as Birmingham (one hundred). There was, inevitably, some looting and stealing. According to the Chief Constable, whereas until the beginning of November there had been no cases of looting, by the time of his report (23 November) there had been eighty-seven suspected cases, with twenty-four leading to prosecutions. He does not specify the date of these arrests. Not all, perhaps, occurred on the night of the big raid, but it seems probable that most of them did.

Those awaiting proceedings the week after the raid included three soldiers, three men from the Auxiliary Fire Service, two girls and four youths. Most were accused of stealing from pre-paid gas meters in private homes.[24] The *Midland Daily Telegraph* reported some of these crimes when they finally came before the Police Court. The youths (three of them seventeen years old) were sentenced to three months' prison with hard labour, while a twenty-one-year-old deserter from the Royal Dragoon Guards, who had acted as lookout, was given six months. The three AFS men, who were all from an out-of-town crew that had been sent in to help fight the fires during 'Moonlight Sonata', were convicted of stealing goods from a bombed-out tobacconist's shop, including cigarette lighters. They were likewise sentenced to six months with hard labour.[25] Another man, who said he had come from Loughborough 'for some A.R.P. experience' in Coventry, had been given three months' hard labour by Coventry Magistrates a few days earlier for stealing a two-hundred-year-old church register from the ruins of the Cathedral. He claimed he had simply taken it 'as a souvenir', to which the Chair of the Magistrates, Alderman Mrs Griffiths, retorted that 'Coventry is passing through difficult days, and it is not manly for people to come here to collect souvenirs'.[26]

It is possible that many thefts were not reported to the authorities. Gwendoline Holmes recalled that when her family finally got back to their severely damaged house in Beanfield Avenue, on the far outskirts of Coventry:

> . . . it had been looted. They found the settee and, oddly enough, the atlas I had been using for the essay (which we still have) but that was about all. None of our personal possessions or clothes or family photographs and documents survived. We had a huge collection of Stevengraphs (we were related to the family – Mrs Stevens was my grandfather's step-sister). In particular there was a large and beautiful woven silk picture of Greyfriars Green, but they had all been destroyed or taken.[27]

16

'Are we down-hearted?'

There were no trains to Coventry on Saturday morning; the line was still being cleared. Therefore the city's most distinguished visitor could not travel by rail, as he usually did.

Admittedly, King George VI's usual rail travel experience differed radically from that of all but a tiny number of his subjects. The royal train, in its original form created for the use of Queen Victoria, had been updated and improved just before the war. Coated in bullet- and splinter-proof steel armour, it provided one coach for the monarch and another for his queen, each with accommodation for them and their maids or valets, plus a personal dining area. However, when the King decided to show himself in Coventry on 16 November, instead of arriving in this considerable splendour he had to be content to be driven up in one of the royal cars. George VI duly reached Coventry at 9 a.m., to be met by a small delegation from the city, including Herbert Morrison, who had stayed overnight for the occasion.

For all that Coventrians always took pride in being nobody's fools, this was a less cynical age. The sight of the King walking the devastated streets that Saturday morning caught many people by surprise. Morrison had been informed of the King's intention, which had been expressed the previous day, but one of the few local officials who were forewarned seems to have been the Mayor, Jack Moseley. The Mayoress, Mrs Moseley, also let in on the secret, was said by her daughter to have burst into tears and exclaimed 'something like: "Oh dear! Doesn't he understand we're in too much of a mess and have so much to do without him coming?"' A hasty phone call was made, conveying roughly this message on behalf of the entire council, and explaining that they could not entertain the King in anything like a fit manner, in answer to which his majesty's equerry had replied that the royal party would bring its own sandwiches.[1]

There are many stories about how the King, a slight man of only a little above average height, at times wandered unrecognised, despite being accompanied by a considerable entourage of smartly dressed and uniformed gentlemen. There is a photograph of the King walking along a rubble-strewn street, flanked by the Mayor on one side and an alderman on the other, with the pugnacious, thickly bespectacled Morrison and Chief Constable Hector, a rangy figure with his thin military moustache, just behind. The King is engaged in animated conversation with Jack Moseley. On the left of the monarch is a burly, bowler-hatted man who looks like the royal bodyguard. He is looking slightly worriedly at a young woman with a wicker shopping basket, who has come very close, and looks somewhat eager to get closer, with a young man behind her who is looking slightly puzzled, though not unfriendly. Two worlds meeting in the ruins. Another encounter involved a little girl and her father on a tour of their own through what remained of the city centre. She remembered more than sixty years later:

I think the thing I can most remember was the smell of burning and the awful taste of dust; everything tasted dusty. We were going towards the cathedral and, when we got there, there were probably eight, nine men in long dark overcoats with bowler hats on, and in the middle of these people was a man dressed as a soldier. And I remember saying to my dad, what's that soldier doing, shouldn't he be at war? And my dad said, that's the King! King George VI. And I said, no! Kings have crowns on, that's not a King! And my mum said, you know, what was it like and all the rest of it, and I said, stones and things, they kept going in my shoes. And she said, who was there, and I said, there was this man that dad said was the King, but I don't think it was.[2]

Of course, the King visited the still-smouldering ruins of the Cathedral. Provost Howard was not expecting him:

The King's arrival took me completely by surprise. To the sound of cheering he entered the south-west door. I went forward to be presented to him and he shook hands with me. I stood with him watching the ruins. His whole attitude was one of intense sympathy and grief.[3]

The symbolism of the Cathedral, and the presence of the tall, ascetic-looking Provost Howard, standing in the ruins with his monarch, was powerful enough to set off a dozen camera shutters.

Other meetings are not recorded in pictures but in words. The King visited a rest centre in St George's Church in Barkers Butts Lane, in the suburb of Coundon. It was one of the six remaining centres out of the thirteen existing before the bombing – these places had been hit hard. Inside, the royal party came upon some dejected homeless and elderly residents, who had been resting on their bunks prior to their arrival. Suddenly they seemed transformed, reportedly hastening to their feet and giving a slightly uncertain chorus of 'God Save the King'. At a WVS mobile canteen, the staff were reduced to tears of joy, and a lady in her seventies went to embrace the King and declared: 'God bless you, lad, you've got more pluck than that Hitler bloke.'[4]

It was said to have been the King's own idea to come to Coventry, and it was certainly something of a master stroke. Even though his person represented the very pinnacle of the English class system, the monarch's appearance in this working city among ordinary people symbolised something about the unique face – democratic and aristocratic all at once – that Britain showed to the world and which would sustain it, in its own eyes and those of others, until the struggle was finally over. King George was generally agreed to have an affable, approachable and modest demeanour, and to be unafraid of 'mucking in' under difficult circumstances. By contrast, Hitler – the elderly lady had been right – refused to visit badly bombed cities such as Hamburg or Cologne. Especially later in the war, when Allied air attacks on Germany became heavy, he preferred to journey by night in *his* personal train with the blinds pulled down over the windows. Once, travelling with the blinds open, due to a mistake by his aides, Hitler's train stopped directly by a hospital train. Its waggons were full of wounded German soldiers; in some agitation, the Führer called for the shades to be lowered immediately.[5]

As in all stories about great events, especially those told at some decades' remove, the ether is full of half-truths and downright legends about the King's visit. A perfect example is the tale of how he came to Coventry. This has Ellen Moseley, the Mayor's wife, sweeping up the last of the damage to their terraced house in the inner suburb of Earlsdon on the morning of Saturday, when there is a knock on the door. She calls for the visitor to 'Go round the back!' A couple of minutes later, she cries out to her husband, the Mayor: 'Jack, there's a gentleman in naval uniform coming down the back garden path!' To which he replies, 'Heavens above, it's the King! We'd better look sharpish!' We know that firstly, they were forewarned the previous evening, and, second, that throughout his visit the King was not wearing a naval outfit but an army field marshal's uniform. All the same, the story is charming and shows affection both for King George and for the mayoral couple. It exists in at least two variants.[6]

By no means everyone saw the King, but enough people did, and they told others. The news spread rapidly. In any case, after a morning of such exertion, King George needed lunch. We do not know if any of the gentlemen-in-waiting were carrying sandwiches, but in the end lunch was indeed supplied. It seems to have been true that the councillors had nothing to offer to assuage the royal appetite. The problem, so the story went, was solved when Lord Dudley, going beyond the strict call of duty, had his butler bring some cold collations

from Himley Hall, the Earl's stately home, roughly an hour's drive
west of Coventry. The party, including Morrison, consumed these
welcome supplies in the Mayor's Parlour, a room without windows
within the Council House, with candles stuck in beer bottles to light
their table while they ate.[7] Refreshed, the King emerged from the
Council House to be greeted with tremendous applause.

Actually, the King did visit Jack Moseley's house during his day
in Coventry. And he did come in round the back, so that part of the
story was true. While driving around the city, the King had asked the
Mayor how things were at home, and Moseley had told him of their
street's travails during the raid. His Majesty promptly insisted that
the Chief Constable, who was in the car with them, direct the royal
driver to the Mayor's address. The account says 'they could not enter
the front door' – apparently it had been blown out on the night of the
raid and replaced by boards. The blackout shutter in the living room
had been put back in its place, to keep out the cold, which meant
that the room was dark and lit only by a few candles. Jack Moseley's
daughter told Norman Longmate what happened next:

> My sister . . . was perched on the end of the kitchen table chatting to
> the other two sitting by the range when she suddenly caught sight of
> dad's bowler hat – followed by a khaki flat cap – passing the window,
> and in a split second dad pushed the door half open and announced,
> 'His Majesty the King!' First shocks over and introductions made,
> King George went round the house with mum . . . He was very
> friendly, natural and kind.[8]

Later, according to her account, the King was given a rousing
send-off by the entire street, with the local people, largely women
at that time of the day, standing on piles of cleared rubble or lean-
ing out of shattered windows. There were many loud cheers and
some tears.

The relief of the authorities at the success of the King's visit was
considerable. Chief Constable Hector's report to the Home Office
on the mood after the raid reveals the difference the King's presence

made to morale. It was the first of many visits that the monarch was to undertake as Britain's provincial cities came under increased attack that winter, and probably the most famous.

'The visit of H.M. the King to the City on the 16th instant completely set aside any doubt I had as to the attitude of the inhabitants,' Hector wrote in his confidential report, inadvertently betraying a temporary unease that he could never have publicly admitted, 'and I was able two or three days after this to dispense with the Military assisting in maintaining Law and Order.'[9]

The reports of the visit, and the photographs of King George among his people in their hour of need, were, of course catnip to the press both in Britain and, crucially, in the United States.

Call it PR, or call it propaganda, but a narrative was rapidly being developed of what had happened to Coventry, how its people were said to have reacted, and what had been the British government's response to the disaster that had befallen the city. This narrative would find its way right round the world.

Coventry was about to become a symbol. The Luftwaffe may have carried out its most devastating raid yet, but in the war of words that was just beginning Germany was poorly armed and even more poorly led.

As the British media quickly noted, the triumphalism of the German press and radio, orchestrated by Goebbels' Propaganda Ministry, was extraordinarily blatant. The official government radio mouthpiece, the *Deutschlandsender*, declared on 16 November:

Coventry is proof of the fact that the German Air Force can strike harder yet. For the attack on Coventry was as strong as the strongest air raids on London, in comparison with which Coventry is only a small town. If 500 German bombers appear over the huge London area that is certainly a terrible thing. But it is more terrible yet for a town of 170,000 [sic] inhabitants, where one factory abuts the next. Every single German bomber dropped 1,000 kg of bombs, so that one is justified in speaking of Coventry as having been smashed completely. This implies immense losses for British war production, chiefly in aircraft but also in tanks. The British Minister for Home Security went to Coventry yesterday to inspect the damage wrought in retaliation for the non-military attack against Munich. Morrison saw fields of ruins and heaps of wreckage, as the American press reports today. UP declares that a large part of the town of Coventry has been annihilated. The English themselves reckon that 1,000 people have been killed. This figure is only explicable if it is assumed that work was still proceeding in the Coventry factories when the German air raid started.[10]

Another broadcast ('Topics of the Day' from Breslau) told a similar story. 'Today,' it announced, 'the whole of Coventry is a mass of rubble. Factories which produced plane engines, aeronautical instruments and electro-motors will not work again. Thirty-six hours ago the so-called shadow factories really became shadows. This was a total, not partial, destruction of Coventry.' This was not true. Actually, the shadow factories had remained largely unharmed, but as a rhetorical flourish it proved irresistible.

There were, however, already indications that Berlin realised how easily the trumpeting of this apparently easy victory could rebound on its authors. Later that evening, after the King's visit and especially his tour of the Cathedral's ruins, German propaganda subtly changed tack. No less a figure than Hans Fritzsche, Goebbels' press chief, later 'Plenipotentiary for German Radio', and such a key figure in the Third Reich's propaganda machine that he would stand trial at Nuremberg, gave a talk on the *Deutschlandsender* about Coventry. His tone might still have been laced with the habitual wild hyperbole, but so far as the content of the broadcast was concerned he switched to a more nuanced approach, laying heavy emphasis on the raid as a tit-for-tat response to the RAF's attack on Munich:

That retaliation was carried out the night before last. It was carried out against Coventry, a city which is the seat of a bishop, like Munich, and has buildings of historic interest – though to a much smaller extent – like Munich, but which consists today almost exclusively of small, larger and biggest armaments factories . . .

. . . we Germans have often enough explained that German retaliation is not based on the Jewish principle of 'an eye for an eye and a tooth for a tooth', but that retaliation would be taken if the British Air Force planned an outrage which was irreconcilable with decent methods of warfare, even if it was unable to carry it out . . .

. . . the retaliation against the Munich raid was . . . directed not against the workers' quarters and not against shrines in England which are worshipped by the people, but against industrial plants which are important for the war effort. If other buildings should have suffered as well, this is an unintentional but occasionally unavoidable consequence of the relationship for which the English themselves are responsible.

. . . this decent and soldierly punishment for an unsoldierly deed. . . .

. . . we know from American sources that 1000 people were buried under the ruins of an aero engine factory . . .

Part of the cause for Fritzsche's new 'reasonableness' (if one does not count the claim that a thousand workers had been killed in just one factory) may have been the realisation that in America, above all, the Luftwaffe's attack on Coventry was by no means a propaganda victory for Germany. Rather to the contrary. In the *New York Times* of that same day, for instance, with the early editions coming out around the lunch hour, Berlin time, there had been clues even in the early reporting. 'Revenge By Nazis', the headline declared. 'CATHEDRAL IS DESTROYED'. 'Homes and Shops Bear Brunt of Mass Assault – Military Damage Is Minimized'. Underneath, there was some mention of the industrial role of Coventry, but these headlines were what held the attention. That, and the description of 'the bruised and battered face of Coventry, a little Midlands city that was the victim of one of the worst bombardments from the air since the Wright brothers presented wings to mankind'.[11]

The next day, when more considered reports started to cross the Atlantic, things got worse for the German cause, so far as public opinion in America was concerned. The *New York Herald Tribune* set the tone: 'The gaunt ruins of St Michael's Cathedral, Coventry, stare from the photographs,' it said, 'the voiceless symbol of the insane, the unfathomable barbarity, which had been released on Western civilization. No means of defense which the United States can place in British hands should be withheld.'[12] On 17 November, the *New York Times* reported King George's visit in glowing terms:

> Coventry – victim of Germany's self-styled greatest air raid in history – was today displaying another kind of greatness by arising from the misery and ashes of yesterday's punishment to heal its wounds and regain the normality valued so highly in all walks of English life.
>
> King George joined the people today around the smouldering ruins of the ancient peaceful city. The emphasis of the tour was directed to the measures being taken to restore everyday life after attending to the immediate needs of the suffering ones.
>
> Once again evidence of the mutual respect for courage was exchanged between the monarch and his subjects. His prompt appearance in the city was appreciated by the populace . . .

Elsewhere in the paper, the story of his triumphant arrival at the Council House for his cold lunch was repeated:

> The cry went up: 'The King! The King!'
>   Then a cheer: 'Hip, hip, hooray.'
>   The King smiled. Saluting, he made his way through the throng as a red-faced policeman yelled:
>   'Are we down-hearted?'
>   'No,' the crowd roared.
>   'Will we knock Hitler's block off?'
>   'Yes.'*

---

* The *Midland Daily Telegraph*, Monday, 18 November, reported this exchange as occurring when the King emerged from his visit to the Mayor's home earlier that morning. Perhaps a misunderstanding of 'Council House' by an American reporter.

The *New York Times'* editorial on that day must have prompted purrs of pleasure in British government circles:

> The disaster at Coventry is a clear warning to America to rush that material aid which we are pledged to give and which our people overwhelmingly desire to give. There is not time for us to send it at our leisure. The British are more than ever dependent on us now for the increase in airplane strength which can, in time, defeat the Hitler challenge to the world. The inevitable loss in aircraft production at Coventry will have to be made good in American factories . . .[13]

On Monday, 18 November, the paper reported that, after what *The Times* had described as a raid 'superlative in its frightfulness', discussions were already under way in Washington to raise the quota of American aircraft production that could be exported to Britain above the current 50 per cent.*

A curious phenomenon immediately after the raid was the appearance of some articles in the British press that, far from portraying the German attack as a raid on an innocent city, in fact (and accurately in most respects) classified it as indicating a switch to a more calculated strategy of attacking British industry in a more deliberate way. Bizarrely, one was in the *Midlands Daily Telegraph* on 16 November. While elsewhere in its pages the paper carried on condemning the Luftwaffe for its cruelty and deliberate targeting of civilians, under the by-line 'By an Air Correspondent', the first part of the rather soberly-written short article read:

> Attacks like those on Coventry, suggest that Germany is changing her night tactics, and has realised that the haphazard and indiscriminate bombing she has carried out during the last few months has completely failed.

* That is, potentially exported. In the same article, *The Times* estimates that out of monthly US production of aircraft amounting to around 2,000, only 300 or so were, in fact, being exported to Britain.

> This new phase in night warfare may mark the beginning of wide-
> spread raids on the industrial parts of England.[14]

The writer then proceeded to deliver 'good news' in arguing that,
firstly, by this the Germans were being forced to imitate the R.A.F.'s
allegedly more discriminating bombing, which had 'achieved their
object in seriously hampering and impeding the German war effort',
and second, that in the case of Thursday night's raid on Coventry,
this method had been unsuccessful. Apart from the fact that neither of these assertions was really true, the overall message could
not help but be confused, and such articles did not appear often.
From this time on, the general emphasis was much more on Nazi
barbarity. The image of the King among the ruins of the medieval
cathedral, surrounded by his brave and loyal people, was far better
suited to the impression that the government wished to create, at
home and abroad.

Mass Observation's report was not published while the war was on,
for obvious reasons, but there was trouble in store for Tom Harrisson,
his organisation – and the BBC – nonetheless. Their problem arose
from the high-level decision to counter confusion about what exactly
had happened at Coventry. This required an eyewitness account from
an experienced broadcasting professional who had been there in the
city in its hour of despair. Harrisson, having spent an uncomfortable
night from Friday to Saturday in his car and then a day in the field with
his teams, returned to Birmingham on the afternoon of 16 November.
Later that evening, he was installed in a BBC Radio studio there, script
hastily written, ready to report his experiences to the nation.

Harrisson's talk went out at nine o'clock in the evening in the
popular five-minute 'Postscript' slot that followed the main radio
news bulletin.[15] Whatever effect it may have had on the general public, plenty of people in authority were horrified by it. The tone was
by no means as uncompromisingly gloomy as Mass Observation's
(confidential) report on Coventry might have led us to suspect,
and ultimately it gave out a positive message about the efficiency

of the civil defence services and the city's keen urge to rebuild. However, by the standards of the time, and given the situation the government perceived the country to be in, the gritty realism of some of Harrisson's remarks was considered shocking. It was really the first part of the talk that caused most of the trouble. Harrisson began:

> I have spent a good deal of life listening to other people talk, but I've never heard people talk less than in Coventry yesterday. Many walked through the city rather blankly looking at the mess, and the commonest remark was simply: 'Poor old Coventry.' . . . I've been chasing air raids in this country ever since they began: often I've heard awful stories of the damage and then arrived to find them grossly exaggerated. But about Coventry there hasn't been much exaggeration: in fact the centre of the town reminded me more than anything of the photos of Ypres in the last war . . .[16]

This and similar observations stood in sharp contrast to the usual government promoted stereotype of the permanently cheery Briton, whether Cockney or Coventrian, defying Hitler to do his worst and assuring the world that the nation 'could take it'.

In fact, it seems that Harrisson was merely telling the story as he found it, at a particular moment. There was no doubt from Mass Observation's own researches that, by the end of that weekend, the population of Coventry was starting to recover from the shock, aided by several nights' respite from the Luftwaffe's attentions. The King's visit had helped. It was also becoming clear that the damage to the factories was less terrible than had at first been thought. A certain pride in having been singled out by the Germans, and surviving nonetheless, was becoming apparent.

All the same, Harrisson's talk caused a major conflict between government and BBC. At the War Cabinet meeting on Monday, 18 November, several ministers joined in to complain about its tone and to express their resentment (in some cases, including that of

Churchill, long harboured) at the failure of the national broadcaster to deliver a properly patriotic message. 'This had been a most depressing broadcast,' the Secretary of State for War (at that time, Anthony Eden) remarked, 'and would have a deplorable effect on Warwickshire units.' There was widespread agreement.

Churchill himself thought that something should be done. As the official account of the meeting stated:

> The Prime Minister said that he did not suggest that the decision to give prominence to the Coventry raid was wrong. The effect had been considerable both in the United States and, from a different point of view, in Germany. The enemy seemed to be alarmed at the publicity given to this raid and to have taken the unusual course of announcing that they had lost 223 dead in our raid on Hamburg on the following night. Unless the publicity in the press had had a bad effect on our morale, he doubted if it had done any harm. Nevertheless, he wished to be assured that the decision as to the degree of publicity given to raids of this character was entrusted to an officer of high standing. He would be glad if the Ministers concerned would consider the present procedure from this point of view.[17]

The Minute that followed the account of the War Cabinet meeting showed exactly the implications of what Churchill had said. Referenced in the margin as 'Broadcasting. Constitution and Management of the B.B.C.', it said:

> In connection with the previous Minute in which the account given by the B.B.C. of the position in Coventry was strongly criticised –
> The War Cabinet –
> Invited the Chancellor of the Exchequer, the Home Secretary and the Minister of Information to examine and report to the War Cabinet what changes, if any, were necessary in the constitution and management of the B.B.C. in order to ensure its effective control by His Majesty's Government.

Luckily, what might have turned into a campaign to exert direct government control over the BBC resulted in the appointment early in 1941 of two government 'advisers', one on foreign and the other on domestic policy, to whom the BBC was supposed to pay attention. Technically, if these outsiders felt they were being ignored they could request their ministers (Foreign Secretary and Minister of Information) to intervene, but they don't seem ever to have done so. The home affairs adviser, though seconded to the Ministry of Information, was, in fact, drawn from the BBC's own management. A close friend of the Prime Minister was also appointed to the Corporation as a Governor, but since that close friend was the impeccably Liberal Violet Bonham-Carter, this hardly amounted to a Goebbels-style takeover of the airwaves.[18]

The relative peace that Coventry enjoyed over the next few days could be ascribed, in good part, to the cloudy, damp weather that had greeted the survivors when they emerged from their shelters on the morning of 15 November and continued to hang over the city. Most locals experienced this as a curse, given the lack of shelter, warmth and basic utilities. In fact, the failure of fate to provide further clear, moonlit skies for the benefit of the German bombers proved a mercy for all.

On Sunday, 17 November, Philip Larkin, then in his first term as an undergraduate at Oxford, hitch-hiked home in the company of a fellow student, a distance of a little under sixty miles. He was worried about his parents, from whom he had heard nothing since the raid. His companion and old friend from Henry VIII Grammar School, Noel Hughes, also sought news of his family. First they went to the Larkin family's pleasant inner-suburban home on Manor Road, not far from the station. The house seemed intact, but no one was there.

So isolated was his difficult family from their neighbours that Larkin knew only one who might provide information of their whereabouts. Larkin was distraught when he drew a blank there, too, but the two young men pressed on with their mission. They next went to the

Hughes family's house, entailing a trek through what was left of the
city centre. There they also found no one – but Hughes managed to
track down a cousin, who assured him that his parents were all right
and had just got out of the city to avoid any follow-up German raids.
The young men got a lift back to Oxford that same night. Fortunately,
there was a telegram waiting for Larkin at the college lodge from his
parents, Sydney and Eva. They were safe. Eva had gone to stay with
Sydney's brother in Lichfield, and he had found refuge at a colleague's
house, from where he could commute into the city to continue his
work with the council.[19]

Wandering his shattered, though still familiar home city during
those desperately anxious hours, the young poet became aware, as
never before, of the fragility of human existence and the full horror of
what technology could visit upon an apparently predictable domestic world. In June 1941, his parents finally moved to Warwick, from
where Sydney commuted into Coventry until he reached retirement
age in 1944. Apart from visits during university vacations, Philip
Larkin would never return to Coventry for any substantial length of
time. His poem 'New Year' gives a sense of how it felt that Sunday,
returning 'home' and finding no one there, and of how it must have
felt for hundreds and thousands of others:

> These houses are deserted, felt over smashed windows,
> No milk on the step, a note pinned to the door
> Telling of departure . . .

The Quick and the Dead

It was clear from the first – apparent, in fact, even while the bombing was going on – that the German attack on Coventry had inflicted very heavy casualties. At 6 a.m. on 15 November, the Home Office was told that figures of dead and seriously injured would be 'very high, probably six hundred'.[1] The figure for overall casualties was rapidly revised upwards, becoming a thousand (dead and injured) later that day (a figure deliberately misconstrued by German radio, which announced that 'the English themselves reckon that a thousand people have been killed'[2]). On Saturday the figure of confirmed dead was increased to 'over three hundred', with seriously injured now estimated at eight hundred.[3]

Meanwhile, recovery of bodies was continuing. By Saturday morning, a few fires were still smouldering, notably at the RAF Stores in the Daimler Works, Triumph in the city centre, and the railway goods yards at Lythalls Lane and Coundon Wharf.[4] Rescue parties had nonetheless been able to get into many wrecked and ruined buildings to retrieve the dead and, in a few fortunate cases, survivors who were still buried under the rubble. By then there were only four sites left in which people were thought to be trapped but alive.[5] There was no shortage of rescue parties – forty-four in total, with twelve coming from outside the Midlands region (including Manchester).[6] In fact, as Captain le Grand had scribbled as early as noon on Friday, 15 November: 'Borough Engineer states that he does not need any more rescue parties.'[7] The main problem seems to have been the lack of experience and technical training of many rescuers. Equally, there was a shortage of the right equipment, especially heavy lifting gear, needed for removing massive girders and masonry, to give access to bombed sites.

By Monday evening, according to a message received by the Home Office, 380 bodies had been recovered and moved to mortuaries. The same report estimated that there remained thirty-eight incidents where it was thought that bodies remained to be recovered.[8] By the end of the week, the number of confirmed dead had risen to 502 with, again, over eight hundred so seriously injured as to require hospitalisation. Hundreds more had been treated on the spot or treated and sent home. Records of the lightly injured were not especially well kept.[9]

The honouring, identification, and proper counting of the dead was problematic and painful enough. It was made even more difficult by a succession of grisly accidents that upset the authorities' quite careful planning for the event of heavy air raid fatalities. The city's swimming baths had been the first choice as a place to store the dead after an attack. By ill luck, however, the baths had been hit early in the night, before they could be put into use. It was fortunate that, before the big raid, Dr Arthur Massey, the city's Medical Officer of Health, had decided to convert a large, nondescript shed near the old gas works, not far from the city centre, into a second emergency mortuary. Just in case. A medical colleague recalled:

> Dr Massey had made provision for a mortuary for 500 bodies (to the quiet amusement of several colleagues, who thought he was overdoing it). It was in a building adjoining the gasometer . . . Racks had been erected with runners, which took an ambulance stretcher and was in fact several layers deep, the upper layers being quite high to load. The routine practice for ambulance and stretcher personnel . . . was to tie a luggage label on to the body, stating where it had been found, whether the identity of the body was known, and the number of the ambulance which had taken the body to the mortuary. These particulars were written with an indelible lead pencil.[10]

By a further grim mischance, the main gasometer – holding three-quarters of a million cubic feet of gas – was also hit during the raid, and exploded, 'like a huge firework'. This blew the corrugated iron roof off the mortuary shed, though it left the building itself intact. During the first weekend following the bombing, there was a downpour of rain, which soaked the bodies stored there, washing most of the writing off the labels. The original identification information was thus lost. As a consequence, because all the deceased had to be identified before a burial certificate could be issued, the medical authorities began bringing in relatives to effect this distasteful but essential task. This process was not a success. Especially in the case of victims who had suffered the full effect of a bomb blast (a civil defence report estimated that between 40 and 50 per cent were 'unidentifiable owing to mutilation'[11]) this proved almost impossible. The dead were often enough 'claimed' by several different families.

The procedure was quickly abandoned. A sign outside the mortuary now read: 'IT IS GREATLY REGRETTED THAT THE PRESSURE AT THE MORTUARY IS SUCH THAT IT IS NOT POSSIBLE FOR RELATIVES TO VIEW ANY OF THE BODIES.'

Another system was found. Clothes, belongings, jewellery and watches, and so on, were removed and placed in one bag, and each body put into a coffin supplied by the Regional Office, care being taken to label bag and coffin with the same unique number and enter the number in a register.

It was gruesome work, which was done by the stretcher party personnel. A bottle of brandy was very useful at the outset . . . Subsequently the bodies were identified by their clothes, jewellery, etc., and . . . there were very few who were not finally identified.[12]

Clearly, all this presented a serious danger both to public health and to morale. One survivor, a girl of eight at the time, had been evacuated to the country shortly before the raid along with her mother and siblings, while their father stayed in the city. The day after, they were told he had been killed:

> My mum . . . had to leave us and go back to identify him. She went into the Council House. She told us everything, I think that's how she coped. They had a little sandbag and they emptied it up and they said, do these belong to your husband? It was . . . I can see his grey overcoat now. And they said, d'you want it? And she said no. And I remember thinking, why didn't you bring it back?[13]

Before long, the authorities decided to undertake a step which had not so far, in the course of the air war, been contemplated: the imposition of mass burials for the victims of bombing. On the negative side, this could be seen as carrying the stigma of an anonymous 'pauper's grave', a final indignity genuinely feared by working- and lower-middle-class people. For them, this harked back to the world of beggary and the workhouse, which in 1940 lay not so far in the past. On the positive side, it enabled a lot of bureaucratic labour to be avoided, and obviated the need for a whole succession of private funerals, drawn out and painful for those involved and for the city as a whole.

In the end, the vast majority of families went along with the scheme. Officially, it was not a mass burial but a 'civic funeral', for which the council handled the formalities and – a strong inducement for most ordinary working families – also assumed responsibility for the expenses (which it then claimed back from central government).[14] This solution also meant, though this was not admitted, that any mistakes in identification – which, given the numbers of dead and the amount of mutilation to many bodies, remained inevitable – would carry no practical consequences for the authorities.

While the big mass funerals were being prepared, the survivors had to be protected. In the immediate aftermath of the raid, more than half of the entire city was without clean mains water. In most practical ways, for the general public, this was a worse problem than the lack of electricity or gas. A teenage boy from rural Coleshill, who had cycled the ten miles or so into the city after the All Clear to check that his best school friend was safe, described the scene that met his gaze:

> I can see now the water pipes, all bursting forth with water running down the street, and electric cables blown apart. There was just no power, no electricity, no water, no nothing. No traffic moving around at all, I mean it really was a total disaster.[15]

Citizens were warned to boil all water, through street signs and travelling loudspeaker announcements. Heavy amounts of chlorine were added to what was left of the mains. Potable water was soon being brought in from outside on large lorries, including big tankers usually used for milk collection, and the population was encouraged to fill buckets and kitchen utensils. Some mains water was available by Sunday, though at low pressure, but this brought with it a new problem. Despite a heavy chlorination programme aimed at minimising the risk of water-borne disease, cracked and broken sewer pipes might well, so it was thought, be leaking waste into the city water supply. The Medical Officer of Health quickly initiated a programme of vaccination against typhoid. There was a systematic campaign through the civil defence services and the local press to induce the population to protect themselves. Thirty thousand inoculations were administered in the next few days, often en masse in reopened factories. Not a single case of typhoid was reported in Coventry, which blazed the trail for successful prevention in other bombed cities, a fact of which Dr Massey was justly proud, and for which he credited the timely use of chlorine.[16]

The disruption of the water supply was one thing, and perhaps for most individuals and families the most pressing immediate problem. Besides this, the destruction of the gas and electricity supply in central Coventry and out into the suburbs was almost total. This was especially so in the case of gas, where gasometers had been destroyed, and 150–200 direct hits on the city's extensive network of gas supply pipes had been reported, along with damage to other delivery equipment.[17] This disruption was hard on citizens who had spent the night in foetid shelters and then come out to dust, smoke, rubble and damaged or destroyed homes. The lack of hot water was keenly felt. As one young woman put it: 'Then when we'd sorted everything out, I realised my legs were just black, with all the dust and everything I suppose. So I thought, oh I'll go up and have a bath. But we'd got no gas and so no hot water.'[18]

The vast majority of households in Coventry cooked with gas. Preparing hot meals was therefore, for the moment, impossible except over fires or coal-fired stoves. Even a simple cup of tea needed boiled water (and boiling, which citizens were being told was essential even for basic drinking purposes, also needed power). These latter inconveniences could be offset by field kitchens and WVS mobile canteens, which appeared quickly, first in the city centre and then, as more were brought in from outside the city, spreading out into the suburbs.

Later, a municipal café was opened in the Congregational Church and schoolroom in Well Street, miraculously serving up to a thousand meals an hour, with seating for five hundred to 'eat in' if desired. A main course of meat and two vegetables cost 6d, a sweet course 2d, and cups of tea and coffee 1d each.[19] Before these things became available, people made do. In some cases, perfectly respectable Coventrians, without food and apparently with nowhere to get any, ended up engaging in what was probably, from a strictly legal point of view, looting. As one eyewitness shyly recounted:

Only yards away from the shelter there was a cooked-meat shop. And my dad went to the front of the shop and knocked on the door, and he got no reply. So he went round to the back of the shop, tried the back door, and he couldn't get it open, but he forced it open. And there was some cold faggots. Then the owners of the shop came back. The lady was really angry about us being there. But her husband calmed her down, and he said to my dad, if I'd have been in your situation I'd have done exactly the same. My dad would never have done that otherwise, he'd be mortified that I was telling people about it really.[20]

So far as the city's war industries were concerned, while they also needed water both for hygiene and various production processes, the lack of gas and electricity was the thing that really laid them low. It affected them far more decisively than any HE bomb crashing through a factory roof, or incendiary starting a warehouse blaze. Eric Bird's initial report made it clear that the physical damage to industrial buildings and plant was highly variable. Only time would tell exactly how crippling the raid had proved for Coventry's industrial capacity. As things stood, however, such calculations were temporarily irrelevant. As the Friday after the raid dawned, almost all of these factories, whether intact or not, had no power. Nothing worked.

Mr Eric L. Bird, of the Home Office's Research and Experiment branch – a leading expert on the effects of fire on buildings who made a rapid but amazingly thorough inspection of Coventry over the weekend of 16/17 November – summed up the early view of the damage in a report that he dictated and submitted the following Monday:

Coventry contains factories of all sizes, from very large, both new and old, down to quite small factories mainly in back streets and employing a few dozen workmen. At a very rough estimate one-third of the factories in the city have been either completely demolished or so damaged as to be out of commission for some months. One-third have sustained considerable damage which will hinder production for some weeks and about one-third have been only slightly damaged. A few escaped altogether.

This rough estimate is concerned only with the number of factories, not with their relative importance. It is noteworthy that two very large new Shadow Factories on the outskirts of the City were entirely undamaged. It is not, however, possible at present to obtain anything

like an accurate picture of the hindrance to Coventry's war effort
which the raid has achieved, except to say that it is considerable.[21]

Bird noted, in his punctilious way, that the water, gas and electricity
supplies were near-non-existent. Apart from the old gas holder
in central Gas Street, a large electricity distribution centre near
the hard-hit Daimler Works in Sandy Lane had also been put
out of action by two relatively small 50-kg bombs. Their impact
completely destroyed the somewhat delicate switching gear and
caused serious fires, though elsewhere the basic infrastructure of
the electricity supply turned out to have survived better than the
gas, water or sewage pipes.[22]

   As for public transport, this was, for a short while, almost at a standstill. Coventry's thirteen-mile system of tramways was completely
put out of action, the metal rails extensively destroyed by bombing,
along with the overhead lines on which the electric trams depended.
Decades later, numerous eyewitnesses still spoke with horrified awe
of seeing 'tramlines twenty feet up into the air', 'a tram burnt out and
all the tram wires . . . all over the road', 'the tramlines all bent up.
Like a U, U-shaped . . . '[23] The recurring image of jagged, twisted
rails, of which these are just a few examples, was set perhaps even
more firmly into the collective memory because, after that day, the
once-familiar trams never ran again in Coventry. It was considered
too expensive to restore the network, with its steel rails set in the street
and its vulnerable overhead power cables.

   The large-scale destruction had forced this decision on the council,
but the abrupt demise of Coventry's trams was not so surprising.
The system had symbolised a transport revolution when it began
running in the mid-1880s, initially under steam power but during
the 1890s switching to overhead electricity. By the 1930s, however,
it had begun a gentle but decided decline.[24] The era of the tram had
begun to turn into the age of the bus. And soon to come, of course,
that of the car. Of the city's 181-strong bus fleet, six were completely
destroyed and seventy-seven damaged by the Luftwaffe.[25] All the

same, that left a hundred or so still running, hindered only by the failure of some drivers to report for work and, especially in the city centre, by the rubble and crater-strewn streets. They carried evacuees out of Coventry to the surrounding countryside and towns from the early hours after the raid, as the police and relief organisation records show. Not that there were really enough to cope. Ten-year-old John Harris, trudging out of Coventry with his mother and his two sisters, heading for their grandfather's in Nuneaton, saw a crowded bus go past and then suddenly stop: 'People started rushing to it, and the driver shouts out, no, no, I'll take the lady with the three kids! That was us, you see.'[26]

The railways had been brought to a complete halt, as the King's forced arrival by car so vividly proved. Damage to station buildings, to track, fences, embankments, bridges and so on, was considerable. The main line to Birmingham had been hit by seven bombs, and the Nuneaton–Coventry–Rugby route by twenty-two. The goods line known as the 'Coventry Loop Line', which left the Nuneaton–Rugby route to the east of Coventry centre and curved round to join the same line going north near Foleshill, thus avoiding the congestion around Coventry station, was especially badly hit, attracting forty-five bombs and a parachute mine.[27] It served several major factories. The suddenness and thoroughness of what happened to the railways, and especially to Coventry Station, was evidenced by the account of a woman who worked in the plotting room at a fighter base. They relied on 'live' reports from around the country for their work:

I recall a friend of mine . . . she was on Coventry, the Coventry station, when it was bombed. And she was plotting from there, and it just went dead. And . . . you see, you're plotting from different areas all round the country. But you did get things like that which really brought it home with a bang. But then you didn't appreciate . . . I mean, just a line going dead. You know something's happened. But it was not long after that I came through Coventry and I saw for myself.[28]

Almost everything was difficult in post-Blitz Coventry, and most particularly any forms of even moderately long-distance communication. The telephone network was all but dead, with more than three-quarters of the city's 6,500 subscribers cut off. The telephone exchange in Hertford Street had survived, as had the postal sorting office in the same building.* This latter apparent stroke of good fortune was not all it might have appeared to be. The GPO itself lay within the restricted city centre zone closed off by the military for the entire first week after the bombing. Sorting work had to be carried out in neighbouring towns.

As in all environments where normal communications had largely broken down, rumours were rife. Information about progress in searching for the living and retrieving the dead from the ruins, for instance, was sporadic. Radios, in the age before transistors, were overwhelmingly run from the mains, which meant for some days after the raid most homes could not listen to news or entertainment programmes. The most important route for information – apart from gossip – was the local papers, in particular the daily *Midland Daily Telegraph*, which despite being printed, for now, in Birmingham, had skipped only one edition since the night of 'Moonlight Sonata'. So it was that, just over a week after the raid, the *Telegraph* felt itself called upon to put one particularly pervasive rumour to rest:

The 'Midland Daily Telegraph' is able officially to deny rumours that large numbers of people still remain trapped beneath central buildings that collapsed as a result of the big air raid.

In the last few days it has been widely stated that not only are many bodies still buried beneath piles of debris and that in some cases central shelters are being sealed up, but that a number of people trapped on the night of November 14 are still alive, and being fed regularly by tubes.

Such statements are authoritatively declared to be incorrect.[29]

* This juxtaposition was not uncommon. The British telephone network was, of course, run by the General Post Office until 1980, when it was hived off as British Telecommunications (BT), which in turn was privatised four years later.

There followed a reporter's account of a guided tour of central buildings and shelters, including those 'about which the rumours had been most rife'. The *Manchester Guardian* also dealt with the rumours, citing popular belief that victims continuing to be trapped in air raid shelters, specifically in the crypt of the Cathedral (which had actually been evacuated during the raid) and under the Barrack Square (near the A. C. Wickman Machine Tools factory in the city centre, and famous for its market). The paper reprinted the official emergency committee announcement:

> All air raid damage incidents and particularly public shelters have been thoroughly investigated, and there is no ground for believing that large numbers of bodies remain to be recovered. It is pure rumour. To believe it is playing Hitler's game.[30]

Other rumours included one that said four hundred men remained buried under the enamelling shop at the Standard Works (a secret funeral service had allegedly been conducted within the ruined factory, with priests blessing the piles of rubble), another claiming that further hundreds of dead had been secretly sealed in the deep shelter at the Courtaulds factory after it received a direct hit, and so on.[31] Even three-quarters of a century later, with communications more than adequately restored, it is nonetheless possible for online commentators to entertain the possibility that the authorities were lying when they stated that all bodies had been found and given decent burial. The stories of lost corpses and sealed shelters have, apparently, still not been put conclusively to rest.[32]

Six days after the first Heinkel 111s had dropped their marker incendiaries on to the centre of Coventry, signalling the start of the terrible night that followed, the first of the 'civic funerals' of its victims was held. The location was the large municipal cemetery on London Road, three-quarters of a mile south of the city centre. The authorities announced that the grave site would be turned into a memorial to Coventry's suffering once the war was over.

The date set for the first mass burial was Wednesday, 20 November. With bodies still being recovered from the ruins and others not yet identified, two ceremonies were planned. Earlier in the war, a section of the cemetery had been quietly set aside for the interment of possible air raid victims. It was in this area that a mechanical digger had been employed, during the first part of the week after the attack, to excavate two deep and long trenches. After nightfall, scores of coffins, some draped with Union Jacks, had been laid out in these trenches, ready for the ceremony. Wednesday dawned grey and damp, but this did not deter relatives, families, well-wishers and sightseers, or the national and international press. These were ordinary people being consigned to the earth, but from the outset this was going to be an extraordinary event.

An account written by one of the clergy who officiated at the ceremony, a Congregationalist Minister, described the grim but solemn scene at the burial site before the ceremony. Clergy and civic officials, and the Regional Commissioner, 'strained and tired', gathered there first and waited for the mass of mourners to arrive:

When all was ready we moved in order towards the gate to meet the crowd of mourners, who were led up the road through the cemetery by a contingent of police, firemen and wardens. Then, at the top of the rise, the bishop and clergy, followed by the civic officials, took the lead to the graveside. It was a quiet and solemn procession. The soft beat of the rubber boots of the firemen, the measured tread of the police and wardens, marching in step across the gravel path seemed to accentuate the silence.

At the graveside it was possible to turn back and look over the long line of mourners still approaching. It was a pathetic sight; women carrying wreaths; here and there a child with a bunch of flowers; the black suits and dresses relieved occasionally by a splash of colour of the uniform of a husband, a son or a brother on compassionate leave. It seemed as if there were no end to this long dark line, which moved slowly across the grass. At last the great crowd was gathered around the graves.[33]

The attitude of the British press turned out to be a mixed one. The Labour-supporting *Daily Mirror* ran it as a front-page splash ('HUNS RAID AS 172 ARE BURIED') with more on page twelve, and a photo section on page seven.[34] The *Daily Express* scarcely carried the story at all on the day following the funerals, relegating it to an inconspicuous spot on page three. Under the headline '73 Words of Comfort' (Old English script in the original), it supplied a quotation from the Bishop of Coventry's address 'at the funeral of the 172 people killed in the raid last week'.[35] The London *Times* confined the story to a dignified but unquestionably brief paragraph at the bottom of page two, beneath 'TWO HOSPITALS HIT IN LONDON'.[36] It seems that the further to the left the paper stood, the more coverage. The *Manchester Guardian* ran a quite lengthy article, albeit well inside the paper, under the headline: 'COVENTRY BURIES HER DEAD: A Strange, Simple, and Moving Service at the Graveside'.[37]

The story really took wing in the American newspapers. Ray Daniell, the London Bureau Chief of the *New York Times*, who had filed such lively and moving copy immediately following the raid, submitted a powerful article that also appeared on the day after the London Road funerals. 'All of them,' he wrote, 'were buried in one grave – a long, narrow, deep gash cut in the red earth by a steam shovel and shored up with rough boards so that it looked like an excavation for a water main.' He continued:

Beside this ugly sepulchre stood some 800 to 1,000 mourners, almost every one clutching a bunch of chrysanthemums, dahlias, or carnations. Most of them were dry-eyed, but thin-lipped and grim-faced. A few wept, but they were bitter tears in which hatred was mingled with sorrow. I saw the same look in the eyes of a woman at a mass funeral in Chicago for thirteen steel workers killed by the police one December day in 1937 . . .

. . . After dust and ashes had been sprinkled on the coffins by a half dozen assistants, those who come with wreaths of flowers filed past the open grave and laid their floral offerings in a line along the edge. Only one woman in that long line broke down and wept, and had to be supported by friends. Others bore their grief silently and inwardly in the traditional British fashion. There was no singing, no music, nothing to alleviate the stark ugliness of what was more like a soldier's burial on the field of battle than anything else.[38]

Underneath this substantial report, the paper noted that 'the foregoing article . . . was heavily censored without explanation. One statement deleted from Mr Daniell's dispatch was allowed to be used in the British press.' The ways of the Press and Censorship Bureau remained mysterious.

The second mass funeral, this time involving 250 victims, was held on the Saturday following, 23 November. Although the number of dead was substantially greater on this occasion, it received little attention in the national and international press. The *Manchester Guardian* gave notice of this on the day before, Friday, but only as part of a Coventry round-up also dealing with progress in the clearing of wreckage in the city centre, the opening of the Well Street municipal cafeteria, the New Zealand Commission's gift of £100 to the Coventry Mayor's Relief Fund, and some ambulances donated by the St John and Red Cross organisations.[39]

In the meantime, after a relative lull, due to the bad weather, the Luftwaffe's bombing war had once again switched direction, and recovered its momentum. In the days immediately after the raid on Coventry, the city had been the centre of the national attention. Help had flooded in, from the centre but also from other provincial cities. Birmingham, in particular, had helped her little sibling city, Coventry, during this traumatic time. Coventry's newspaper, the *Telegraph*, had been printed in Birmingham. Staff from Birmingham's Registry Office had been brought over to Coventry, half an hour's drive away, to help their colleagues there deal with the sad but pressing task of issuing hundreds of death certificates for those killed in the attack. Then, five days after the Coventry raid, the outside staff were hurriedly withdrawn. They had even more urgent business at home.

On the night of 19/20 November, 440 German bombers attacked Birmingham. Four hundred and fifty people died. Lucas Industries, GEC (whose cable factory in central Coventry had also been all but destroyed), and Birmingham Small Arms (BSA) were badly hit, as were whole streets of workers' housing. The grim caravan of the Luftwaffe's Blitz against the British provinces had moved on.

The positive factor in all this was that Coventry would be spared more pain, at least for the moment. The city's people, already recovering their nerve, could begin to think about rebuilding. First the utilities, then the factories, and then their homes.

18

Coventrated?

There could be no doubt that the attack on Coventry, in its ruthlessness, scope, and – it must be admitted – level of success, represented a new departure in the air war. Nonetheless, during the attack and the days that immediately followed, when journalists, politicians and ordinary men and women looked for a word to sum up what 'Moonlight Sonata' meant, they reached for previously familiar comparisons. One popular word coined to describe Coventry's fate was 'Guernica'd', after the historic Basque town that had been all but wiped out during the Spanish Civil War by dive-bombers of the so-called 'Condor Legion'. This force was composed of Luftwaffe pilots who had 'volunteered' to help the pro-Axis Nationalists, and many of its veterans were now taking part in the Blitz against Britain. The *Midland Daily Telegraph*, for its part, latched on to another horrific air raid and dubbed the German attack 'Coventry's Rotterdam night', referring to the devastation of the Dutch port's picturesque city centre by Luftwaffe bombers six months earlier, in May 1940.[1]

Then, quite quickly, there arrived the verb 'to Coventrate' – in German, 'coventrieren'. It was a curious coinage, obviously triumphalist and relying, like a political or comedy catchphrase, on a worldwide public's ability to make an instant connection with the terrible thing that had happened to the city. It meant, of course, a thoroughly wrought work of urban destruction, executed from the air. The word was also, of course – for all its quasi-jollity – a not especially subtle threat. The Luftwaffe, it implied, could do the same thing again.

Other British cities and towns would soon share Coventry's now notorious fate.

The actual origin of the term is somewhat obscure. Its first verifiable use, at least as a verb in German, is on a German photograph, issued as a propaganda document a short while after the raid. This shows an aerial view of the bombed Midlands city, accompanied by a prominent headline saying: 'Coventry – coventriert'. The full text reads:

> On 15 November 1940 the German High Command issued this communiqué: 'The non-stop attack of strong formations under the command of Field Marshals Kesselring and Sperrle was particularly powerful and successful. Bombs of heavy and very heavy calibre were dropped on numerous factories making engines and extensive plant serving the aircraft industry, as well as other facilities of military importance, causing the utmost devastation. Gigantic conflagrations, fed by burning stores of raw materials, which were visible from as far away as the Channel coast, completed the work of destruction . . .' After this massive attack by the German Luftwaffe, which was in retaliation for a British attack on Munich, the English invented a new verb, to 'coventry' (coventrieren). With this word, which could be translated as to 'completely destroy', they admitted the success of the German attack, whose effects can be seen clearly from this photograph taken by a German reconnaissance aircraft.

Curiously, this is presented in Britain as evidence of the origin of the word 'coventrate'. In explanations of this document (which is kept at the Herbert Museum and Art Gallery, Coventry), the 'new verb' invented, allegedly, by the British, is given as 'coventrate', whereas in the actual text the term used is 'to "coventry"'. The word 'coventrate' does not appear at all, anywhere. Nevertheless, in one British publication the text is even translated with the words 'to coventrate' substituted, without explanation, for the actual words used: 'to coventry'.[2] Perhaps it is because the German text in the document is, in reproduction, tiny and best read with the aid of a magnifying glass, that this mistake has arisen. The fact is interesting because the phrase 'to coventry' is more plausible as a native British coinage than 'coventrate', which sounds . . . well, as if it was translated from German. 'To *do* a Coventry' would sound even more plausible ('to do a Dunkirk' was already common usage by the winter of 1940[3]) but is not suggested by the German author.

Nonetheless, it seems almost certain that the word 'coventrate' itself, however hard its originators might try to persuade us that the awestricken British had made it up in acknowledgment of German superiority, and whenever it was actually invented, should be credited as a creation of the German propaganda machine. Most contemporary accounts indicate that 'Lord Haw-Haw' used it first in a broadcast shortly after the raid, though no recording of this seems to exist. However, at least one published diary contains a reference connecting Germany's most notorious English-language radio propagandist with the phrase ('She came along this morning with the news that Lord Haw-Haw last night promised to "coventrate" Ipswich'), recorded only two weeks after the big raid on Coventry.[4]

The phrase's implicit evocation of 'devastate' or 'obliterate' further underlines its unpleasantness. It does not sound like a word that a British person of the time would have thought of, and which might have spread out from an original British source, as did the word 'Blitz' as shorthand for the bombing war against Britain. That 'coventrate' as an expression was, nonetheless, to some extent accepted by the British public seems more in the nature of a defiant gesture, of the kind that defuses a threat by turning it into a joke (much as racial and socially insulting epithets are sometimes deliberately adopted by the people affected, as a way of turning their malicious energy against the abusers). Use in British newspapers and in the government's own propaganda (especially in America) certainly successfully exploited its unattractive implications. This is not just clumsy 'Teutonic' humour, was the implication; behind it lies a dark brutality.

Was Coventry, then, really 'coventrated' on the night of 14/15 November 1940? The raid was spectacular, terrifying and extremely destructive. Germany's air force inflicted a great deal of damage within an extensive urban area, and killed hundreds of human beings, while itself suffering the absolute minimum of losses (in the shape of the one aircraft lost near Loughborough). The Luftwaffe air crews' skill and determination, not to mention the excellence of German aeronautical and radar technology, were convincingly demonstrated. The German specialist magazine *Luftwissen* (Air Science) engaged in distinctly less than scientific braggadocio in its first issue after the raid on Coventry:

In the space of a few hours the squadrons of General Field Marshals Kesselring and Sperrle dropped 500,000 kg. explosives and 30,000 kg. of incendiaries over Coventry and flattened to the ground the city with its factories, which were irreparable as far as England's air craft industry was concerned. A few days later, attacking planes found that the city, or what was left of it, was like a desert. No A.A. shells rearing upwards, no searchlights sweeping the sky. The English city was truly wiped out. Even the venomous inciter in the ecclesiastical vestments of the Archbishop of Canterbury, who had demanded the extermination of German women and children by British bombs, was silent then. American commentators announced that Coventry's inhabitants especially did not wish for reprisal raids on Germany as 'they could take all the horrors of war without flinching'. People had finally admitted that Germany possessed air superiority if not complete mastery. What frantic deliberations the warmongers on the Thames had (after this realisation) on the carrying on of the war, is impossible to imagine. The last 10 days of November bore witness that German strength was by no means weakened after the attacks on Germany.[5]

The last part was true. Once the weather had sufficiently improved, the Luftwaffe launched major attacks on Southampton (17 and 24 November), Birmingham (19 and 23 November), Bristol (25 November), Plymouth (27 November), and – once again – Liverpool (29 November). There were then two more raids, on successive nights

(30 November and 1 December), against Southampton. What the Germans did not do, however, was to press home their advantage against Coventry. They did not attack again for some weeks, at least not in any significant force.

The oddity of this has been commented on often enough since, and was certainly reflected in Mass Observation's report during the immediate aftermath, when it said: 'If there had been another attack, the effects in terms of human behaviour would have been much more striking and terrible.' Thirty years or more later, Tom Harrisson, who saw the city at its most dejected, before it began to bounce back, called on the Prime Minister in support of this view. 'Churchill thought the place could have been knocked out,' he wrote, quoting the great man: '"They would have done much better . . . to have stuck to one thing at a time".'

It was not to be. Instead of hitting Coventry again quickly, and hard, after the massive November raid, the Germans carried out no comparable attack on the city for another five months. There was no follow-up. The next major German raid, on 17 November, was against Southampton, a slightly smaller town. It represented an abrupt switch from the industrial Midlands down to the south coast. Harrisson commented further:

> The erratic pattern in the German blitzes . . . seems in retrospect to be nearly senseless. The sequences show no logic, no discernible theory of what such attacks – more or less indiscriminate bombing all structures within a few limited areas nightly – were supposed to achieve; nor any reason why one place was left alone for weeks or months, while another was given serious assault, though still never with any consistency. This very uncertainty was . . . one explanation of the lack of pattern. No one in Britain could know or predict where the next bombs were to fall . . . But the meagre evidence indicates that this uncertainty was also considerable in the minds of those responsible for target decisions at the Luftwaffe end.[6]

Southampton, with a population of 180,000, had already been raided a number of times, most notably in late September, when the

Supermarine Spitfire aircraft factory was all but destroyed. Fortunately, the authorities were already well advanced with the dispersal
of production to shadow factories elsewhere in the country, including
at Castle Bromwich near Birmingham. October was relatively quiet
for a while after that. Then the Hampshire town was subjected to four
major raids, between 17 November and 1 December. Each time, the
attack involved a substantial number of German bombers (159 on 17
November, 121 on 23 November, 251 over the two successive nights
of 30 November and 1 December).

Although a quite large number of aircraft were involved on 17
November, the later attacks on Southampton were much worse in
their effects. Destruction to the port, the centre of town, and most
notably the large and much-praised Civic Centre, which had been
built shortly before the war and also housed an art school as well as
municipal offices, was very severe. A number of art students were
killed, along with their tutors.[7] This degree of devastation was arguably as bad as that inflicted by 'Moonlight Sonata'. People on that
part of the south coast certainly thought so, and by the end of the
devastating sequence of raids many were apparently claiming that
their experience was 'worse than Coventry'.[8] Coventry had quickly
become the proverbial measure of airborne horror.

The local historian of the Southampton Blitz, Bernard Knowles,
called the port's ordeal 'indescribable . . . even the most savage
convulsion of nature could convey no idea of the universal uproar
and clamour. Every possible form of terror was used. Every second or
two the town was shaken to its foundations.'[9] Knowles's account was
an otherwise conventional 'Britain can take it' version of the story.
In fact, there seems to have been genuine evidence of political and
social breakdown. Mass Observation's representative there, a young
man by the name of Len England, declared that 'the human and
morale problems of Southampton are being left to local resources
and local personalities which are, in this case, inadequate'. Later, it
would be argued that England was young and inexperienced and had
misinterpreted or even misrepresented the situation.

It was not just one Mass Observation reporter who criticised the authorities' response to the emergency, however. In an official report, Southampton's Mayor was described as 'a poor creature . . . [whose] sole concern was to be out of town as soon as possible in the afternoon', the Chief Constable went off sick (quite legitimately, it seems), and the Town Clerk was 'entirely unsuited' to playing any kind of role in the crisis. All this was contained in a document signed by Wing Commander E. J. Hodsoll, the Home Security department's Inspector General of Air Raid Precautions. Hodsoll was a man of great experience and considerable Whitehall heft who had also submitted a (favourable) report on the use of the military in Coventry three weeks earlier.[10]

Sometimes even the toughest of populations could come close to cracking under the strain. Liverpool, the most bombed city after London, suffered terribly, for the most part with great courage and resilience. Sir Frederick Delve of the nascent National Fire Service nonetheless used Merseyside's experience as an example when he told an interviewer of the damage to morale that could be wrought by repeated and persistent bombing on a provincial city. Successive raids on Liverpool had – in his view – at one point almost brought the city to its knees. Then, abruptly, the Germans turned their attentions elsewhere:

Very, very fortunately, I think it was after the sixth night, the raids stopped. We were very relieved when that happened because I had formed in my own mind that had those raids continued, there would have been riots in Liverpool. The people, you could see . . . the reactions of the people. They'd had enough.
How did it show in their reactions?
Various ways, their panic and this that and the other . . .
But of course that happened in London, did it not?
No. It happened very exceptionally. London is a very large area. Bombs are dropped in Wandsworth one night, East Ham the next. They don't know anything about it, you see. But here it was the same streets night after night.

This was the special terror of the provincial raid in a nutshell. Aubrey Lewis, a psychiatrist, who wrote a wartime article for the medical journal the *Lancet* on the mental damage inflicted on civilians by bombing, summed it up at the time:

Plymouth or Coventry, more unified, small and concentrated, can be so devastated that every citizen is affected, and the interference with essential services – food, warmth, light, water – serves to intensify depressive and other neurotic reactions.[11]

Tom Harrisson put things more frankly:

I know from personal experience that it is ten times more unpleasant to be blitzed in a place the size of Coventry or Bristol, where every bomb is personal and every piece of damage is a disaster to one's own town, instead of the great agglomeration of town which is called London.

In fact, although there was understandable depression, fear and sometimes panic among the populations in all the towns and cities bombed by the Luftwaffe during the winter of 1940/41, the civilians affected also showed a surprising capacity to absorb the terror and carry on with life. The Coventrian version of this phenomenon was different only in detail. The sunny propaganda view that 'Britain can take it' is not so much untrue as unnuanced. The nation did, after all, ultimately 'take it' and survive. British city-dwellers during those years suffered all the inevitable negative, pessimistic feelings that difficulty and tragedy breed, but were buoyed up by the positive and optimistic ones that are also part of any human experience, however painful. In particular, a powerful sense of common purpose and mutual aid came to the fore. Afterwards, of course, when times improved, they tended to forget the bad parts of the experience and highlight the positive ones.

Almost everyone who reported on Coventry in those first days after the big raid noticed, to some extent or another, the stunned, temporarily disheartened attitude of most of the population. They also, however, noticed that within a short while, and certainly by the end of the first post-attack weekend, the population (or the part of it that had stayed in the city) had started to cheer up. 'Out of the rubble,' as Harrisson wrote, 'began to grow local pride.' If we are to believe that there was indeed some adoption of the German coinage 'coventrate', that would also be down to a defiant, to outsiders often perverse-seeming assertion of self-respect that is typical of the West Midlands, as it is of industrial mid- and north Britain in general.

The enormous publicity that the government allowed to be given to one particular raid could have backfired, as was obvious from the slightly anxious discussions inside the War Cabinet about the decision to name Coventry as a bombed city instead of just 'a Midlands city' or a similar formulation. The curious thing was that after this the authorities went back, for the most part, to their habit of not naming bombed communities, so that – judging from the *Daily Mirror* on 18 November – Southampton became 'a southern town' or 'a south coast town'. However, when Liverpool was bombed on 18 November – that same day – the city, like Coventry, was specified in government communiqués.[12] This fact, and the brevity of the press's mention of a quite large raid, must have contributed to Southampton's undoubted perception of its own invisibility, of being ignored in favour of more 'glamorous' cities that had somehow been adopted by the authorities as symbols of courage.[13]

If the Luftwaffe had decided to take a bombing tour of provincial England according to no obvious plan, British government policy in regard of identifying afflicted cities was also clearly all over the place. In retrospect, the policy of keeping locations of bombed areas mostly secret seems faintly ludicrous (as if the Germans didn't know which towns they had bombed on particular nights). In fact, moreover, there is evidence that being named in the national (and international) press helped to an extent to aid psychological healing in bombed provincial cities. (London, as ever, was *sui generis* in this regard because of its size and obvious worldwide visibility.) As Coventry's Chief Medical Officer of Health, Dr Massey, told American reporters four years later: 'World-wide publicity through the daily press helped the people of Coventry keep up their morale during and after the terrific air raids on that English city in November, 1940 . . . Not a single case of "shell shock" occurred, so far as he knows, although the people of Coventry were enduring front-line conditions.'[14]

Allowing for wartime exaggeration, Massey's very positive remarks held a strong element of truth, with the King's visit a little over twenty-four hours after the raid undoubtedly a strong element in that equation. His assertion would find an echo, though a strangely negative one, in the authorities' view of Coventry over the next few years, when, in fact, the 'special' status of the city and its people would become something of an irritation.

Of course, one other important element was the fact that Coventry had been, and remained, a city of industry. When the first Monday after the raid came around, it was time to return to work. Apart from the fact that there was a war to win, Coventrians also needed to earn a living.

Working people in Coventry had many problems to face, as they emerged back into what passed for real life the morning after the raid. They had survived, and of course that was the main thing, but unless they had money already in the bank or the savings account, one difficulty that featured high on the priority of many was a simple, practical one: it was Friday, and Friday was pay day.

There were cases where factories, or factories' office areas, had been totally destroyed by German bombing. Banks were closed, too. Those who made it into their places of work that were at least part functioning were usually given a 'sub' (i.e. a payment on account) to get them through the weekend. Others, as Longmate records, who wanted out of the city or (in the case of Irish and other immigrants) out of the country altogether, demanded their wages due in full, and there were some ugly scenes. At the Daimler engine works in Allesley, on the outskirts of the city, a 'visibly shaken' chief wages clerk and his staff were forced to accede to the workers' demands and hand over substantial sums from the cash in the office safe.[15]

A new verb, to 'trek', was already in existence, denoting (usually in a pejorative sense) the flight of large sections of the civilian population of large towns under air attack to places of refuge and perceived safety, in the countryside and the surrounding smaller towns. It had begun in London in September, when frightened civilians from the East End, heavily bombed because of its proximity to the docks, took to camping out in Epping Forest overnight. As the fifty-seven-day Blitz on the capital continued, the nocturnal movement of people spread west and north as well, with 'trekkers' turning up in Reading and Oxford and Windsor (where 'Jews or children' were forbidden), as well as Hertfordshire and Bedfordshire.[16] The 'trekking' of large proportions of the population on the day after the Coventry raid was, of course, even admitted in news accounts (although no photographs were published).

Whether this betrayed poor morale among civilians (which the Ministry of Home Security and the Ministry of Information certainly feared) or (as recognised by most psychiatrists at the time and just about all historians writing three-quarters of a century later) a rational response to danger, 'trekking' did not, so it seems, permanently damage the social or economic functioning of the cities affected. Especially in Coventry and Birmingham, the 'trekkers' often turned out – at least in the case of the breadwinners – to be not deserters but commuters. Moreover, the phenomenon seems, in the overwhelming majority of places, to have shown a close correlation to the actual damage done to homes and neighbourhoods. As a Ministry of Home Security report, based on field studies in bombed towns, stated:

> The relation of absenteeism for personal reason to the percentage of houses destroyed and the casualties per thousand, and possibly the effective density of the attack, should give the best indices on which to base conclusions as to the relative morale of the various towns.[17]

In other words, if a lot of people's homes had been destroyed or badly damaged, they were more likely to leave the city. Not just fear, then, but practical necessity. After all, they had nowhere to live. Both Sydney Larkin, City Treasurer, and the Mayor, Jack Moseley, became commuters in the time after the raid. Unlike Moseley, Mr Larkin did not even have the excuse that his house had been devastated. Some continued to commute. By 1941, Midland Red buses were carrying five thousand more passengers into the city at clocking-on time every morning than they had before the raid.[18] This did not include people travelling in by car – quite common in England's 'motor city' – with car-sharing overcoming problems with petrol rationing. Then there were those who walked, or travelled in by rail, once the line was repaired, or by bicycle. After being bombed out of Coventry, the historian Adrian Smith's father undertook a lengthy commute in from his parents' house, across the border in rural Northamptonshire, every day by bus or motorcycle to his job at Armstrong Whitworth's Baginton works.[19]

In the case of the West Midlands, including Coventry and Birmingham, if some did leave for good, they were, in any case, rapidly replaced by new immigrants attracted by the prospect of steady, highly paid work in the booming war industries.[20] The main problem, then, for what was left of Coventry's industries, was not labour shortage. During the first days, with the city in confusion and the centre still cordoned off, there was little enough for many employees to do anyway. In fact, for the first time since the Depression, provision had to be made for substantial public support of unemployed workers in Coventry.[21] The qualifying period usually needed before unemployment assistance became payable was suspended because of the special circumstances.[22]

Nevertheless, in those factories that had not been totally devastated, people were quickly returning to their places of work, soon in ever-increasing numbers. Some had managed to get in on Friday, and had some idea of the task ahead. Len Dacombe, who had lived through the raid while on night shift at Coventry Climax, remembered:

When the management started arriving in the morning, I showed them round all the damage that had been done, and the boss called a meeting, and said, well, there's not much we can do. Report to work on Monday and we start clearing up.[23]

After a few hours' sleep on the sofa at home, Len then persuaded his fiancée, Cecilia ('Cis'), to get on his motorbike and come with him to untroubled Northampton 'for a rest' ('The sirens went, and nobody took any notice!'). After being stopped six times at police checkpoints during their journey home on the Sunday, it was back to work on the Monday – at least for him. As Cecilia had already discovered the day after the raid, her place of work, Bushill's, a large firm of printers, stationers and box makers, had been burnt to the ground and would never reopen.[24]

The clearing up took time, depending on the state of the factories concerned. This often turned out to be appreciably less desperate than had at first been thought. The main problem in a lot of places was loss of electricity, gas and water, but factories had priority in getting these resources restored. Once electricity, in particular, was back, some production could restart. There was still no gas citywide at 6 p.m. on Monday, 18 November, however. The danger of gas leaks and consequent explosions was an enormous hindrance. A gloomy note from the Ministry of Aircraft Production about the gas supply in Coventry, received by the Prime Minister's office on 19 November, admitted: 'No definite information as to ultimate restoration. Hoping for one-third reasonably quickly, one-third some weeks later, and remaining one-third extremely uncertain.'[25]

On the plus side, 50 per cent of the electricity grid was by then back in operation. Substantial parts of the water system had been temporarily disconnected at the weekend, to isolate damaged stretches that might have become infected from cracked and broken sewage mains. By the beginning of the new working week, citizens were still being advised to boil water, but the situation had now 'improved' and 'all pumping stations were in operation'. Units of the Royal Engineers had laid eight miles of temporary water piping. The weekly report circulated at the Ministry of Home Security on 20 November, detailing the situation, noted that, whatever the

Germans said, 'industry in Coventry . . . has not been brought to a standstill'.[26]

It was true that some factories were definitely finished. Triumph in the city centre had been totally destroyed, and also the nearby GEC cable works. The Triumph plant would not be rebuilt in Coventry, but transferred to new premises at Meriden, near to what is now Birmingham Airport. There it would resume production, operating for the rest of the war and well on into the 1970s. A substantial part of the Herbert Machine Tool complex had likewise been wrecked, a serious blow to factories all over the country as well as locally, along with Daimler in Sandy Lane, the old Alvis plant off Holyhead Road, and Humber (where the three-man bomb disposal team and their company guide had perished). The Singer factory just to the east of the city centre had been very seriously damaged, along with a host of smaller companies, some of them like the unnamed foundry 'in the city centre . . . which contains stock of very great value'. These last were more essential than would at first appear, since they had contained stores of castings and master moulds, which – like machine tools – were less easy to replace than plant and machinery. British Thomson Houston in Alma Street, a centre for the production of magnetos, which were key to the functioning of motor vehicle and aircraft engines, had 'two shops gutted; considerable glass and roof damage', and much work had already been transferred to Rugby. At important factories such as Rootes, Riley, Morris, and Standard, however, damage had already been repaired, and in some cases production had been resumed as early as the day after the bombing, Friday, 15 November. Even at the GEC Telephone and Radio Works in Copsewood, on the outskirts of Coventry, although 'half of the general assembly shop' had been destroyed, in the rest of the factory work had begun again on Friday afternoon.[27]

Coventry's industry had been seriously hit, no question about it, but as early as Monday, 18 November the War Cabinet had agreed that 'damage to munitions production was less extensive than feared'. The initial 'preliminary and rough' report of the Coventry Reconstruction Committee, chaired by Lord Rootes, the motor industry magnate, gave an accurate and quite detailed rundown, factory by factory, of the state of things. In many – surprisingly many – cases, the real harm caused by what had appeared to be a totally devastating raid was relatively superficial. One page (p. 19), picked at random, is more typical in its findings than the few points in the report where total destruction is described:

COURTAULDS LTD., FOLESHILL ROAD
No damage to plant.

Generate own power.

Roof damage prevents working nightshift. Hope to finish repair by this weekend.

MAUDSLEY MOTORS
Only machine tool damaged is an old Herbert No. 1 Flat Turret with bar equipment.

Section of roof approximately 40 ft. square badly damaged under which machines are suffering from water.

Roof lights broken in other parts of factory, but repairs to these are in hand.

No power.

VALVES LTD.
Plant damaged – about 6 Plain Turning Lathes, one Double Ended Pedestal Tool Grinder.

End of two bays demolished.

Will be at 85% production by Wednesday, providing power is available.

S.S. CARS*
Plant damaged – negligible.

Whole of roof shattered on 5 bays.

* Later Jaguar Cars.

Temporary cover been applied.

2 phase current promised tomorrow (Old Works)

3 phase current promised sometime this week (New Works Machine Shop)

Approximate stoppage of production (part) – 1 week.

Gas – outside help required on heat treatment (mainly gears)

We to recommend suitable firm.

COVENTRY MOTOR PANELS

No damage to plant.

Functioning 100% day and night.

Continuation of this controlled by gas supply at present cut off.

After Wednesday this lack of gas will affect production 20%.

Have arranged to overcome this by sending work to Boulton & Paul, Wolverhampton, but this it is considered will not be necessary.

GEO. WILSON GASMETERS, FOLESHILL ROAD

No damage to plant.

75% production tomorrow (Tues.) on machine parts (Aero). Labour disorganisation and transport = 25%.

Power O.K. (electric)

Gas off (mains)

Water on.

Sheetmetal Shop

Whitley* Petrol Tank production 75% O.K.

Tank Repair 100% O.K.

Sheetmetal assembly stopped. Expect to be functioning partly within a week.

An important element in the German leadership's understandable but ultimately mistaken triumphalism was the lack of really accurate

---

* The medium Whitley bomber, used by the RAF for attacks on Germany and on anti-submarine work for Coastal Command, from 1936 until its 'retirement' in 1942.

aerial photographs taken after the raid. Rain, cloud and still-drifting smoke hindered the reconnaissance crews in their work. Likewise, the horrific photographs of urban destruction that were wired around the world lent the scene in Coventry an apocalyptic quality that was visually shocking, but actually the real, structural damage to the working city (as opposed to the city as a pleasant place to live) was nowhere near as great as it appeared. As both sides would learn when the air war escalated further, almost any town that had been subjected to a large scale of bombing would invariably look broken, as if no one could have survived, and as if a continuation of anything like normal life in such a shattered environment would be impossible. Almost always, even in the worst cases – such as the bombing of Dresden – these things proved not to be the case. This truth applied even more acutely when it came to war industries and munitions production. Factories tended not to burn as well as old houses and inner-city apartment blocks. Apparent obliteration was not all it seemed.

At the end of December, the Rootes Committee submitted a report detailing the damage, how and to what extent it had been dealt with, and listing its recommendations. In general, it recommended appointing after any raid on a city or town 'a small body of resolute men, acting in association with Regional Commissioner, including Government Officers having complete powers to determine priorities, to allocate materials, to requisition property and to settle problems of finance'. Lord Rootes' men of resolve had actually voted themselves out of existence well before Christmas. A little more than a month after what most observers had thought to be a totally annihilating raid on Coventry, their job was considered done.

In Coventry, the Committee was able to adjourn *sine die* four weeks to the day after its first meeting, secure in the knowledge that every serious problem had been tackled and that facilities for production were to a very large extent restored and were growing every day. Electricity, gas, water, and telephones had then been restored to all factories engaged in war production.[28]

On the weekend of 15 and 16 November, Tom Harrisson and his two Mass Observation reporters had supplied the original portrait of Coventry's post-raid shock (although careful also to note its people's rapid return to something close to optimism). As it happened, another co-founder of MO also arrived in the city that same day. The film-maker Humphrey Jennings had been shooting a morale-boosting short documentary to be entitled *The Backbone of Britain*, concentrating largely on the resilience of ordinary folk in the north of England. This project found him, in mid-November, among the hills of the Lake District with his fellow members of the GPO'S Crown Film Unit, constructing a sequence around the hardy lives of fell-dwellers. Then the news of the bombing came through. Sensing the importance of what had happened, he and his crew set off down to the Midlands in Jennings' Standard Ten saloon. They began filming in Coventry early on Saturday, about the same time as King George arrived.

Almost needless to say, the monarch's mood-enhancing visit fails to feature in Jennings' documentary, any more than it does in Harrisson's account of his own visit to Coventry. They were, after all, both very much men of the political left. The film does contain some striking and moving footage of Coventrians among the ruins of their city, as well as an appearance by the energetic director of Coventry's WVS, Councillor (later Lord Mayor) Pearl Hyde, a publican's daughter and Labour Party stalwart, who did a lot to banish the image of the organisation as a stronghold of middle-class Lady Bountifuls. In a cameo that would bring her fame all over the world, especially in America, she spoke feelingly about the work of the women who operated the WVS canteens in the devastated city centre, succouring the victims and keeping up the strength of the rescue crews and the firemen:

> You know you feel such a fool standing there in a crater holding a mug of tea . . . until a man says 'it washed the blood and dust out of my mouth' and you know you really have done something useful.

Jennings was not in Coventry for an especially long time. He carried on filming elsewhere in the country, but a month later returned to shoot what would turn out to be the closing sequence of the finished documentary. This time he did not set himself up in Coventry city centre but at the Armstrong Whitworth aircraft factory on the outskirts, at Baginton. The note on which the film ends is positive, expressing the swift recovery of Coventry from the effects of the Luftwaffe's attack (Baginton had, fortunately, been unaffected by the bombing). Men in overalls go purposefully about their work for the war effort, fitting doors and hull sections to skeletal aircraft fuselages, tapping and winding and screwing. In a few final frames we see a completed Whitley bomber, manufactured at Baginton, taxiing on to a runway at the works airfield and then taking to the air. It is an image of soaring optimism, but also of intention to strike back.

By now, Jennings' much-altered film, with its new focus on Coventry, had been retitled *The Heart of Britain*. The final, somewhat grandiose words of its commentary, spoken over these images and a choir singing the 'Hallelujah Chorus' from Handel's *Messiah*, are clearly ones of revenge for what the Luftwaffe has done to Coventry:

Out of the valleys of power and the rivers of industry will come the answer to the German challenge, and the Nazis will learn, once and for all, that no one with impunity troubles the Heart of Britain.

19

Defiance

Vera Miles and her fiancé, Stan, were due to get married on Saturday, 16 November, only a little more than twenty-four hours after the end of the German attack on Coventry. He worked at the Rootes car factory, she at GEC.

In October, after German bombs demolished a house in Catherine Street, not far from where she lived in Swan Lane, and her place of work also suffered a direct hit, they decided this was the 'last straw'. They found refuge with family in Nuneaton. Stan and his father cycled into work every day, a ten-mile commute each way. It was from the relative safety of Nuneaton that they witnessed the big raid on their home city. They were, however, still due to marry two days later at St Peter's Church in Charles Street, a couple of hundred yards from Swanswell Pool and close to where they had grown up. The fact that Coventry was 'in ruins' had failed to diminish their determination not to let the Luftwaffe stop them from celebrating the big day as they had planned.

Stan's step mum, Gladys, and his dad, they went around to see if someone had got a car that would bring us over to Coventry. Turned up with the car and got us as far as the outskirts. And the police stopped us. They said, where do you think you're going? I said, we're going to get married. They said, you'll be lucky. Stan said, they want Swan Lane, so they said, OK, we'll let you through.

So I turned up at my mum's. We all hugged one another. We were so pleased to see them. They'd had a terrible night. I went upstairs and put my wedding dress on. As I was putting it on, a landmine went off up the road. A good way away, but it was enough to shake us.

We didn't know what we'd find when we got there. It was just a chance we took. The soldiers were in the churchyard, and they were clearing the pathway up to the main door. That's when they offered to help us up. They did lift the little girls around, but I said, no, I'll walk. We saw Paul Stacey coming along. Minister that was going to marry us. He was dirty and bloody. My goodness, he said, I wasn't expecting to see you. It's lovely to see you, he said, in such a desperate situation. Hang on, he said, and I'll go and get changed and get ready for you. And he married us.[1]

It was a proud day for the young couple, and a remarkable achievement under the circumstances, even though there were only cheese sandwiches for the reception.

In fact, on Friday, courtesy of the Ministry of Food, rationing was temporarily abandoned for Coventry. True, without gas or electricity, and with so many shops (between four and five hundred, according to the Regional Food Officer) destroyed or otherwise put out of action by the bombing,[2] most Coventrians found it hard to cook the unrationed food even if they could get it. For the first forty-eight hours after the raid there was not necessarily that much to eat, on or off the ration, but the move was undoubtedly good for morale. Gwendoline Matthews, a teenage diarist in suburban Stoke, wrote in her diary a description of events on the morning of 16 November:

Mother and I went out to buy food. Mother stood in a queue in the King William Street Co., while I went on to the Co-op Bakery. This building was burned to the ground, but the men were just rescuing what bread they could. There was a terrible scramble to get loaves. I succeeded in getting three after waiting a long while.[3]

The suspension of rationing meant that, like the girl and her mother, people were not confined to the shops where they were registered for ration purposes, but could roam from retailer to retailer, looking for availability, and the best choice or value.[4] A touch of peacetime in the midst of the worst that war could inflict. As supplies improved, this became a genuine pleasure.

Dr Clitheroe of Holy Trinity expressed the slow return of hope and determination to Coventry:

We had neither gas, electricity, nor water. But very soon water at least was available in most places. The Municipal Authorities worked with energy and devotion. Soldiers came to clear the debris. Gas, telephone, and electricity speedily began to be available at least in parts of the city. Food was always at hand, even though the shops did not exist . . .

. . . Dr Massey, in charge of public health, took measures which safe-guarded our lives and kept us free from epidemics. Indeed, we actually seemed to thrive in the amazing conditions under which we had to live, and never were colds and common ailments less notice-able. Even my old ladies in the Widows' Court seemed to lose their rheumatism. I lost two stone in weight, and felt better than ever in physical health. Hearty thanks to Dr Massey, who told us that the one sin any of us could commit at the moment was not to boil water.[5]

The Reverend Dr Clitheroe was no Pollyanna. His little book, *Coventry Under Fire*, also contained passages about combating gloom and depression after the bombing, and was criticised at the time for it. By the middle of the next week, however, all the reports confirmed that there was 'an abundance of food in Coventry'. On Tuesday, a Divisional Food Officer's Report said: 'Bread from Birmingham being eased off. It is possible too much bread went into Coventry yesterday.' The main problem was not so much quantity, as distribution. A lot of meat being shipped in was frozen or canned, which people did not necessarily like – this applied especially to corned beef – as even Lord Woolton, the Minister of Food, was prepared to admit.[6]

Within days, in fact, well-known chain stores had begun to reopen in temporary premises. For instance, Marks & Spencer, formerly in Smithfield Street, were (in the words of the *Midland Daily Telegraph*) 'playing their part in defying the activities of the Huns by opening up in Whitefriars Street' in part of a garage that had been hit in the raid.[7] The Co-operative store was reopened in new central premises in Corporation Street (where, seven and a half decades later, it still has a large branch). Construction quickly began on a temporary shopping centre in Corporation Street, composed of prefabricated huts (asbestos panels in timber frames), designed to accommodate forty or so 'essential retailers'. The businesses were in operation by 23 November, according to a civil defence report.[8]

Rationing was reimposed on 26 November, which indicated a certain rather gloomy return to something like normality. All the same, a caricature of the time entitled 'The Spirit of Coventry' showed an unshaven man, wearing bits of an ARP uniform standing in a ruin (with Coventry's famous Three Spires in the distance) and frying bacon and eggs over a candle flame. He holds a kettle in his other hand, presumably waiting to put it over the flame in turn so that he can have a cup of tea with his breakfast.[9]

For obvious, hard-headed wartime reasons, priority for restoration of utilities was going to the factories. Stan Morris reported that his family got no gas or electricity back in their house until around Christmas.[10] Some utilities had still not been reconnected in the first days of the new year. The schoolgirl from Stoke noted that after the 14 November raid 'we had no water for four weeks, no gas for six weeks, and no electricity for seven weeks'.[11] During these weeks, bathing and washing facilities were opened to the general public at municipal baths, factories, first aid posts and even colliery pit heads.[12]

Those who still had a roof over their heads could somehow improvise – if not quite as amusingly as the comical ARP man with his frying pan. Luckily, most houses were still heated by coal fires, not electricity or gas. All the same, there was a horribly large number who did not enjoy such basic good fortune. Of the 66,000 houses within the Coventry city boundaries, more than half (37,274) were registered as having suffered some sort of damage. Twenty thousand (almost a third of the total) were considered uninhabitable in the immediate aftermath of the raid, with 2,500 of these described as 'completely wrecked, or had to be demolished'.[13] Yet again, the numbers showed how uniquely devastating the raid had been – at least for that stage of the war. They also underline the rational choice that so-called 'trekking' represented. Fear was, understandably, ever-present, but it was by no means the only motive.

As in other parts of Britain during the Blitz, mutual help and comradeship, overcoming individual anxiety and resentment, played a great role in the recovery of the people's spirit. Even Mass Observation, much criticised for its reporters' supposedly misleading reports on morale in Coventry just after the raid, were happy to admit that within a couple of days this had changed for the better. 'There was one thing about the Blitz,' as one survivor, put it. 'People really helped one another. And people who'd got a home with windows in and a roof on the top, very often took in almost complete strangers to give them somewhere where they could sleep.'[14]

All the same, the biggest problem, once the shock of the bombing had been overcome, was the sheer lack of accommodation in the city. True, a lot of people who had hitherto lived and worked in Coventry, often not far from their homes, had now moved to the outskirts or even to towns and villages within commuting distance. On 16 November, the Ministry of Health declared Coventry an 'evacuation area'. This was a step that put Coventrians seeking accommodation outside the city on a par with Londoners, who since the heavy raids in October had been eligible both for travel vouchers and financial aid with out-of-town billets, so long as they were considered 'priority' individuals – children, pregnant mothers, the elderly and infirm and the homeless.[15] More than three and a half thousand children were officially evacuated (or probably, in some cases, re-evacuated) in the ten days or so following the big raid.[16]

The huge problem of housing shortage in the city after 14 November was in part overcome by just the community and family spirit exemplified in the sentence 'people really helped one another', but even the most generous attitude on the part of family and friends was not enough to cope with the sheer numbers involved, especially if the homeless had no connections in the city.

Temporary prefabricated camps were put up for construction workers and other craftsmen who were being imported into the city to help repair factories and homes. Given the widespread damage to roofs, tilers and slaters were especially in demand. Huts for 2,000 men were quickly erected by the Ministry of Works on the edge of the city, and by Christmas such accommodation for a further 6,000 was being investigated. The Reconstruction Committee wrote that 'Accommodation on this scale is in our view essential in order to house some of the many thousands more men and women whom the Ministry of Labour must bring into the Coventry district if the factories there are ever to achieve their full production'.[17] Tellingly, the accommodation had to be on the outskirts, because many of these outside relief workers were unwilling to spend the night in the city proper.

Once the reconstruction effort had got underway (with the priority, as ever, given to factories and essential utilities), things moved fast. First, buildings were protected and made watertight ('We wish to emphasise the urgent need for tarpaulins, of which there cannot be enough'[18]), and then the repairs began. Houses were soon being repaired at the extraordinary rate of 500 a day. Within six weeks of the raid, just over 16,000 had been made habitable once more.[19] This was due not only to the outside help supplied by the government and city authorities. There were reports of men touring neighbouring streets in their spare time, seeking out those who needed help to patch up their roofs or make broken windows weatherproof.[20]

With the surviving factories rapidly returning to full or almost full production, the labour market tightened again. The greatest difficulty the factories had was to attract workers to do the night shifts. After dark was the time when the bombers had come on 14 November (and in the October raids, too). Men understandably felt vulnerable, even where big, deep factory shelters existed. All it took was one direct hit. Night work, men knew, also meant leaving their families to cope by themselves in case of another major raid. Slowly, however, workers were coaxed back on to the long night shifts. Black-out precautions were restored with special care; steps taken to improve staff morale (including extra efforts to secure the support of the unions and the shop stewards); and transport improved so that the workers could be sure of getting to and from work at unsociable times, if necessary by sequestering buses and drivers from other towns and cities.[21]

It was a measure of Coventry's importance to the British war effort that its factories had to be kept working, and the city's workforce kept, if not happy, then at least operational, just about no matter the cost. Humphrey Jennings' final image in *The Heart of Britain*, showing the Coventry-built Whitley bomber taking to the skies, was both an admission of Coventry's importance and a morale-boosting fillip to the city's bruised and battered workers. It was they who had to be kept at their benches and machines in order to provide Britain with the guns, vehicles, aircraft and machines that she needed to stay in the war and – who was to say? – one day even to win it.

The clear return of defiance to the Coventry mind-set, once the shock of the raid had faded, may or may not have been connected to a thirst for revenge. Almost everyone in a city this size, where (by a final but still not quite confirmable count) 568 people had been killed and another 863 seriously injured, knew someone who had been a casualty of the Luftwaffe. If we accept the wartime population of Coventry as around 238,000, this means that between 7:15 p.m. on Thursday, 14 November and about 5:15 a.m. on 15 November 1940, roughly one in 166 of the city's inhabitants had been killed or badly wounded. If the number registered as 'lightly injured' is added, this figures goes up to one in 130, which excludes the almost certainly large numbers of people not seriously hurt, who may have been patched up but had no formal note taken of them in the confusion of hard-pressed first aid posts and unlit out-patient rooms. As Norman Longmate points out, the average civilian rate for death and serious injury in the United Kingdom between 1939 and 1945 was one in 272. The chance during that one night in Coventry of becoming such a casualty was 60 per cent higher than for the rest of the country during the entire Second World War.

Nonetheless, Mass Observation quickly ascertained that, although there was little sign of fanatical patriotism in the city, 'It should be stressed that *no sign whatever* was found of anti-war feeling.' It continued:

> . . . The first effect of violent and sudden raids is easy to increase people's interest in the personal and local aspects; they seem unable to associate such instances with the war as a whole or with external events. There was, however . . . very little feeling in favour of reprisals.[22]

Harrisson repeated this assertion in his short radio broadcast on 16 November:

> I see some reporters stressing the fact that Coventry is clamouring for reprisals. This wasn't borne out by my own observations; for, after all, this was a reprisal, according to the Germans, and it only makes Coventry realise that this sort of thing doesn't end the war and only makes it more bitter.[23]

In an article for *The Cambridge Review* in May 1941, entitled 'A Public Demand for Reprisals?', he would become even more specific. In this piece, Harrisson criticised the sort of language used by BBC News ('The evening's best news of the war in the air – particularly for the people of Coventry – is that . . . British bombers last night made a terrific raid on the city of Hamburg'), but especially singled out the notoriously belligerent Beaverbrook press (*Daily Express* and *Sunday Express*). Hilde Marchant of the *Daily Express*, for instance, who had

written immediately after the raid of the 'young airman' in the ruins
of the Cathedral the morning after the raid and his call for 'God' to
'avenge' what had been done, also wrote, among other things: 'The
whole of Coventry cries: "BOMB BACK AND BOMB HARD!"'

Harrisson disputed this claim to speak on behalf of an entire city
('Quite how a city of two hundred thousand inhabitants cries out as a
whole, I do not know') and produced a powerful sample of evidence
from his researches, and those of his reporters, that contradicted
the popular press's presumptions. It was not so much that no one
was prepared to think of reprisals for German attacks, more that it
wasn't in the forefront of people's minds. They had to be prompted,
which was most effective, as Harrisson remarked, obviously referring
to Marchant, if 'a charming lady journalist made one of those typical interviews in which she gives the lead and the rather flattered,
slightly shy, 'man-in-the-street' says the sort of thing he thinks will
get into print'.[24]

Marchant, who countered the word 'Coventrated' with a somewhat
awkward coinage of her own – 'Berliminated' – to describe the process
of Britain 'BOMBING BACK',[25] was, of course, also doing the will of
her proprietor, the Conservative press baron and Minister for Aircraft
Production. Harrisson's concerns – though he declared in the matter
of reprisals that he did not 'care one way or the other' – were also in
part conditioned by his general view of the world, and there may have
been an element of psychological projection in his opinions about
the supposed lack of belligerent patriotism among ordinary people.
On balance, though, his view rings truer, at least at this point. In
May 1941, opinion polls, in which people in various parts of Britain
were asked whether they wanted reprisal bombing against civilians in
Germany, indicated a narrow nationwide majority in favour (53 per
cent for, 38 per cent against, and 9 per cent undecided). However,
if the figures were broken down into regions, Inner London, which
had been bombed most heavily of all, actually had a majority *against*
reprisals, and while the Midlands and the Scottish industrial belt,
which had been hit hard, still registered in favour (by 49–40 per cent

and 53–43 per cent respectively), the biggest majority in favour of bombing civilians was to be found in rural north-western England (76 per cent), which had scarcely been bombed at all. Likewise, the rural valleys of Wales were strongly in favour, but the principality's coastal ports, which had already been visited by the Luftwaffe, less so. In fact, according to a Mass Observation survey in London, 26 per cent of respondents did not even know what the word 'reprisal' meant, but, if that is true, it could redefine the argument either way.

Moreover, as Harrisson pointed out in the same article in which he quoted the poll figures, a few months after the bombing of Coventry and Birmingham there had been a by-election in the suburban Birmingham constituency of King's Norton. By then, the entire West Midlands had been even more badly bombed than ever. Still, a 'Reprisals' enthusiast (popularly known as the 'Bomb Berlin' candidate), who insisted that Britain should be 'striking indiscriminately at all German towns and cities', received only just under 1,700 votes from an electorate of nearly 60,000. This was not many more than the other independent hopeful, a representative of the pacifist 'Peace Pledge Union'. The overwhelming winner, unopposed by the other major parties, was a Conservative, Captain Peto, who had until recently served as ADC to the Governor of Bombay. A curiosity of the campaign was that the pro-reprisals man was supported by Jack Moseley, Labour Mayor of Coventry, in a move that apparently did nothing for Moseley's popularity – in part (according to Harrisson) because people there feared that if they made too much fuss of that sort the Germans would bomb the city again.

Also out on its own in its attitude to the bombing – though for different reasons – was the Communist Party. Relatively unimportant in Coventry compared with strongholds such as the East End of London, 'Red' Clydeside, and the mining regions of Scotland, north-east England and South Wales, the Communists managed to garner some support from their campaign for better shelters and their campaign against conditions in the area's factories.[26] According to the *Manchester Guardian*'s parliamentary reporter, Willie Gallacher,

representing West Fife as the solitary Communist MP, quickly took
to his feet in the House of Commons to confirm the party line on
the German bombing of the Midlands:

> . . . [He] declared that the shelter provision in Birmingham and Cov-
> entry was 'a scandal, a shame, and a disgrace.' Wealth came spouting
> out of these places, but when it came to the defence, care, and welfare
> of the people there was not another part of the country so neglected.
> The important question was how to bring this monstrous war to an
> end at the earliest possible moment . . .[27]

Gallacher was isolated, along with his party, hog-tied by the ambiv-
alent attitude to the anti-fascist war effort forced on them by their
masters in Moscow because of the Nazi–Soviet Pact. He was not, however, the only critic of the government's perceived failure to protect
Coventry from the German bombers. The response of the *Midland
Daily Telegraph*, a broadly conservative paper, probably expressed the
(mixed) feelings of its readers quite well. In a sober but startlingly
frank editorial on 22 November under the headline 'Reprisals', it
questioned the right of 'one of our leading . . . national newspapers'
(the publication was not named) to pass comment on Coventrians'
attitude towards this issue. In doing so it conveyed a few of the things
that bothered the city's people rather more than the question of the
revenge bombing of Germany:

> Coventry is rather too busily engaged at the moment in the sheer task
> of living to worry very much about reprisals. If Coventry is demand-
> ing anything at all of our belligerent forces, its thoughts are directed
> towards the Fighter Command. If Coventry has any complaint at all,
> it is that the city was left 'to take it.'
>
> Coventry has waited in vain for the cheering sound of droves of
> night-fighters. We know, and we have explained all the answers to
> this complaint: the simple truth is that Coventry does not accept
> them. Coventry refuses to believe that night-fighters are helpless on

a bright, moonlit night, and will refuse to believe it until someone decides that the time is ripe for a demonstration.

Coventry is not bewailing its lot; it bewails only that part of which it supposes to have been capable of prevention. The outside world may also accept our fullest assurance that Coventry's morale is sky high. There has never been the slightest suggestion of panic or disorder.

To-day, there is not even a sign of nervousness. There has been no more marked effect of Thursday's carnage than the grim and purposeful resolution it has produced to see this thing through. Coventry feels that Hitler has done his worst, and Coventry knows now that it can 'take it'.[28]

Likewise, in all the recollections of survivors represented in this narrative, none includes an indication that they or their parents or relatives expressed a thirst for revenge in the aftermath of the raid on Coventry. This is not a scientific sample. It does not mean that they didn't express such a thing, nor that plenty of people didn't privately think it, nor that people weren't angry at the Luftwaffe. All the same, it tends to imply that Harrisson's instinct was the truer, and tit-for-tat revenge was perhaps not foremost in their minds. Based on this sample, sadness, fear, regret, defiance and a stoic determination 'to see this through' seem to have come first, and these were, as most opinion agrees, the things that enabled Britain to survive and fight back during these, its darkest days. In that, Coventry was wholly representative.

So far as the military and political elite was concerned, Coventry did represent a watershed in the development of their attitude towards bombing. Under Chamberlain, bombing had been confined strictly to military targets, while once Churchill came to power the whole distinction between civilian and military started to get fuzzier. This attitude rapidly filtered down the hierarchy, if we are to believe a British bomber pilot of the time:

Right up to about November, I think until after Coventry, we were still very much under instructions to bomb specific military targets.

There was no question if, I mean, the theory was that if you couldn't find your target you might be given an alternative, but in theory you then bring your bombs back. In fact, we seldom if ever did, but on the other hand we did endeavour to pick out the so-called target, which was usually a marshalling yard or an aerodrome or a factory or something. And it was only after Coventry that we were literally told, OK, if you can't find your targets you just lob 'em down on the town, which made a lot of difference. I mean, we went to Hamburg and we went to various other places and generally then if conditions were that bad you would simply bomb on ETA if you could see it or you went into the middle of the flak and you bombed that.[29]

There seems, however, little doubt that Coventry was an excuse rather than a direct cause. The higher echelons of the RAF had been eager since the outbreak of war to bomb Germany to the maximum of their bomber force's ability (which admittedly would for some time turn out to be distinctly doubtful), and had been held back mostly by political considerations and the limitations of the aircraft at their disposal. As early as October 1939, a War Cabinet paper admitted that if, as the RAF wanted, the Ruhr industrial area of Germany was to be bombed without restriction, the population 'might be expected to crack'. However, this would involve 'a heavy casualty role among civilians, including women and children'.[30] The barrage of publicity given to Coventry may or may not have caused a wave of public demand for ruthless revenge, but it did harden opinion, both domestic and foreign – particularly in America – in favour of less-discriminate bombing of Germany, should this become a consequent policy.

Coventry, though shaken, had not 'cracked'. All the same, the celebrations of the city's ability to 'take it' and the big, optimistic headlines declaring the success of retaliatory raids against Berlin, Hamburg, Essen and so on, and the superiority of Bomber Command, did not necessarily reflect the private opinions of all the RAF's decision-makers. In a minute written five days after the raid, Air Commodore Donald Stevenson, Director of Home Operations at the

Air Ministry, had actually floated the idea of abandoning the game of to-and-fro of 'anti-morale crash concentrations' (i.e. intense and localised raids with substantial numbers of aircraft aimed at undermining the popular will to resist) that was now being played with 'the Boche', as he referred to the Germans. These types of raids, he argued, carried serious risks at this stage of the war, especially as 'during the dark period' (i.e. the long winter nights) the British ability to intercept German night attacks was still poor. It would remain so until developments in AI allowed night fighters the ability to find and shoot down enemy bombers.

> At present . . . we have to be careful that our great centres of production and industry and that the great spirit of our people is not irreparably harmed by the concentrated effort of the German long range Bomber Force being laid against places like Coventry, Birmingham, Sheffield, Liverpool and Glasgow.[31]

He made an interesting admission in the course of his argument:

> *We started the practice of concentration* [my italics] and it is inherently sound, provided we can reasonably withstand the enemy counter action to our stroke. We have beaten up Berlin, Munich, Essen and Hamburg in this way. On the night of 8th/9th we did Munich. On the 9th November instructions were issued to the G.A.F. [German air force] to carry out the crash concentration plan 'Moonlight Sonata'. We thought it was a reprisal for our attack on Munich and the Führer confirmed this in the German High Command communiqué after the attack on Coventry. Under this Plan he 'Namsosed'* Coventry with 300 bombers in a single night. The damage to the war potential and to the morale of the people in Coventry is considerable.

---

* Though now forgotten, at the time 'to 'Namsose' was yet another expression, like 'to Guernica', implying a devastating air attack. It referred to the Luftwaffe's bombing of the small town of Namsos in the north of Norway during the Anglo-French-Norwegian campaign against the German invaders in April/May 1940. The wooden town was totally destroyed by incendiaries.

The implication was clearly that, in his opinion, the British were coming off the worse in this contest. Stevenson was therefore in favour of easing back on these types of raids, at least for the moment, in the hope the Germans would do the same. Instead, the RAF should be targeting 'our oil and industrial objectives'. There followed another admission of the Luftwaffe's relative superiority. Stevenson's final words, in particular, would never have appeared in the *Daily Express*:

On balance it pays us more than it pays him [i.e. 'the Boche'] to relinquish the crash concentration until we have solved the night interception problem, because the German scale of attack operates over short distances against our industry concentrated within very narrow limits, whereas we must reach to great distances in Germany *with a Bomber Force which is inferior to his* [my italics].

Both the Chief of Air Staff and his Deputy were polite in their replies, and followed Stevenson's logic, but demurred. They obviously shared his concern at the effect of the Coventry raid and other German 'concentrations'. However, the DCAS thought that there was 'a lot – but not enough' in DHO's arguments:

I feel that the Boche doesn't like crash concentrations any more than we do. Perhaps not as much. Ours are as good as his in quality, if not in quantity, and we should be able to do nearly as much to say Hamburg in two nights, as he can do to Coventry in one.

I feel therefore, why should we stop first? If he keeps on, then we must, I feel, retaliate, and if he likes to stop first, then it will be time enough to consider whether we will follow suit on the principle of letting a sleeping dog lie.[32]

The DCAS's only concession was that 'if, in fact, we suffer more "Coventrys" within the next week or so . . . then no doubt we may have to reconsider any and every means – not excluding pandering to the Boche – to persuade him to lay off'. 'The conclusion,' he added, 'is therefore, no change for the immediate present.'

The discussion between these two views of bombing – between more or less legitimate military targets or 'crash concentrations' – would rumble on throughout the war. With hindsight, it always seemed likely that the 'crash concentration' advocates, among them Harris and his boss, Portal, would win the day. There was concern about the Luftwaffe's current effectiveness, and whether the RAF could match it, but there was also a feeling in elite British circles that the German population was indeed weaker in its capacity to bear the brunt of a big bombing campaign than its British counterpart. This sense may have been founded in the experience of 1914–18, when the suffering of civilians had been a key contributory factor to the outbreak of revolution in Germany at the beginning of November 1918, and the consequent final collapse of the country's war effort. The actual response of the Air Staff to grim events such as Coventry, therefore, was to conduct an investigation of the Luftwaffe's recent raids – especially on London, Coventry and Liverpool – to see how the RAF could inflict more destruction on German cities than it had hitherto been able.[33]

This persistence in an aggressive approach to German morale may have been helped by the fact that the Deputy Chief of Air Staff, who had replied to Stevenson on 25 November – only one day into the job, which he had officially begun on 24 November – was forty-eight-year-old Air Vice-Marshal Arthur Travers Harris. A year and a half later, Harris would be put in charge of Bomber Command, where he – far from 'pandering to the Boche' – would gain both glory and notoriety as the great advocate of ruthless area bombing.

Harris would later write in his usual brisk, analytical way, of 'Moonlight Sonata': 'The Germans again and again missed their chance . . . of setting our cities ablaze by a concentrated attack. Coventry was adequately concentrated in point of space, but all the same there was little concentration in point of time . . .'[34]

The nearest the Germans would come, in fact, to duplicating Coventry was a little over a month later. Much the same techniques were used. On 29 December 1940, the Luftwaffe attacked the City of London. At about seven o'clock on the moonless evening of that Sunday after Christmas, the first enemy aircraft arrived over London's historic heart, marked on the air crew's maps as target area 'Otto'. *X-Gerät* beams previously locked on to the docks, further east, had been redirected to cross there. The pathfinders of K.G.100 dropped their special marking incendiaries, and by the time the main force arrived the area was already well alight. A total of 136 aircraft were involved in this wave, and because they were operating on short hops from their French bases – much shorter than in the case of Coventry – they could save fuel and devote yet more cargo space to bombs, including large quantities of incendiaries. The German plan was that they would return again and again, as they had in their attack on Coventry.

It was an exceptionally low ebb tide that exposed the muddy shores of the Thames. Firefighters had to wallow through a quagmire as they attempted to reach water for their hoses – and often failed, as had Chief Cartwright's men on the fatal night of 14 November. In the City of London, on 29 December, hundreds, and then thousands, of small fires began to break out. Individual incendiaries were generally easy enough to douse, with the aid of a bucket of sand, and fires could be tackled with a stirrup pump. As in Coventry, it was the sheer quantity of them that made it impossible to get on top of the situation before it was too late and larger fires formed. Since the attack happened on a Sunday in a district where there were few residents but many places of work, there was also the problem that many empty buildings were locked.

The author of a book titled *Britain Under Fire* described the night that many considered to be the worst of the entire London Blitz:

But though the flames licked its very walls, as buildings on each side of the Churchyard blazed, a southerly wind and the Fire Brigade saved the [St Paul's] Cathedral. Fifteen firebombs that fell on the historic Guildhall were dealt with promptly by the ARP staff. But an unchecked fire in Gresham Street spread to the church of St Lawrence

Jewry, which was locked and unattended, and from the belfry of which sparks were carried to the Guildhall roof. Among the famous buildings gutted were the churches of St Bride's Fleet Street; Christ Church, Newgate Street, and six other Wren churches; Girdlers' and Barbers' Halls; the Cathedral Chapter House; Dr Johnson's house in Gough Square; Trinity House on Tower Hill . . . when the City returned to work on Monday, the whole area north from St Paul's, including Paternoster Row, Amen Corner, long stretches of Newgate Street and Cheapside and northwards along Wood Street, were smoking ruins.[35]

The attack had been planned as a nine-hour operation, which might have caused truly huge destruction, but it was abandoned after three hours. Dense cloud had developed over the bombers' home bases in northern France, making the intended shuttle operation impossible. The weather worsened further overnight, eventually turning to snow and grounding the entire German bomber fleet.

London was lucky, luckier than Coventry. Due to the curtailment of the raid, and the fact that, because it was a weekend, the City was virtually uninhabited, casualties were relatively low. The British capital suffered 160 civilian dead, plus twenty-five firefighters. And, of course, lost much of the irreplaceable core of its history.

Afterwards, Arthur Harris, normally an unemotional man, as befitted a technocrat of aerial warfare, recalled:

I watched the old city in flames from the roof of the Air Ministry, with St Paul's standing out in the midst of an ocean of fire – an incredible sight. One could hear the German bombers arriving in a stream and the swish of the incendiaries falling into the fire below. This was a well-concentrated attack . . . the Blitz seemed to me a fantastic sight and I went downstairs and fetched Portal up from his office to have a look at it. Although I have often been accused of being vengeful during our subsequent destruction of German cities, this was the one occasion and the only one when I did feel vengeful . . . Having in mind what was being done at that time to produce heavy bombers in Britain I said out loud as we turned away from the scene: 'Well, they are sowing the wind'. Portal also made some comment to the same effect as mine, that the enemy would get the same and more of it.[36]

20

'Thank goodness you're alright'

The people of Coventry had feared that the German bombers would come again, just as they had begun to rebuild their city. In the end they were right.

By the new year, the utilities had been restored, food was as plentiful as it was going to get during wartime, and the factories, apart from a few that had been relocated, were in full production again. So far as the wider war was concerned, the 'weak link' of the German Axis of alliances was proving to be Fascist Italy. Its attempted invasion of Greece in October 1940 had been repulsed, and the Greeks were pushing forward across wintry peaks into the rocky interior of Albania, where Mussolini had established control the previous year. In North Africa, the Duce's armies had been driven back into his Libyan colony by the British and Commonwealth forces. There the Italians were soundly defeated, losing more than a hundred thousand men as prisoners of war.

Hitler's plans to attack his supposed friend, Stalin, were well advanced. At the same time, the Luftwaffe was still striking at Britain, apparently more fiercely than ever. It was true that the night-fighter-against-night-bomber problem was slowly being solved. German bomber losses, negligible the previous year, were now slowly mounting. Nevertheless, in the first months of 1941, British towns and cities were still very much under attack.

There had been a number of smaller raids on Coventry after 14 November 1940, from the tiny, scarcely noticed single visit on 16 November to a slightly larger one on 19 November (two dead), coinciding with the big attack on Birmingham, another on 11 December, then 7 January 1941 against the Standard Works (killing six), on 8 January with no fatalities, and then on 11 March (one civilian killed).[1] All these were rather along the lines of the 'disturbance attacks' with which the Luftwaffe had begun its campaign against centres of industry back in the early autumn of 1940.

In any case, from early February 1941 the emphasis of the German bomber war had switched, in obedience to a new directive (No. 23) from the Führer, away from the Midlands industrial cities to the ports – Southampton, Portsmouth, Plymouth, Bristol, and especially Liverpool. This switch was part of the Germans' attempt at a counter-blockade of Britain. Learning from the experience of 'Moonlight Sonata', the Luftwaffe began using more and more incendiaries in its attack mix. During this period, the ratio of high-explosive bombs to incendiaries reached 1:1. The effect on the ports, especially the historic ones such as Plymouth and Bristol, which contained many concentrations of old buildings, was quite devastating. London, the centre of power within the British Empire and also its most important port, was, as ever, considered a priority target. The British capital, and especially its docklands, had been hit hard through the winter but experienced a comparative lull until the middle of March. After that, it suffered terribly once more.

If it was impossible to break British morale by a few hammer blows, as Hitler and other members of the Nazi leadership now reluctantly accepted, then the enemy must be starved of food and of weapons of war produced in America and Canada.[2] The main burden of this strategy fell, of course, on the German U-boat fleet, which at this point in the war – before the British had developed viable anti-submarine technology – was operating with very considerable success, sinking hundreds of thousands of tons of shipping heading across the Atlantic to the United Kingdom.

'Opportunistic attacks' on the British aero industry were therefore a less important priority, and this was reflected in the pattern of Coventry's reduced vulnerability during the mid-winter months and on into the early spring. Birmingham, too, was subjected to serious bombing only once during this period (like Coventry, on 11 March). Sheffield had been heavily attacked in December, twice, and then the pressure eased off. By April, things must have seemed relatively quiet.

Hitler and the German High Command were, at this time, secretly preoccupied elsewhere. The time was approaching when Nazi Germany would launch its attack on the Soviet Union, which had been in preparation since the previous autumn. Originally the invasion had been scheduled for late May. Then, in early 1941, the Germans had been forced to deal with two extra problems. The first was the failure of the Italian war in Greece, followed by the arrival of British troops there. The second was the situation in Yugoslavia.

On 27 March 1941, the Yugoslav government, dominated by Prince Paul, uncle of the seventeen-year-old King Peter, had signed a pact in Vienna making his country an ally of the Axis. The response in Yugoslavia was massive street demonstrations and a military coup – favoured, though not actually engineered by, the British – in which Paul and his co-Regents were deposed and the young monarch declared fit to rule. Although the new government tried to assure the Germans that it had not reneged on the 27 March treaty, it was demonstrably planning a more independent role for the country than the Germans felt comfortable with. The mood in Yugoslavia, or at least in the Serb part, was strongly anti-Axis, under the motto, 'Better war than the pact, better the grave than a slave!'³ A furious Hitler issued Directive 25, instructing that Yugoslavia be treated as a 'hostile state', and a few days later Directive 26, ordering preparations for war. Yugoslavia and Greece, hostile hindrances to the south of the Führer's path of advance into Russia, had to be crushed before he could begin his great, longed-for blow against Bolshevism.

German, Italian, Hungarian and Bulgarian forces moved into Yugoslavia before dawn on Palm Sunday, 6 April 1941. On 3 April, a pro-Axis Croatian officer of the Yugoslav Air Force had defected to the Germans and betrayed vital details about the country's air defences. Almost immediately after the Axis forces crossed the border, German aircraft bombed Belgrade, in an operation that was given the codename *Strafgericht* (literally, Criminal Court, but usually translated as 'Retribution'), indicating clearly Hitler's view of it as punishment for Yugoslav 'treachery'. The bombing by up to 500 aircraft, many transferred from northern Europe expressly for the purpose, continued in waves for two days. The weak Yugoslav air defences were overwhelmed, and within hours the country's government and military command structures had been effectively destroyed, further facilitating the rapid Axis victory in the ground war that followed.[4]

The physical damage, including the total destruction by fire of the Serbian National Library, containing thousands of priceless books and manuscripts, was appalling. The human suffering more than equalled it. Estimates of the deaths range wildly – from 1,500 to 30,000 – and there still appears to be no generally accepted figure for casualties.[5]

The bombing was carried out under the command of Colonel-General Alexander Löhr, C-in-C of Air Fleet IV. After the war – unique among air force commanders – Löhr would be executed as a war criminal by the Communist government in Belgrade. The reason was that, on the outbreak of war, the Yugoslavs had declared Belgrade, along with Zagreb and Ljubljana, capitals of the Croat and Slovene parts of the country respectively, as 'open cities'. Designed to protect buildings and populations in major cities, it was a status already claimed so far in the war by Brussels, Paris and Oslo, when it became clear that they were about to fall. All had been given up to the Germans without a fight and remained intact.

The bombing attacks on Belgrade were noted in the British press, but not yet their full extent. Communications with the Yugoslav capital were seriously interrupted (as had been the Germans' intention). In *The Times* of 8 April, the paper's Aeronautical Correspondent wrote with a hint of complacency that 'the need to transfer aircraft and ground staff to Rumania and Bulgaria has no doubt affected the size of the force maintained in Holland, Belgium, and Northern France for operations against this country'.[6] The Luftwaffe might indeed have seemed, so far as his readers were concerned, to be operating with awful destructive power far away in the Balkans, and to have put a lot of its eggs in that particular basket. If so, a correction to this view was not long in coming.

On the evening of the same day, just after dusk, German bombers returned to Coventry, with a vengeance.

The raid, by 230 aircraft, lasted almost seven and a half hours. Two hundred and ten tons of bombs were dropped (compared with 500 tons on the night of 14/15 November) along with 25,000 incendiaries. Two hundred and eighty-one people died. Courtaulds suffered severe fire damage, and 15 acres of buildings at the Daimler No. 1 Shadow Factory were destroyed.[7]

Again, an examination of the available details of individual deaths shows that the overwhelming majority of those killed were civilians, in civilian shelters, whether of the Anderson or the public type. The exceptions, if war workers are indeed exceptions, were the six night-shift workers who died at the heavily bombed No.1 Daimler aero-engine works a little under two miles north of the city centre, and the three at the Alvis Works off Holyhead Road, where the old factory had been obliterated the previous November. Two also died at the huge Herbert Machine Tool factory to the west of the canal.

There were two places of refuge in which many civilians died. The Coventry and Warwickshire Hospital, which had survived the 14 November raid with some damage and with its power cut, but had been repaired and re-equipped in the aftermath, was this time bombed heavily. It has been suggested that the Germans might have mistaken it for a factory.[8] The hospital suffered ten direct hits, laying the buildings to waste. Twenty-one patients, seven nurses, two doctors, and three St John Ambulance Brigade stretcher-bearers were killed. Just about every window in the hospital was shattered. Despite attempts to fight the fires with water pumped out of the nearby Swanswell Pool, the hospital was put mostly out of action for the rest of the war. Where there had been several hundred beds, there now remained around sixty, mostly accident and emergency. In the immediate aftermath, there was no heating, power or water. By a bitter irony, however, the worst (because cruelly unexpected) came after the All Clear.

As Dr George Forrest, a survivor of the November raid and still working at the hospital the following April recalled that night more than sixty years later:

This was at the entrance and there was a round crater, just had appeared from somewhere, we didn't know where, just outside the main door. It was about, I suppose six feet broad, two or three feet deep and somebody had got a bit of wood and put it across and we were walking across this thing. And then of course the All Clear went about seven in the morning or something of that kind and I remember meeting one of the nurses called Clarke, she was the staff nurse on the medical ward which I was on, and we went up to the roof to have a look at the town, and as we went up we passed some of my fellow house surgeons and nurses in various side wards, you know, just on the way up and 'Oh, thank goodness you're alright' and that kind of thing. We were on the roof and looking round the town to sort of see where the smoke, where the fires were, and suddenly there was a tremendous noise and everything shook and dirt and stones began to descend from the heavens on us. This crater which I've mentioned had been the entrance point of an unexploded bomb, delayed action. And it went off when we were on the roof and actually the roof cracked underneath us. That's a bit of a surprise, but this bomb had taken a cone out and all it had done to the roof where we were was cracked it, but it had destroyed that cone and it killed several of the doctors that I'd been talking to on the way up, and nurses.[9]

Dr Forrest and his colleagues rushed down and did what they could for the dead and injured. When he went back into the hospital, and decided to check on what was left of the children's ward, he found two young probationary nurses washing newborn babies, as the day's routine demanded. He had no idea where they got the water – or the courage.

The second major scene of carnage that night was in the basement beneath the Barras Green Social Club, in the suburb of Stoke Heath. This was about a mile north-east of the city, and close to the Morris Motor Engine Works as well as a number of other factories. A survivor, Adrian Macey, who was fourteen at the time, remembered it vividly because his family of five, through sheer luck, escaped death that night. He was the eldest. His then baby brother, Howard, was almost fourteen years younger, but many years later knew the family story well and helped fill in the details:

Adrian Macey: The Germans dropped a lot of bombs in our area. A lot of the damage was from anti-aircraft shells. The shrapnel from when they exploded. The shrapnel had to come down. You used to hear it clattering on the roofs. Eventually the air raid [warden] came round and told us we'd have to get out of the area because of the unexploded bombs.

So we got out and we went to the Barras Club for shelter, because it was a big building and it had got a cellar. We went down in the cellar. Of course, my mum had got small children – Howard was a little baby – went down in the cellar and it was absolutely packed with people, all puffing away at cigarettes and the baby, Howard, started coughing with the cigarette smoke, and my mum said, we can't stop here with all this fag smoke, you know. She said, we'll get out and go somewhere else, you know. We moved out and moved away towards where we lived, in Camden Street.

Howard Macey: After the All Clear we started to make our way home.

Adrian Macey: There was the club where we'd been down in the cellar the night before. Got a direct hit by bombs. Practically everybody in it killed, you know. The club was wrecked, you know.

Howard Macey: The bomb went straight through into the cellar. I don't think there was any survivors. Adrian always tells the story it was me who saved all the family's lives. Because I was coughing.[10]

The Barras Green Social Club was a community centre and its cellar used as a shelter for the area. Its destruction and the deaths that night of those seeking safety beneath it was traumatic for the working-class suburb. Another survivor, then in her mid-twenties, saw the tragedy from a more adult, matter-of-fact point of view:

A woman across the road to us, she was one of the stewards in the Barras Social Club. She was there all night. She got killed. And her daughter. Only a girl . . . About ten of them I believe got killed there. [Actually twelve.]

The next day we had a service on the Common. They said it was a thanksgiving service. I said, I can't see what we got to thank God for this lot for. But I suppose they meant, thank God for them people what were still alive. My dad went back to work. He had to get back. He worked at the Daimler and that got bombed.[11]

Also bombed were other places that had somehow survived 'Moonlight Sonata', including the Central Police Station on St Mary Street, opposite the now-ruined Cathedral, and St Mary's Hall, which lay between it and the Council House. Several policemen, including the Commandant of Special Constables for the city, Arthur Frederick Matts, MBE (awarded for his efforts on the night of the big raid), were killed. Another loss was Christ Church – the third of Coventry's famous 'Three Spires' – most of whose early Victorian structure was destroyed that night, although the medieval tower and spire survived. This left the city with only one intact church in its centre (Holy Trinity, thanks to the heroic efforts of Dr Clitheroe and his firefighters) but, since the tower of the Cathedral had also escaped destruction, still three spires. The 400-year-old Henry VIII Grammar School, just down from the station and close to Sydney Larkin's house, was largely

obliterated. Fortunately, its students and staff had already been moved
to a safer temporary home at Alcester, in rural Warwickshire, just as
the equally venerable Bablake School had been evacuated to Lincoln
after the November raid.

On the night of 8 April, the main havoc was wrought, all the same,
in the suburbs, with their factories and workers' housing. In this, it
was distinct from the November raid, which had concentrated so
heavily on the central part of the city. But, as so often, survival or
death came down to luck.

Thelma Green, then seven years old, had been evacuated at the
beginning of the war, and so had missed the November Blitz. She
had returned to be with her parents in their home to the west of
Whitley Common just two days before the April attack. Her father
was an auxiliary fireman. 'If he could have got back to the factory
he was serving in, he would have been safe,' she says. 'They weren't
touched that night.' The family were eating their evening meal when
the bombs started to fall. 'He pushed mummy and I and he grabbed
one of the portable gas coppers and he pushed us under the stairs.' Her
father then left the house to help the neighbours put out incendiary
bombs. That was the last time they saw him. He was in an alleyway
between two houses, where a neighbour's shed had been set on fire,
when another German bomber did a run over the area, dropping
high-explosive bombs.

And you can almost trace that stick of bombs because they went
through the cemetery and then came through the field at the side of
us. Whether that was the last one that was dropped, I don't know.[12]

They heard the blast. It was three doors away at number 108.

Mummy could hear them shouting for an ambulance and . . . he
never came back. He never came back to see if we were all right after
he went out to see this garden shed . . . we must have been four or
five hours under the stairs and . . . she must have realised who the
ambulance was for.

It was two days before they could be certain:

And we had a local hospital close to us so she automatically went there and they said, no, there was nothing, and they sent her to another hospital and he wasn't there . . . he was never likely to be there, obviously, with the injuries he'd taken . . . and then they let her go looking around, and then someone had got a record somewhere that he'd been taken to the mortuary.

Her husband was identifiable only by his brown hair and some things he had in his pockets that night. On his death certificate, Mrs Green said, stood the words 'Unknown Fatality'.

The terrible thing was that, by the time Mrs Green found and identified her husband's remains, Coventry had been hit yet again. On Thursday, 10 April – the night before Easter – a slightly smaller German bomber force came against the city.

Gwendoline Matthews, the teenage diarist who chronicled the November raid, had been evacuated the next week to her grand-mother's in Worcester, the ancient cathedral city thirty-five miles south-west of Coventry, where she enrolled in a new school and prepared to take her School Certificate. Early on the morning of 9 April 1941, the day after her school in Worcester had broken up for the Easter holidays, she set off home to visit her family. On the radio before she left Worcester, she heard that a 'Midlands city' had been raided during the night, and assumed it must be Birmingham, which was awkward because her mother was supposed to be meeting her there. During the bus journey, the conductor told her that it had been Coventry. As a result, when the bus arrived in Birmingham, and her mother was nowhere to be seen, she decided to make her own way. Though carrying two heavy suitcases, she got on the first bus to Coventry. Unlike after the November raid, the police had not set up road blocks to stop people going into the centre:

There were ambulances and buses along the Holyhead Road. The town was in a dreadful state. I could not carry the cases home from the meadow, so I waited for a Stoke Heath bus outside the Hippo-drome.* After waiting twenty minutes in the cold I got a Binley bus as a Stoke Heath one did not arrive.

I got off at Gosford Green and onto a Stoke Heath [bus].

When I got off, at the top of Clay Lane, I was surrounded by unexploded bombs.[13]

When she got home, her mother was not there either, and so she went to the nearby home of her aunt, who told her 'that she did not know where Mother was, and that we had had an incendiary bomb in my bedroom. I waited until Mother arrived at three o'clock.'

The next night, Thursday, 10 April, 'we had another raid, but it was heavier at Stoke than in this district'. On Friday morning, with the bombers gone, Gwendoline and her mother felt safe enough to visit an Aunt Alice in Stoke. This proved a mistake, for reasons the diarist calmly went on to describe:

We left Auntie Alice's and went along Hollis Road. Suddenly, very close to us, a large bomb exploded. No one knew it was there and it killed four people. We turned and ran and we were very fortunate as I was only hit in the back by flying rubble.[14]

Eight members of one family are recorded as killed at 7 John Grace Street, in Lower Stoke, near the London Road Cemetery. At least fourteen people died in a shelter at Warwick Row, in the centre of the city, with another eight fatalities a hundred yards away in Gros-venor Road. Five died in the shelter at the Smith's Stamping Works (forging and stamping for aircraft and motor vehicles) in Lower Stoke near Humber Avenue.[15] The GEC Works on the eastern outskirts of

---

* 'The meadow' is Pool Meadow, where the bus station was situated. The 'Hippodrome' was the site of the old theatre and music hall across the street from it, which was demolished shortly before the war and replaced by the 'New Hippodrome', an Art Deco building in Trinity Street. Clearly the bus stop was still named after the vanished building.

Stoke, was again attacked, making it the main industrial victim of the Luftwaffe's second night's work. Here a VHF radio link system with automatic changes of wavelength was being manufactured for the RAF. Oil-based incendiaries destroyed a third of the large factory complex, hitting production hard. Dispersal of production for these key devices to a remote part of Yorkshire was already under way; knowing how much the air force depended on them, the authorities accelerated the dispersal process after the Easter attack.[16]

The press accounts of the raids were relatively cursory, to an extent concentrating on successes by night-fighter pilots against the bombers.[17] No figures for dead were given. The only indication that these two raids, taken together, were almost as serious in terms of casualties as those of 14 November, came in a report in *The Times* of 16 April. On page two, this contented itself with saying: 'A large number of Coventry's air raid victims were buried yesterday in a common grave and the funeral was attended by 3,000 mourners. Others will be buried later.'[18]

The rest of the report was given over to enumerating the clergy officiating (Roman Catholic, Church of England and Nonconformist) and paraphrasing a defiant address by the Bishop of Coventry. In November, the *Manchester Guardian* had given the first mass burial some prominence; in April there was no sign of a report.

The popular press was a little more forthcoming. The *Express*, as usual represented by Hilde Marchant, who had reported on the November Blitz, initially concentrated on the deaths of the nurses at Coventry and Warwick Hospital, and the death of Mr Matts, Commandant of Special Constabulary. After the second raid, it ran the headline 'THE GOOD FRIDAY MIRACLE OF COVENTRY'.[19] The story concentrated on the Good Friday service being held in the ruins of Coventry Cathedral; it was heavy on spiritual strength and exhortation rather than detail. Its mass-market competitor on the left, the *Mirror*, had likewise confined itself almost exclusively to the deaths of the nurses when reporting the first raid. For the second, it also carried the story about the Good Friday service, with a photograph of the congregation in the Cathedral ruins, on page five. It quoted Provost (recently appointed Archdeacon) Howard, who told his audience: 'These ruins are full of a strange power. It does not matter when we die. It only matters how we die.' On page two of the same edition, the *Mirror* concentrated on the story of a bride-to-be who had been killed in a raid on 'a West Midlands town' when an enemy bomber crashed into her family's house. Another story on that page once again featured Provost Howard. He and his family had turned their home by the Cathedral into a dressing station, presumably for the victims of the bombs on St Mary's Hall and the police station, among others. The article directly below it was headlined 'THOUSANDS OF HUN HOMES HIT'. It detailed a radio talk by an air commodore in which he had declared that 'tens of thousands . . . maybe hundreds of thousands' of homes in Germany had been demolished or made uninhabitable by the RAF.[20]

The *Express* carried nothing about the mass burial that followed the Easter Holiday, but the *Mirror* did. Unlike *The Times*, it described not just the service, but how 'many women broke down and, sobbing, had to be led away. Others, distracted, threw their wreaths onto the coffins, which were covered in Union Jacks.'[21]

One hundred and fifty-three tons of bombs were dropped and 170 people killed on the night of Maundy Thursday in Coventry. This second death toll brought the total of fatalities in April 1941 to 451, with 702 seriously wounded. The figures, spread over two nights as they were, easily bear comparison with those of the infamous November attack. Yet, for ever after, these would be called 'the forgotten raids'. A few eyewitness accounts, recalled over a distance of some seventy years or more, by a trick of memory conflate the two, identifying events that occurred in April as having taken place during the November Blitz. In some historical works on Coventry, the April raids are scarcely mentioned.[22]

The Luftwaffe never returned in force. There would be some devastating raids elsewhere in Britain between April and June 1941 – in May, Birmingham again, and also London's most costly yet in terms of deaths. However, already ever more numerous German air force units were being transferred to the east, ready to support the massive invasion of the Soviet Union, now planned for 22 June 1941. Hitler may well have continued his aerial assault on the United Kingdom through these weeks – in the case of London, seemingly with more fury than ever – in good part simply to fool Stalin into the belief that he was still so preoccupied with defeating the British that he would not think of turning against Russia.

Following April's new devastation, there were actually only six more relatively small 'disturbance' raids against Coventry, accounting for a total of ten deaths. The last German bombs fell on the city on 3 August 1942, a little less than two years since the first, once more striking the industrial and working-class area of Stoke Heath, close to the big Morris Works. No one was killed.

For the city of the Three Spires, the time of destruction was over. Reconstruction – or at least thinking about reconstruction – could at last begin.

21

Resurgam

A familiar claim is that this or that German town or city was chosen by the British as a 'revenge target' for Coventry. Perhaps the most often named is the historic city of Dresden, bombed to destruction just eleven weeks before the war ended, almost four and a half years after 'Moonlight Sonata'.

In the narrow sense, however, this claim can be true only of the Rhenish city of Mannheim. Together with its sister city of Ludwigs-hafen, on the opposite river bank, their total population was almost 400,000. An elegant town that had long been the residence of the Princes of the Palatinate, Mannheim was attacked on the night of 16/17 December 1940, just over a month after the November raid on Coventry. In the aftermath of the Luftwaffe's intensive and apparently indiscriminate bombing during November, and particularly the levelling of Coventry and Southampton, the British cabinet had for the first time authorised a large-scale attack aimed specifically at the centre of a provincial German city rather than its industrial or military districts.

Originally, the plan was to send 200 bombers over to Mannheim. In fact, only 134 made the journey, of which between eighty-two and 102 actually dropped bombs.[1] Eight Wellington bombers, carrying full loads of incendiaries, were first over the target, a kind of British imitation of KG.100's pathfinder group. The Wellingtons had been told to create clear marker fires in the city centre, as the Luftwaffe had done in Coventry, so that the main force could wreak concentrated destruction there. Unfortunately, their targeting was not accurate and fires appeared in other places outside the ostensible bombing zone. The result was that the attack ended up a scattered disappointment.

According to the RAF's report, 240 buildings in Mannheim were destroyed or damaged by incendiary bombs and 236 by high explosives. Thirteen commercial premises, a railway station and office, a school and two hospitals, including a military hospital, were included in these estimates. Not all were seriously damaged. At the Military Hospital, there were injuries to staff and inmates caused by flying glass. Four barges or river steamers were reckoned to have been damaged. Casualties were estimated at thirty-four dead (thirteen male civilians, one soldier, eighteen women, and two children), eighty-one injured, and almost 1,300 bombed out of their homes – appreciably more than two hundred of the latter group in Ludwigshafen, on the other side of the Rhine (and a legitimate target because of the huge BASF chemicals works). Two Hampden bombers and one Blenheim were lost to the enemy defences, while four crashed over England on return.

The truth was that, at this point, Bomber Command was incapable of equalling the Luftwaffe's capacity for destruction even when it tried. Between June 1940 and June 1941, the German bomber fleet killed 43,384 people in Britain. In 1940, the total death toll in Germany from RAF raids – the same ones that the British press expended so much printing ink on celebrating – was only 975. Both sides were inaccurate in most of their night bombing, though the British record was worse. At least the Germans had their beams, until these were jammed, and bent, and consequently abandoned. A survey of British bombing by Patrick (later Lord) Blackett, one of the government's leading scientific advisers, calculated that the Germans killed around four times as many per ton of bombs as the British at this time.[2]

Bomber Command would nevertheless keep up this campaign for almost exactly a year after the destruction of Coventry. Only when Mr D. M. Butt of the Cabinet Office carried out a detailed and searching investigation, based on photographic and documentary evidence, did it become clear exactly how ineffective the British bombing effort had been and continued to be. Most British bombers didn't get within three miles of the target – as few as one in ten in the Ruhr raids – and, on examination, it turned out that a high proportion of aircraft officially credited with 'hits' had in fact dropped their bombs in open country. His report was rejected in high circles as too 'pessimistic', but by the summer it was clear that, not only was he right about the inaccuracy of the RAF's targeting and bombing, but German air defences were improving and so Bomber Command was starting to lose unconscionable quantities of bombers. The stark fact was that more air crew had been lost over Germany since the beginning of the war than German civilians had been killed on the ground.[3]

On 13 November 1941, the day before the first anniversary of 'Moonlight Sonata', Bomber Command was instructed to halt long-range operations until further notice. It was a serious admission of failure. Their efforts were turned, on Churchill's instructions, principally against the German sea raiders and their bases at Brest.

Only when Air Marshal Sir Arthur Harris, that great defender of 'crash concentrations', was placed in charge of Bomber Command, towards the end of February 1942, did the situation change. He had in mind to create scores of German 'Coventrys', with full support from the government – which had by then decided to relaunch the RAF's aerial assault on Germany, with official permission to bomb more or less indiscriminately. This he achieved, in an escalating campaign that used and improved the techniques originated by the Luftwaffe in 'Moonlight Sonata', and saw almost every German town of any size 'coventrated'. Harris's relentless campaign would end only in April 1945, when the Reich lay all but defeated. The destruction of the centre of Dresden, on 13 February 1945, costing up to 25,000 overwhelmingly civilian dead, was its awful culmination. It was in that sense, and that rather tenuous sense only, that Dresden's fate could be seen as Britain's 'revenge' for the destruction of Coventry.

It is commonly believed that all the enchanting streets and buildings commented on by J. B. Priestley in 1933 were destroyed by the German air force. In fact, a substantial part of that medieval street pattern had already been demolished in the years before the war on order of the city council.

Like all historic cities, during the period immediately before the Second World War Coventry found itself faced with a serious practical (and to some extent socio-economic) problem. With the rapid growth of motor traffic, public and private, the narrow, winding, cobbled streets, with their central gutters, were becoming a serious barrier to free movement. At that time, even the proud royal city of Dresden found itself levelling centuries-old streets in its historic core. A radical programme of further clearances, specifically to make the city fit for the motor vehicle, had been planned before war intervened.[4]

In Coventry's case, unlike Dresden's, there were no plans to build a gigantic headquarters for the *Gauleiter*, but a blueprint for drastic change did exist, and was likely to be acted upon even before the first siren sounded over the city. The demolitions in the mid-1930s had included St Agnes' Lane, picturesque Butcher Row (by Holy Trinity Church), with its overhanging Elizabethan houses and alleyways, and the Bull Ring – all winding, cobbled streets of the ancient sort, filled with pretty (if often insanitary) dwellings and crooked-fronted shops out of a Dickens novel. They were replaced by a new, wide thoroughfare named Trinity Street, creating much easier access to and from the city centre. It was on Trinity Street that the steel-framed, five-storey structure of the new Owen Owen department store rose proudly to symbolise a new era of modern consumerism in Coventry. This was seen both as a rational improvement of the street plan and (with some justification) as slum clearance. When cutting the ribbon at the opening of Trinity Street in 1937, the Mayor referred to the now gone Butcher Row as a 'blot on the city'.[5]

The election of a majority Labour council in 1938 saw the process set to accelerate. Previous councils had been keen enough to rationalise the city centre, but Labour had an ideological commitment to improvement. It appointed Donald Gibson as Coventry's first City Architect and Town Planner – a rival, in many ways, to the City Engineer, who had previously presided over such matters. In May 1940, before the first bomb had fallen on any British city, Gibson and his eager, radical young team of modernists – Le Corbusier was a great influence – staged an exhibition, 'The Coventry of Tomorrow', which clearly signposted the intention to undertake yet more definitive change on the city centre. It envisaged clearing most of the medieval and Georgian buildings around the Cathedral and Holy Trinity, building a museum on Earl Street by the Council House, and the creation of a big open space enclosed by civic buildings 'in long, sinuous four-storey blocks'.[6]

Six months later came 'Moonlight Sonata'. Gibson famously described it as 'a blessing in disguise. The jerries cleared out the core of the city, a chaotic mess, and now we can start anew.' Later, the City Architect recalled professionally heady times amidst the horrors of the Blitz: 'We used to watch from the roof to see which buildings were blazing and then dash downstairs to check how much easier it would be to put our plans into action.'[7]

Gibson's plan was duly accepted by the council in February 1941. A local paper commented: 'The City Architect has tolerated no barriers, has refused to concern himself unduly with the preservation of ancient features, has disregarded the lines of ancient streets insofar as they complicate his scheme, and has certainly not permitted questions of cost to cramp his inspiration.'

One of the chief reasons why the drastic rebuilding of the city centre had posed so many problems before the war was that private landowners had to be persuaded and expensive matters of compensation considered. Now, however, the government had taken steps to enable reconstruction of British cities under terms much more favourable to the local authorities. On 8 April 1941, by coincidence the day of the first April raid on Coventry, the Minister of Works and Buildings, Lord Reith (former head of the BBC), told reporters that Coventry, Birmingham and Bristol local authorities had been invited to prepare a plan for reconstruction of their cities. 'We told them to do it boldly and comprehensively,' he added, 'and not to bother about questions of private ownership and private property.'[8]

In 1944, the Town and Country Planning Act made extensive allowance for powers of compulsory purchase by councils. Coventry could not just rebuild, but build new.

Towards the end of the war, the Town and Country Planning Association published a booklet which defined attitudes towards city rebuilding, with particular reference to Coventry, where plans already existed and the devastation had been so severe as to create an exemplary case for modernist reconstruction. The booklet was entitled *Resurgam* (Latin for 'I Shall Rise Again'). As it happened, the *Midland Daily Telegraph* had published a defiant editorial with exactly that same word as its headline following the 14 November raid and the King's visit, encouraging Coventrians to take heart:

> Coventry's fine old Cathedral has gone. Its streets are a shambles and some of the things Coventry has loved for centuries have been destroyed in a night. Those who walked the littered streets to-day, who saw the cheery smiles of those who toiled to clear the debris, and who heard the cheers of enthusiasm which greeted the arrival of H.M. the King, know full well that Coventry cannot be beaten this way, and that its people will someday enjoy the task of raising in a greater and finer style the things that have been beaten down.[9]

One thing that was decided quite soon after the end of major bombing raids against Coventry was that the Cathedral would be rebuilt. However, according to the diocesan resolution of 16 May 1942, the new St Michael's would stand alongside, rather than completely replace, the ruin of the old one. It would be built in the red Midlands sandstone characteristic of many historic buildings in Coventry, including the old Cathedral, as well as the town walls and gates (some of which are preserved), and the old Grammar School on the corner of Hales and Bishop Street.

Originally, a well-known establishment architect, Sir Giles Gilbert Scott, had been invited to submit designs for the new Cathedral, which he did in 1944. It was on the basis of these that an appeal was started for the rebuilding. Scott, then in his sixties, was most famous for the neo-Gothic anglican Cathedral in Liverpool, begun in 1910. There were arguments about the scale of the proposed work, whether it would fit on the site, and whether it was too old-fashioned. After the war, opposition within architectural and artistic circles grew, and rejection of his designs by the Royal Fine Arts Commission led to Scott's resignation.[10]

In 1950, a competition for a new design was held, attracting over two hundred entries. As a result, the prestigious commission was awarded to Basil Spence, an uncompromising modernist.

Because of post-war shortages of building materials – and the pressing need to provide housing and commercial buildings in the largely bombed-out city centre – the new Cathedral was not consecrated until 1956, and the building itself not completed until 1962. In the end, the shattered outer walls of the old Cathedral were left to enclose a garden of remembrance next to the new structure. The new one rose a score or so yards to the north of it, partially on land that had once been the medieval church's graveyard. At Provost Howard's urging, the words 'Father Forgive Them' were carved in the stone behind the ruined altar. The spire tower, which had survived the bombing and was one of the city's famous trio, was left in place.

The Cathedral was controversial at the time because of its modernism. 'A horror', 'an aesthetic outrage', and 'super-cinema' were a few of the furious comments hurled at the building by members of the public. Apparently, it was even referred to as a 'concrete monstrosity', despite the fact that it was constructed entirely of red sandstone.[11] The new Cathedral, which Spence rather saw as a 'plain jewel casket with many jewels', nevertheless soon became a much-loved building and a symbol of the city's revival. As Spence's 'jewel casket' remark implied, the interior was graced, among many other fine things, by a stained-glass window by John Piper and an enormous tapestry, *Christ In Glory*, by Graham Sutherland.

Outside, fixed to the wall, rose a large bronze sculpture, *St Michael's Victory Over the Devil*, by Sir Jacob Epstein. The great sculptor's last completed work before his death in 1959, it faced towards the city and the world, expressing, as Provost Howard put it, 'Flashing brightness, Strength and Beauty, Freedom from malignity, Confidence'. The Cathedral made Spence's reputation, earned him a knighthood, and led to many more commissions, equally prestigious but not necessarily very sacred. These included the British Embassy in Rome and the thirty-three-storey Hyde Park Barracks in London, completed in 1970 as a home for the Household Cavalry and, unlike Coventry Cathedral, still widely disliked.

The legacy of 'Moonlight Sonata' gave Coventry a particular international status as a symbol of the effects of Nazi barbarism, but this also gave those who desired to heal the war's wounds a great opportunity to spread their message. Provost Howard became a powerful promoter of international reconciliation in the post-war period, especially with the former enemy and bomber of Coventry. For a while after the destruction of the Cathedral, he had held services in his home nearby, and the Holy Trinity Church had also extended hospitality to the Cathedral's congregation. Occasional services had been held in the Cathedral ruins, some of which were broadcast. The city established itself as a centre for Peace and Reconciliation.

As early as 1946, Howard had conducted a service in which the bishop of the badly bombed German city of Hamburg had also participated via radio link. The next year, the city of Kiel in what would become West Germany, established a society of Friends of Coventry, which rapidly acquired 800 members, leading to the establishment of a reciprocal organisation in the British city, and a regular exchange arrangement that has persisted ever since. In the 1950s, Councillor Pearl Hyde, formerly of the WVS and now Lord Mayor, visited Dresden, in the first important recognition of the tragic connection between the two cities, and the relationship grew in the 1970s. After the fall of the Berlin Wall, and the reunification of Germany, an appeal was launched to rebuild Dresden's own symbolic church, the Baroque Frauenkirche, which had been destroyed by fire in February 1945 when the city was bombed by the RAF.

Unlike their counterparts in Coventry, Dresden's citizens chose to build a near-replica of the former church, based on the original plans of its early eighteenth-century architect, Georg Bähr. It was reconsecrated in 2005. Dresden and Coventry remain closely connected. Delegations exchange visits, especially on the anniversaries of each other's fatal bombing raids. The Bishop of Coventry is a patron of the Dresden Trust, as was, until his recent retirement, the Canon Emeritus of Coventry Cathedral, Paul Oestreicher.

A further reminder of unity in suffering, but also of hope, is contained in the name of the 900-seat Belgrade Civic Theatre, built in 1958 on Corporation Street. It was named after the Yugoslav capital, which had been destroyed by German bombers on 6/7 April 1941, the eve of Coventry's second great Blitz, and which was also in the process of post-war rebuilding. When the project was first proposed, after a visit by the Yugoslav ambassador in 1953, the Yugoslavs donated timber from their city for the construction of the theatre. Coventry gave the Mayor of Belgrade a car made in the city. These were, after all, the boom times of the post-war British motor industry, and Coventry remained at its heart.

Throughout the war, and well into the post-war period, Coventry remained a place where good money was earned by working people, and they spent it if they could.

The authorities had not generally approved of this before the bombing of the city, and they continued not to during the rest of the war.

It seems to have been a widespread view in Whitehall circles and the powerful regional bureaucracy that Coventrians were spoiled, both by high wages and also the special attention they had been granted by Britain and the world because of what had happened to the city on 14 November 1940. In an exchange of letters between officials at the Ministry of Food and their counterparts at the Ministry of Home Security in late 1941 this opinion was expressed in the context of complaints in Coventry that there were not enough shops in the city and consequently not enough food. The problem was exacerbated by the fact that a great many women were engaged in munitions or other war work and therefore had little time to go shopping. 'Coventry is a boom town,' the Ministry of Food's report began:

> Little over a generation ago it was a small Cathedral city and it is against the background of phenomenal growth that present problems must be visualised. The working population has been drawn from all parts of the British Isles, there is, for instance, an Irish contingent about 10,000 strong. Coventry labour has a minimum of civic sense. The peculiar employment policy of the motor industry – high wages with an hour's notice on either side – has resulted in the development of a self-conscious labouring class bargaining with the factory managements on an equally ruthless basis at the highest possible price . . .

'The Coventry worker,' the man from the ministry suggested, 'has a great deal of money in his pockets, with no more opportunity than anyone else to satisfy his desires.' He then went on to describe the 'psychology of Coventry':

> After the severe raids of last winter, Coventry came into the news as the supreme example of the Huns' barbarity. The city was held up as the example and proof of the proud claims that 'Britain can take it'. Royalty, foreign personages, politicians and journalists all flocked to the town, saw the ruins and made their speeches. Then the excitement

died down, important visitors became fewer, and Coventry began
to feel neglected.[12]

'Shopping difficulties,' it was said, 'formed a convenient stalking-
horse for more fundamental grievances.' There are other examples,
all pursuing the same line of disparagement, by those born to be
comfortable, of those who have to work for their comforts. The post-
war situation was not judged, from London, to be much different,
since even in peacetime Coventry kept up a certain notoriety from
its wartime suffering.

Meanwhile, within ten years, and certainly within twenty, there
was no lack of shopping facilities. On 8 June 1946, the official Victory Day, a stone was ceremonially laid in the centre of Coventry,
bearing what had become a familiar symbol of the city: the mythical
phoenix, arising from the ashes. Donald Gibson's new city centre,
grouped around what was left of Broadgate and bearing a marked
similarity to his pre-war plans, was a concrete modernist paradise of
courtyards and gardens, largely consisting of what would soon be
called a shopping mall.

Overcoming the resistance of traders, who insisted that if a cus-
tomer could not park his or her car right outside, they would not go
into the shop, beginning with the West Orchard development, the
city planners initiated what amounted in Britain to a retail revolution.
They turned the centre of Coventry into the first urban shopping
area where customers left their vehicles in car parks and then walked
through the precinct to the shops they required. It worked, whatever
the traders said. In any case, within a relatively short time after the
war, car ownership had become so widespread that to have had simple
parking outside individual shops would have been totally impractica-
ble. Also, however sentimental locals and architectural historians may
have viewed the destruction of old Coventry, it was already doomed
before the war. Even without the Luftwaffe's involvement, a lot of the
city's centre would indeed have had to go the same way as Butcher
Row and the Bull Ring, just to accommodate the age of the car.

Not that the near-extinction of old Coventry was entirely due to wartime bombing. The Society for the Protection of Ancient Buildings reckoned that there were 120 timber houses left in the city at the end of the war, and even in 1958 the National Buildings Record found a hundred still standing. Two-thirds of these would soon disappear. Gibson had resigned as City Architect and Planning Officer in 1954, but his successor, Arthur Ling, pressed on with the completion of a ring road and a new building for the Lanchester College of Technology (later combining with the Art School to form Lanchester Polytechnic, and now Coventry University).

Scores of old houses were demolished and their timbers burnt. The local weekly paper, the *Coventry Standard*, ran the front-page headline: 'Demolition Recalls the Days of the Blitz'. Bizarrely, a few buildings that survived were dismantled, moved and rebuilt in Spon Street, around a tiny core of old buildings formed by the old Bablake School and Ford's Hospital. Against Gibson's opposition, this seventeenth-century alms house had been rebuilt in the early fifties.[13] It is now surrounded by transplanted historic buildings as part of a kind of open-air Museum of Quaintness, visitors being directed to it by signs all over the city reading 'historic' or 'medieval' Spon Street. Looming over it all, a short distance up Corporation Street, is a giant branch of IKEA.

Lanchester College of Technology had been named after Sir Frederick Lanchester, pioneer of the Coventry automotive industry. His family company, founded by three brothers in 1895, had produced some of the early twentieth century's finest (and most expensive) sedans before going under in the Great Depression. In 1930, Lanchester became part of the BSA empire, and manufacture was transferred to the works complex that housed another BSA-owned company, Daimler, by which it was ultimately subsumed.

Through the post-war complex of mergers, mistakes and failures that characterised the British motor industry, Coventry kept going, and retained something of the 'boom town' it had been during the war. There were still plenty of fine, proud engineers employed in the city, but, plagued by labour troubles, lethally combined with often incompetent management and out-of-date technology, and finally damaged by international competition, the British motor industry declined sharply in the 1970s, in Coventry as elsewhere. Since Peugeot (formerly Chrysler, which in turn was once the Rootes Group) closed its Ryton factory in 2006, there is no major motor manufacturing in the Coventry area, except for the relatively small-scale LTI company, which makes purpose-built taxis. Peugeot retains its parts warehouse in Coventry, and Jaguar – now owned by the giant Indian Tata Group – still has its corporate headquarters and Research and Development department there, at Whitley. Alfred Herbert Machine Tools, whose main works had once covered 22 acres and employed 4,000 operatives, was forced to ask for state aid from the government financed National Enterprise Board in 1975. This was duly provided, but the international market conditions were by now such that the company had to be wound up a few years later.

The early Thatcher years had seen Coventry at a new low point. Between 1980 and 1983, the West Midlands, including Coventry, experienced the largest contraction of the employment base and the highest long-term unemployment of any English region.[14] The decades of prosperity had helped to bring thousands of immigrants to the city, chiefly from South Asia and the Caribbean, just as the boom in the first half of the twentieth century had attracted the Irish and the Welsh.

Economic collapse brought with it crime and social tension. One iconic local band of the early 1980s, The Specials, reflected the ethnic mix of the new Coventry, in a kind of Ska-Punk fusion music known as 'two-tone'. Their best-known song, the number one hit 'Ghost Town', reflected the drastic nature of the city's economic fall from grace. Coventry had long been used to steady, decently paid work and enthusiastically enjoyed, affordable leisure. 'Ghost Town''s angry feeling for solidarity across the city's (and the country's) divides was very much of that moment.

Coventry between 1940 and 2015 has probably seen more change, in its architecture, its street pattern, its social make-up and its ways of earning a living, than any other city in the United Kingdom. The rapid expansion of its university, with a current student body of 27,000 (of which approximately 30 per cent are international) has transformed the nature of the city, especially in the central and inner suburbs, where many students live. Services, IT, food and entertainment, creative industries, and others, are increasingly replacing what had once been a manufacturing monoculture. The city still has a relatively high unemployment rate, but in 2014 Coventry showed the ninth highest growth in business establishment for the United Kingdom, the seventh highest for employment growth and the second in private sector jobs growth. It is one of only four cities outside the south-east of England where the typical wage is above the national average.

Over the centuries, Coventry has been remarkable for its native ingenuity, its ability to reinvent itself, perhaps more than any other major English city. More peaks, and more troughs. Three-quarters of a century after 'Moonlight Sonata', there are signs and hopes that Coventry is once again on the verge of recovery.

Resurgam.

NOTES

INTRODUCTION

1   J. B. Priestley, *English Journey*, p. 69f.

CHAPTER 1: WOOL, BUTTONS AND MAGNETOS

1   For this and other details concerning Godigfu/Godiva's life, see the entry by Ann Williams in the online edition of *Oxford Dictionary of National Biography*.

2   Richard Goddard, *Lordship and Mediaeval Urbanisation: Coventry, 1043–1355*, pp. 28ff.

3   Ibid., p. 15. This estimate was based on contemporary poll tax estimates.

4   Kenneth Richardson, assisted by Elizabeth Harris, *Twentieth-Century Coventry*, p. 64.

5   To be precise, 69,877. See Richardson, *Twentieth-Century Coventry*, p. 182.

6   Coventry Transport Museum website http://wiki.transport-museum.com/White%20and%20Poppe.ashx

7   For details of Coventry's war-related production in these years, see David McGrory, *Coventry History and Guide*, p. 96f.

8   Richardson, *Twentieth-Century Coventry*, p. 38.

9   See Frederick Taylor, *The Downfall of Money: Germany's Hyperinflation and the Destruction of the Middle Class*, p. 38.

10 Priestley, *English Journey*, p. 74.

11 Ibid., p. 69.

12 Ibid., p. 70.

13 Table taken from Richardson, *Twentieth-Century Coventry*, p. 67.

14 See Neil Hanson, *The First Blitz*, p. 52f., and the article 'Spon Street, Coventry: The Toughest Bullet of the War', at http://www.bbc.co.uk/programmes/p01wtvv6

CHAPTER 2: 'THE BOMBER WILL ALWAYS GET THROUGH'

1   See Letitia Fairfield, CBE, MD (ed.), *The Trial of Peter Barnes and Others (The I.R.A. Coventry Explosion of 1939)*, p. 21f. Also useful, T. Ian Adams, *The Sabotage Plan*, pp. 63ff. Internet sources include 'Coventry IRA bombing: The 'forgotten' attack on a British city', at http://www.bbc.co.uk/news/uk-england-coventry-warwickshire-28191501; also http://www.historiccoventry.co.uk/articles/s-shaw.php

2   For these details see Fairfield (ed.), *The Trial of Peter Barnes and Others*.

3   See the comprehensive list of IRA actions, including the Coventry incidents mentioned, in Appendix 5 to Fairfield (ed.), *The Trial of Peter Barnes and Others*, pp. 260ff.

4   'Bomb Found At A Flat: Charges Against Five Men', in *The Times*, Saturday, 9 September 1939, p. 3.

5   'Man Hunt After Outrage', in *Sunday Times*, 27 August 1939, p. 18. Adams was in fact the uncle of Sinn Fein leader Gerry Adams, and also rumoured to have been prominent in the IRA – even for a while, its 'Chief of Staff'. The report stated that he was also known to use the surname 'Norman'.

6   See also www.historiccoventry.co.uk

7   'Anti-Irish Demonstration in Coventry', in *Manchester Guardian*, 29 August 1939, p. 10.

8   Thirty years later, in the late 1960s, an elderly Irish republican by the name of Toby O'Sullivan from Cork claimed to have been responsible for setting the bomb. He maintained that he had been horrified at being ordered to place the bicycle in Broadgate but feared reprisals from his superiors if he refused. See the report in the *Irish Examiner*, 25 August 2014, http://www.irishexaminer.com/analysis/75-years-since-the-ira-bombed-coventry-283375.html. Also cited in David O'Donoghue's book on the IRA and Nazi Germany, *The Devil's Deal: The IRA, Nazi Germany and the Double Life of Jim O'Donovan*.

9   '1,317,000 Evacuated', in *The Times*, Saturday, 9 September 1939, p. 10.

10 Interview with Mary Evans, courtesy of BBC Radio Coventry and Warwick-shire, from many hours recorded for the award-winning radio documentary, 'Beyond the Blitz: 70 Years On' (2010). These interview recordings donated by BBC and now (as 5-disc DVD set) part of the archival resources at Coventry History Centre (File PA 2815/3/7). Transcribed by the author and used with the permission of BBC Radio Coventry and Warwickshire. Further references indicated as 'BtB', with interviewee's name.

11 Evacuation statistics and photographs in Alton Douglas, Gordon Stretch and Clive Hardy, *Coventry at War: A Pictorial Account 1939–4*, p. 10f.

12 Richardson, *Twentieth-Century Coventry*, p. 74.

13 Coventry History Centre, Coventry City Records, CCA1/4/45, Air Raid Precautions Committee 1938–1939.

14 Richardson, *Twentieth-Century Coventry*, p. 74.

15 Douglas, Stretch and Hardy, *Coventry at War: A Pictorial Account 1939–45*, p. 12.

16 Richardson, *Twentieth-Century Coventry*, p. 76.

17 Audio interview from Imperial War Museum, London (1990) with Sir Frederick Delve (1902–96), Deputy Head of National Fire Service from 1941, later Chief Officer of the London Fire Brigade, available online at http://www.iwm.org .uk/collections/item/object/80011325

18 As recounted by Philip Larkin to John Kenyon, a Professor of History at Hull, where Larkin was University Librarian for nearly thirty years. In Andrew Motion, *Philip Larkin: A Writer's Life*, p. 12. Also for the Nazi regalia in his office and the comments by his deputy, Alan Marshall, regarding Sydney's continuing pro-German sentiments even during the war.

19 This advice and the details about the 'dams', in Richardson, *Twentieth-Century Coventry*, p. 75.

20 Quoted in Frederick Taylor, *Dresden, Tuesday, February 13, 1945*, p. 86.

21 See Richard Overy, *The Bombing War: Europe 1939–1945*, p. 32f.

22 See Nicholas Kristof, 'Okunoshima Journal; A Museum to Remind Japanese of Their Own Guilt', in *New York Times*, 12 August 1995.

23 Taylor, *Dresden*, p. 72.

24 Richardson, *Twentieth-Century Coventry*, p. 76.

25 Overy, *The Bombing War*, p. 147f.

26 Ibid.

27 Ibid., p. 148.

28 Richardson, *Twentieth-Century Coventry*, p. 77.

29 Ibid., n. 8.

30 Overy, *The Bombing War*, p. 139.

31 Ibid., p. 137.

32 Ibid.

CHAPTER 3: BOOM

1 David Edgerton, *Britain's War Machine: Weapons, Resources and Experts in the Second World War*, p. 200.

2 Richardson, *Twentieth-Century Coventry*, p. 65.

3 *Dictionary of National Biography*, Sir Alfred Herbert (1866–1957) by Tom Donnelly.

4 Richardson, *Twentieth-Century Coventry*, p. 71.

5 Ibid., p. 67.

6 Ibid., p. 70.

7 Ibid., p. 68. And for the other details about Banner Lane.

8 Ibid., table on p. 67. Figures are not available for the Rootes Shadow Factory No. 1, which, though sizeable, was basically an extension of the existing plant

in Aldermoor Lane, two miles south-east of Coventry city centre. Without this figure, the workforce (1943) numbered just under 25,000.

9   Except where otherwise stated, for the following details of Coventry companies see Richardson, *Twentieth-Century Coventry*, p. 71f.

10 See Lexa Dudley and Reg Kimber, *A. C. Wickman, A Life Diary*, p. 14. His father was said to have been a Prussian diplomat who died from food poisoning after a lobster dinner when Axel (b. 1894) was two years old.

11 'Great Britain in War-Time V – Coventry's Task: Aircraft and Machine Tool Production', in *The Times*, Thursday, 8 February 1940, p. 5.

12 See Mass Observation report on Savings London and Coventry (online) SxMOA1/2/57/3/D, p. 267.4.

13 Ibid., p. 267.11.

14 Ibid., p. 267.15.

15 Ibid., p. 267.12.

16 Ibid., p. 257.15.

17 Figures from Malcolm Chandler, *Britain in the Age of Total War*, p. 21.

18 Mass Observation report on Savings London and Coventry, as above, p. 267.14.

19 Ibid., p. 267.35.

20 Ibid., p. 267.16. And for the following quote.

21 Ibid., p. 267.17.

CHAPTER 4: WAITING FOR THE LUFTWAFFE

1   Briefly but well described in John Lukacs, *Five Days in London: May 1940*, pp. 205ff.

2   See John Lukacs, *The Duel: Hitler vs Churchill*, p. 184.

3   Churchill speech on BBC Radio, 14 July 1940. Text available at http://www .winstonchurchill.org/learn/speeches/speeches-of-winston-churchill/126-war-of-the-unknown-warriors

4   For a concise and gripping account of discussions among the German leadership and Hitler's own vacillating attitude see Lukacs, *The Duel: Hitler vs Churchill*, pp. 180ff.

5   Herausgegeben von Ralf Georg Reuth, Joseph Goebbels. *Tagebücher*, Band 4: *1940–1942*, p. 1449, entry for 6 July 1940.

6   Hitler's speech in *Verhandlungen des Reichstages 4. Wahlperiode 1939, Sitzungen 1–8, Anlagen Nr. 1–3*, Band 460 S.78 (translation by the author).

7   See Goebbels, *Tagebücher*, Band 4, p. 1455, n. 121.

8   Hugh Gibson (ed.), *The Ciano Diaries, 1939–1943*, Introduction by Sumner Welles, p. 277, entry for 19 July 1940.

9   Ibid., entry for 20 July 1940.

10 Goebbels, *Tagebücher*, Band 4, p. 1456, entry for 21 July 1940.

11 Lukacs, *The Duel: Hitler vs Churchill*, p. 194.

12 Ibid., p. 192f.

13 Quoted from an essay by Hermann Rahne, *Zur Geschichte der Dresdner Garnison im Zweiten Weltkrieg 1939 bis 1945*, in *Verbrannt bis zur Unkenntlichkeit: Die Zerstörung Dresdens 1945*, p. 127.

14 Quoted in Lukacs, *The Duel: Hitler vs Churchill*, p. 188.

15 Goebbels, *Tagebücher*, Band 4, pp. 1458 and 1459, entries for 24 and 25 July 1940.

16 Herausgegeben vom Militärgeschichtlichen Forschungsamt, *Das Deutsche Reich und der Zweite Weltkrieg*, Band 2, p. 377. As we shall see, at that same meeting in the Berghof, Hitler also declared his intention to attack Russia the following spring.

17 Ibid., p. 378.

18 Quoted in Lukacs, *The Duel: Hitler vs Churchill*, p. 221.

19 Stephen Bungay, *The Most Dangerous Enemy: A History of the Battle of Britain*, p. 119.

20 See Overy, *The Bombing War*, p. 74f.

21 Ibid., p. 77.

22 Bungay, *The Most Dangerous Enemy*, p. 118.

23 *Das Deutsche Reich und der Zweite Weltkrieg*, Band 2, p. 382.

24 Overy, *The Bombing War*, p. 78f.

25 *Das Deutsche Reich und der Zweite Weltkrieg*, Band 2, p. 384.

26 See Overy, *The Bombing War*, p. 81.

27 *Das Deutsche Reich und der Zweite Weltkrieg*, Band 2, p. 384.

28 For details on the Ju 87's unsuitability for conditions pertaining during the Battle of Britain, see Bungay, *The Most Dangerous Enemy*, p. 256.

29 Account of the Gosport fiasco in Bungay, *The Most Dangerous Enemy*, p. 229. The Ju 87's abrupt withdrawal from the battle is noted by Overy, *The Bombing War*, p. 74.

30 Overy, *The Bombing War*, p. 82.

31 Bungay, *The Most Dangerous Enemy*, p. 288. And for information about courageous WAAFs.

32 Ibid., p. 232. And for the following.

33 Ibid., p. 224.

34 Overy, *The Bombing War*, p. 82.

35 Herausgegeben und ausgewertet von Willi A. Boelcke, *Wollt Ihr den totalen Krieg? Die geheimen Goebbels-Konferenzen 1939–1943*, p. 93 (23 August 1940).

36 Bungay, *The Most Dangerous Enemy*, p. 304.

37 Ibid., p. 305. And for Göring's reaction.

38 See *Das Deutsche Reich und der Zweite Weltkrieg*, Band 2, p. 386 and Overy, *The Bombing War*, p. 83.

39 Overy, *The Bombing War*, p. 84.
40 This excerpt from Hitler's speech in Rolf-Dieter Müller, *Der Bombenkrieg 1939–1945*, p. 71 (translation by FT).
41 Bungay, *The Most Dangerous Enemy*, p. 308.

CHAPTER 5: BLITZ

1   Johnstone quoted in Bungay, *The Most Dangerous Enemy*, p. 309.
2   Pilot Officer Steve Stephen, quoted in Derek Robinson, *Invasion 1940: The Truth about the Battle of Britain and What Stopped Hitler*, p. 186.
3   Ibid.
4   *Das Deutsche Reich und der Zweite Weltkrieg*, Band 2, p. 386.
5   Overy, *The Bombing War*, p. 86f. And for the mix of bomb loads in the attacking fleet.
6   Boelcke, *Wollt Ihr den totalen Krieg?*, p. 99 (7 September 1940).
7   Ibid., p. 101f. (9 September 1940).
8   Overy, *The Bombing War*, p. 89.
9   Ibid., p. 88.
10 Quoted in Robinson, *Invasion 1940*, p. 190.
11 See Overy, *The Bombing War*, p. 88.
12 See Robinson, *Invasion 1940*, pp. 192ff., drawing on the research of Alfred Price.
13 Quoted in Bungay, *The Most Dangerous Enemy*, p. 336.
14 See Overy, *The Bombing War*, p. 90.
15 Ibid., p. 91.
16 Cited in *Das Deutsche Reich und der Zweite Weltkrieg*, Band 2, p. 392.
17 Ibid., p. 393.
18 Ibid.
19 Ibid., p. 392.

CHAPTER 6: RAIDERS

1   Report of 3 April 1939 for DHO on 'Possible German Courses of Action in the Event of Air Attack on the United Kingdom and Possible Distribution of Attack', Appendix 'A': 'Possible Distribution of German Air Attack', at NA Kew AIR 20/2070.
2   Interview with the Tucker Family, from 'BtB'.
3   See 'Diary of Air Raids in Coventry' by Betty Bokes, August–November 1940 at Coventry History Centre file PA 2516.
4   Richardson, *Twentieth-Century Coventry*, p. 81.
5   See the Movietone News film of the opening, available for viewing at http://oldcoventryonfilm.vidmeup.com/view?q=4f1c061f20211.flv

6 Bokes, 'Diary of Air Raids in Coventry'. And for the following.

7 Bokes, 'Diary of Air Raids in Coventry'.

8 Interview with Michael Logan, from 'BtB'.

9 Interview with Michael Logan, as above.

10 *Manchester Guardian*, 14 October 1940, p. 2.

11 See http://www.historiccoventry.co.uk/tour/fords.php

12 *Manchester Guardian*, 15 October 1940.

13 Richardson, *Twentieth-Century Coventry*, p. 82f.

14 For damage to houses, see NA Kew CAB 80/22/17, p. 105.

15 *Das Deutsche Reich und der Zweite Weltkrieg*, Band 2, p. 393.

16 See Dr Horst Boog, 'A Luftwaffe View of the Intelligence War', in *Air Intelligence Symposium, Bracknell Paper No. 7*, especially pp. 59ff. Available online at http://www.rafmuseum.org.uk/documents/Research/RAF-Historical-Society-Journals/Bracknell-No-7-Air-Intelligence.pdf

17 *Das Deutsche Reich und der Zweite Weltkrieg*, Band 2, p. 394, and for the following paragraph.

18 'Copy of a letter dated 7th November 1940, from the Minister of Labour to the Prime Minister', in NA Kew CAB 80/22/17, p. 73.

19 Annex II to CAB 80/22/17, p. 74.

20 Ibid., p. 75.

21 'Air Defence of the City of Coventry: Report' C.S. (40)922 (FINAL) at NA Kew CAB 80/22/17, p. 102.

22 Ibid., p. 104 and for observations regarding morale.

23 Overy, *The Bombing War*, p. 99.

24 '. . . dass es dem Ost-Ende von London einmal zu langweilig wird und dass Verhandlungen mit Deutschland und vielleicht sogar ein neues Kabinett gefordert wird', in *Das Deutsche Reich und der Zweite Weltkrieg*, Band 2, p. 396.and for the Luftwaffe headquarters staff communication referred to below.

CHAPTER 7: *KNICKEBEIN*

1 R. V. Jones, *Most Secret War: British Scientific Intelligence 1939–1945*, p. 93.

2 Ibid., p.134f. And for the following.

3 Ibid., p.125f.

4 Ibid., p.137.

5 Ibid., p.138f.

6 Aileen Clayton, *The Enemy Is Listening*, p. 79. The author was a German-speaking WAAF officer who served with the 'Y' service, based at Kingsdown in north Kent ('on the Berlin/London 'bus route') picking up and interpreting the Luftwaffe's operational radio traffic.

7 Quoted in Brian Johnson, *The Secret War*, p. 44.

CHAPTER 8: *KORN*

1 NA Kew HW 5/6: Government Code and Cypher School: German Section: Reports of German Army and Air Force High Grade Machine Decrypts (CX/FJ, CX/JQ and CX/MSS Reports) 26 Oct. 1940–2 Dec. 1940, No. 63, dated 11.10.40 (probably in error, should have been 11.11. or 10.11).

2 Jones, *Most Secret War*, p. 201.

3 See https://www.flickr.com/photos/32293736@N04/6974951880/, which also has a link to a photograph of the street as it is today, with the houses involved viewable.

4 'A.I.I. (k) Report No. 878/1940', in NA Kew AIR 40/2401 (INTERROGATIONS OF GERMAN AND ITALIAN PRISONERS OF WAR Oct.–Dec. 1940). And for the following.

5 'To D. of I. From S/L S.D. Felkin, 12.11.1940', in NA Kew AIR 2/5238: GERMAN OPERATIONS 'MOONLIGHT SONATA' (BOMBING OF COVENTRY) AND COUNTER-PLAN 'COLD WATER'.

6 Minute 'Moonlight Sonata' 12.11.1940 by G. W. P. Grant (A.I.1 (w)), in NA Kew AIR 2/5238.

7 See reference to captured map as part of comment on latest German signals intelligence in report CX/J/450 dated 15/11/40 in NA Kew Hw 5/6. No date is given for the recovery of the map material, but clearly this information was already known to Wing Commander Grant two days earlier.

8 Jones, *Most Secret War*, p. 201.

9 See 'Note for the Prime Minister on Projected Operation by G.A.F. – "Moonlight Sonata" and the Counter-Operation by the Metropolitan Air Force – "Cold Water".' 14.11.1940, in NA Kew AIR 8/352.

10 See 'Note on German Operation "MOONLIGHT SONATA" and Counter-plan "COLD WATER"' from DDHO on 17.11.40, in NA Kew AIR 2/5238: GERMAN OPERATIONS 'MOONLIGHT SONATA' (BOMBING OF COVENTRY) AND COUNTER-PLAN 'COLD WATER', p. 1.

11 See 'NO. 80 WING OPERATION ORDER NO. I', 14 November 1940, in NA Kew AIR 2/5238: GERMAN OPERATIONS 'MOONLIGHT SONATA' (BOMBING OF COVENTRY) AND COUNTER-PLAN 'COLD WATER'.

12 This last detail in 'Note for the Prime Minister on Projected Operation by G.A.F. – "Moonlight Sonata" and the Counter-Operation by the Metropolitan Air Force – "Cold Water".' 14.11.1940, in NA Kew AIR 2/5238.

13 See 'Raid Damage to Coventry Cathedral', in *Midland Daily Telegraph*, 14.11.1940.

14 See the transcript of this intercepted message dated 11/11/40 CX/JQ/44, p. 2, in NA Kew H5/6.

15 Clayton, *The Enemy Is Listening*, p. 80.

16 See Jones, *Most Secret War*, p.199f and for the following. For more details see also '80 Wing Periodical Reports No. 11 Appendix – Elektra I' pp. 3ff, in NA Kew AIR 40/2236.

17 See initial reports in '80 Wing Periodical Reports No. 12', p. 3, in NA Kew AIR 40/2236.

18 Clayton, *The Enemy Is Listening*, p. 83.

CHAPTER 9: FINDING THE BEAM

1 Jones, *Most Secret War*, p. 203.

2 BBC interview with R. V. Jones, 1970s, quoted in Johnson, *The Secret War*, p. 47f.

3 Jones, *Most Secret War*, p. 189.

4 See the interview with Mrs Petrea Winterbotham for the Imperial War Museum, London (1984), Accession no. 7463, reel 1, available at http://www.iwm.org.uk/collections/item/object/80007265

5 Audio interview (thirty-six reels) with Group Captain F. W. Winterbotham from Imperial War Museum, London (1984), Accession no. 7462, reels 23–24, including the following extracts, available online at http://www.iwm.org.uk/collections/item/object/80007264

6 Clayton, *The Enemy Is Listening*, p. 83.

7 See David Irving, *Churchill's War*, p. 492. Irving asserts that Lady Tweeddale corroborated this verbally.

8 Agnes Humbert, *Resistance: Memoirs of Occupied France*, translated by Barbara Mellor, p. 20f.

9 'I have little doubt the Official Historians are sitting on them . . .' See his remarks quoted at David Irving's website http://www.fpp.co.uk/History/Churchill/Coventry_1411940/summary_1984.html

10 See Johnson, *The Secret War*, p. 55.

11 Götz's remarks, ibid., p. 48.

12 'HOME SECURITY WEEKLY APPRECIATION NO. 22 FOR THE PERIOD 0600 HOURS 13 NOVEMBER TO 0600 HOURS 20TH NOVEMBER, 1940', in 'Air Raid, Coventry 14/15 November '40', in NA Kew HO 199/178.

13 Richardson, *Twentieth-Century Coventry*, p. 82.

CHAPTER 10: RED ALERT

1 'Report of the Chief Officer of the Fire Brigade on an Enemy Air Attack at Coventry on 14/15 November, 1940' (21 December 1940), in NA Kew HO 187/1780. And for the following references where this source is indicated.

316 NOTES TO PAGES 123–135

2   See 'HOME SECURITY WEEKLY APPRECIATION NO. 22', in NA Kew HO 199/178.
3   See 'First Report on Enemy Operation "Moonlight Sonata"', in NA Kew AIR 8/352.
4   Interview with Dennis Adler, from 'BtB'.
5   Interview with Alan Hartley, from 'BtB'.
6   Teleprinter message, HOME SECURITY FROM BIRMINGHAM, Situation Report to 0600 Hours 15/11/40 in NA Kew HO 199/178.
7   See Radio Counter-Measures: No. 80 Periodical Report No. 12, 'ENEMY ACTIVITY', p. 1, in NA Kew AIR 40/2336.
8   Unteroffizier Günter Unger, interviewed for the BBC and quoted in Johnson, *The Secret War*, p. 51.
9   Peter Taghon, *Die Geschichte des Lehrgeschwaders 1*, Band 1, *1936–1942*, p. 162.
10   Reports respectively no. 934/1940 and no. 938/1940 in 'Air Ministry (A.I.1 (k) Prisoner of War Reports Nos 902–986, 16.1.1940–31.12.1940, Vol. 9', in NA Kew AIR 40/3127. The lake was finally drained in 1941 after the second big raid on Coventry. Coombe Abbey is now a country house hotel and stages regular re-enactments of the night of the Coventry raid based on this story.
11   Interview with Mayselle Swift, from 'BtB'.
12   Interview with Doris Dawson, from 'BtB'.
13   Interview with Stan Morris, from 'BtB'.
14   Interview with Brian Huwson, from 'BtB'.
15   For this and the following, see the recorded interviews with Bertha Leverton and Ingeborg Sadan, both née Engelhard, online at the IWM. Bertha Leverton interview recorded 1997, accession no. 17310 (reel 3) available from the IWM website at http://www.iwm.org.uk/collections/item/object/80016598; Inge Sadan interview recorded 1997, accession no., 17290 (reels 1 and 2) available from the IWM website at http://www.iwm.org.uk/collections/item/object/80016596
16   Bertha Leverton, IWM recording, as above.
17   Interview with Len Dacombe, from 'BtB'.
18   Audio interview with Donald Frederick Thompson, recorded 1999, accession no. 18772, available from the IWM website at http://www.iwm.org.uk/collections/item/object/80017908

CHAPTER II: EXECUTIVE COLD WATER

1   'Telegram en clair', Air Ministry to recipients, 14.11.1940, in NA Kew AIR 2/5238.
2   NOTE beneath Minute to Duty Group Captain, 14.11.1940, also in NA Kew AIR 2/5238.

3 'Operation Instructions for Air Operation 'Cold Water'', dated 14.11.1940, p. 2, in NA Kew AIR 2/5238.

4 See Ulf Balke, *Kampfgeschwader 100 'Wiking': eine Geschichte aus Kriegstage-büchern, Dokumenten und Berichten 1934–1945*, p. 60.

5 Ulf Balke, *Der Luftkrieg in Europa: Die operativen Einsätze des Kampfgeschwaders 2 im Zweiten Weltkrie*, Teil 1, *Das Luftkriegsgeschehen 1939–1941: Polen, Frankre-ich, England, Balkan, Russland*, p. 196f.

6 'Report on Enemy Operation "Moonlight Sonata"', p. 2, in NA Kew AIR 2/5238. And for the following.

7 Stevenson, DHO to DCAS, 12.11.1940, in NA Kew AIR 2/5238.

8 See Martin Middlebrook and Chris Everitt, *The Bomber Command War Diaries: Operational Reference Book 1939–1945*, p. 104.

9 'Bombs on Centre of Berlin. Successful Attack on Railway Station', in *The Times*, Friday, 15 November 1940, p. 4.

10 See section 'Action by special radio bombers', in 'Note on German Operation "MOONLIGHT SONATA" and Counter-Plan "COLD WATER"', 17.11.1940, p. 2, from DDHO, in NA Kew AIR 2/5238. For one German air crew's account of finding 'their' beam had been bombed on the night of 14/15 November, see NA Kew AIR 40/2401 (INTERROGATIONS OF GERMAN AND ITALIAN PRISONERS OF WAR Oct.–Dec. 1940), no. 938/1940.

11 See analysis in '80 Wing Periodical Reports' (based on Prisoner of War Reports), Part I (to 31.12.1940), p. 3, no. 11 (b), in NA Kew AIR 40/2336.

12 Note from Whitworth-Jones (DDHO) to DCAS, 16.11.1940, in NA Kew AIR 2/5238, as above.

13 See '80 Wing Periodical Reports', Part I (to 31.12.1940), p. 5, no. 16, in NA Kew AIR 40/2336.

14 SRA 1048, 'A 653 – Unteroffizier (Bomber W/T operator) Captured 19.11.1940; A 659 – Obergefreiter (Bomber pilot) Captured 24/25.11.1940', p. 2, in NA Kew AIR 40/3072.

15 Recorded interview with John Cunningham (1989), IWM Catalogue no. 10729 (reel 2), available from the IWM website at http://www.iwm.org.uk/collections/item/object/80010506

16 See Cunningham's obituary in *Guardian*, 29 July 2002, at http://www.theguardian .com/news/2002/jul/29/guardianobituaries.nigelfountain. A quiet, modest man, as is apparent from his interview, he was appalled by all the razzamatazz, and especially the propaganda stories that put his success down to eating carrots rather than the new on-board radar technology.

17 Recorded interview with Richard Ronald Mitchell (1990), IWM Catalogue no. 11364 (reel 2), available from the IWM website at http://www.iwm.org. uk/collections/item/object/80011120

18   Air Ministry to Fighter Command, 15.11.1940, in NA Kew AIR 2/7415.

19   See 'Note on German Operation "MOONLIGHT SONATA" and Counter-plan "COLD WATER"', from DDHO on 17.11.40, in NA Kew AIR 2/5238, p. 3.

20   Handwritten note from DHO, dated 15/11, 'Coventry, COS (40) 916', in NA Kew AIR 8/352.

21   For Regimental War Diary of 95th HAA, November 1940, see NA Kew WO 166/2385.

22   'Report of Coventry GOR & Its Communications from 1900 hrs, 14th Nov., 1940, to 1700 hrs, 24th Nov. 1940' from 4th AA Division Signals, in NA Kew WO 166/2143.

23   Richardson, *Twentieth-Century Coventry*, p. 82.

24   Norman Longmate, *Air Raid: The Bombing of Coventry 1940*, p. 143.

25   War Diary of Unit HQ, 34th AA Bde, for November 1940, in NA Kew WO 166/2261.

26   A.I.1. (k) Report 909/1940, 18.11.1940, filed with other Beam Intelligence, in NA Kew HW 14/9.

27   There was, indeed, contemporary research to that effect, which clearly played a role in government provision of anti-aircraft batteries, even if they proved mostly more or less useless. See Edgar Jones, Robin Woolvin, Bill Durodie, and Simon Wessely, 'Civilian Morale During the Second World War: Responses to Air Raids Re-examined', in *Social History of Medicine*, Vol. 17, No. 3, p. 477.

28   Recorded interview with Thomas Ashley Cunningham-Boothe (1999), IWM Catalogue no. 19913 (reel 1), available from the IWM website at http://www .iwm.org.uk/collections/item/object/80018479

29   Interview with John Huthwaite, from 'BtB'.

30   IWM recorded interview with Thomas Cunningham-Boothe, as above.

31   Interview with Alan Hartley, from 'BtB'.

CHAPTER I2: 'A SEETHING MASS OF FLAME'

1   Interview with Dennis Adler, from 'BtB'.

2   Interview with Dr George Forrest, part of Warwick University Coventry and Warwickshire Hospital Project at http://www2.warwick.ac.uk/fac/arts/history/ chm/outreach/cwhp/sitesofmemory/interviews/interview81/

3   'Report of the Chief Officer of the Fire Brigade on an Enemy Air Attack at Coventry on 14/15 November, 1940' (21 December 1940), p. 4, in NA Kew HO 187/1780. This included one professional from Coventry Fire Brigade, seven auxiliary firemen, twelve volunteer firemen from Works Fire Brigades, and six from assisting outside forces, in this last case presumably made up mostly or even wholly of the Stoke-on-Trent firemen.

4 Richardson, *Twentieth-Century Coventry*, p. 83.

5 'Report of the Chief Officer of the Fire Brigade' (21 December 1940), in NA Kew HO 187/1780.

6 Richardson, *Twentieth-Century Coventry*, p. 71.

7 See the account of the canal water being used to fight fires in the Cash's ribbon factory and Courtaulds, both beside the waterway further out of Coventry, in Ronald Tweed's account at http://www.bbc.co.uk/history/ww2peopleswar/stories/96/a4896796.shtml

8 See R. T. Howard, *Ruined and Rebuilt: The Story of Coventry Cathedral 1939–1962*, p. 4. Also the more detailed account of the dissolution in William Page (ed.), *A History of the County of Warwick*, Vol. 2 (Religious Houses of Warwickshire), p. 59, and from a Catholic point of view at http://www.coventry-catholicdeanery.org.uk/html/Benedictine%20Cathedral%20Priory%20Coventry.html

9 Howard, *Ruined and Rebuilt*, p. 8. And for the other pre-raid details.

10 Ibid., p. 10, and following pages for his account of the attempt to save the church.

11 Quote from ibid., p. 13.

12 Interview with Winifred Dales, from 'BtB'.

13 For Dr Clitheroe's account of how he and his team saved Holy Trinity that night, see his account in his book, *Coventry Under Fire: An Impression of the Great Raids on Coventry in 1940 and 1941*, especially pp. 23ff.

14 Ibid., p. 25.

15 See entry for Victor Alexander Satchell in the alphabetically searchable list of Coventry Blitz victims at http://www.familyresearcher.co.uk/Blitz-Victims/Coventry-Blitz-Victims-details-S.html

16 See Les Ryan, *A Coventry Kid*, p. 54, for a description of regular Sunday-night trips to the Gaumont in the early 1930s.

17 See entries for Thomas Lowry, William Lambe, George Edmund Cooke, George Frederick Cooke, Louisa Cooke, and Minnie Stokes, in the list of Coventry Blitz victims, as above.

18 See entries for Anne Audrey Roberts, Audrey Patricia Roberts, Eric Chinn, Vera Maud Chinn, James Cronan, Sara Lavinia Cronan, Arthur Overbury, William Mallard, in the list of Coventry Blitz victims, as above.

19 See entries for Angela Elizabeth Collett, Cyril Ernest Collett, Hugh Wilfrid Collett, Sydney Albert Collett, Henry John Collier, Edith Congrove, Lewis Congrove, Norah Cooper, Mary Ann Graham (née McCann), Alfred Barron, Alfred John Beck, Brenda May Piggon, Clifford David Masser, Horace William Miles, John Cooper Norman, William Robert Lowdon, in the list of Coventry Blitz victims, as above.

20 Interview with Geoff Penton, from 'BtB'.

21 Interview with Thomas Arthur Barnes, from 'BtB'.

22 See recorded interview with former messenger H. G. Miles (1969) on the Coventry University website (Richardson Collection), at https://curve.coventry .ac.uk/open/items/b0047bfb-b9f0–2531–06e0-ad9738af90fd/1/ (045 H.G. Miles .wav).

23 'Report of the Chief Officer of the Fire Brigade' (21 December 1940), p. 2, in NA Kew HO 187/1780. And for the further paragraph below.

CHAPTER 13: DEATH IN THE SUBURBS

1 Felkin's report, 18 November 1940, 'A.I.1. (k) 908/1940', p. 4, in NA Kew HW 14/9.

2 See 'Preliminary and Rough Report' of the Coventry Reconstruction Committee, 18.11.1940, p. 23, in NA Kew PREMIER 3/108.

3 For more details of the destruction of this factory see report of 17.11.1940, HOME SECURITY FROM BIRMINGHAM, p. 4, in NA Kew HO 199/178.

4 For the full list of those who died in Foleshill, including at the shelter and the ARP headquarters, see the Commonwealth War Graves Commission website at http://www.cwgc.org/education/imp_pop/foleshill.htm, and for Gordon Edwards, http://www.blackcountrygenealogyandfamilyhistory.co.uk/131759 .html

5 Interview with Len Decombe, from 'BtB'. See also BBC *WW2 – People's War*, archived at http://www.bbc.co.uk/history/ww2peopleswar/stories/31/a4190131 .shtml

6 NA Kew PREMIER 3/108, p. 35.

7 See Bernard Harbourne, Douglas Hill, Alan Hiscocks, and Alexander (Alex) Thomas McArthur in the alphabetical list of victims at http://www.familyresearcher .co.uk/Blitz-Victims/Coventry-Blitz-Victims-detalls-S.html, as above.

8 NA Kew PREMIER 3/108, pp. 33–5. See also 'HOME SECURITY FROM BIRMINGHAM: Situation Report from 06:00 hours to 18:00 hours', 17 November 1940, p. 3, at NA Kew HO 199/178.

9 See Balke, *Der Luftkrieg in Europa*, p. 196.

10 NA Kew PREMIER 3/108, p. 26. And for the following re: the aero factory.

11 See report, 'Air Raid on Coventry, 14–15 November 1940', by Eric. L. Bird of the Research and Experiments Branch (author of the book *Fire in Buildings*, dictated after 'a visit of inspection to Coventry on 16th/17th November 1940', p. 3f., in NA Kew HO 199/178.

12 See recorded interview with J. J. Parkes (1968) on the Coventry University website (Richardson Collection), at https://curve.coventry.ac.uk/open/items/ ffd6f60e-52b4–5179–0cfe-a6601617ae6e/1/ (110 Mr JJ Parkes .wav).

13 Bertha Leverton and Ingeborg Sadan, IWM recordings, as above.

14 Interview with Gladys Cook, from 'BtB'.

15 Interview with Bill Ward, from 'BtB'.

16 See details (provided by family) of David Wilson Burrows in the alphabetical list of victims at http://www.familyresearcher.co.uk/Blitz-Victims/Coventry-Blitz-Victims-detalls-S.html, as above. He died in hospital on 17 November.

17 Interview with Beryl Brown, from 'BtB'.

18 Interview with Brian Huwson, from 'BtB'.

19 Interview with Sheila Howes, from 'BtB'.

20 Account by Mrs Gwendoline Holmes, née Rylands, at Blitz Story Archive, part 9, at http://www.familyresearcher.co.uk/Blitz-Victims/Blitz-Stories-part-9.html. Mrs Holmes died in November 2014, aged ninety-three. Also for the following quotations from this account.

21 'Douglas Hancox Reminiscences' in Coventry History Centre file PA 2837.

22 Interview with Ann Brooks, from 'BtB'.

CHAPTER 14: THE LONG NIGHT ENDING

1 Interview with Alan Hartley, from 'BtB'.

2 For location of rendezvous post see transcript of Telephone Message to Home Office from Col. Rowles, Acting Inspector of Constabulary, 'Coventry', 15.11.1940, in NA Kew HO 199/178.

3 For Captain le Grand's informal recollections of his role see his letter to the Lord Mayor of Coventry, 28 April 1962, in Coventry History Centre PA 1781. The captain was, curiously, by now resident in Munich. The rest of this account is based on 'Working a Rendezvous Post', a report submitted by le Grand on 22 November 1940, available in NA Kew HO 199/178.

4 Captain le Grand, letter to the Lord Mayor, as above.

5 Quoted in Balke, *Der Luftkrieg in Europa*, as above, p. 197.

6 15 November 1940, 0145, HOME SECURITY FROM BIRMINGHAM, in NA Kew HO 199/178.

7 15 November 1940, 0220, as above.

8 15 November 1940, 0330, as above.

9 Captain le Grand, letter to the Lord Mayor, as above. The rank of Coventry's leading citizen was raised to that of Lord Mayor in 1942 in recognition of the city's bravery.

10 See le Grand's remarks in 'Working a Rendezvous Post', as above, p. 3.

11 Interview with Len Dacombe, from 'BtB'.

12 See http://www.familyresearcher.co.uk/Blitz-Victims/Coventry-Blitz-facts-part-2.html. Allan W. Kurki in *Operation Moonlight Sonata: The German Raid on Coventry* gives the time, from Luftwaffe records, as 5:10.

13 Interview with Roma Buckley, from 'BtB'.

14 Interview with Bill Ward, from 'BtB'.

15 Interview with Sheila Howes, from 'BtB'.

16 Interview with Eileen Bees, from 'BtB'.

17 Author's interview with Reg Kimber, Coventry, 22 March 2012.

18 Interview with Ann Brooks, from 'BtB'.

19 Interview with Cecilia Dacombe, from 'BtB'.

20 Bertha Leverton, IWM recording, as above.

21 Interview with Hazel Keene, from 'BtB'.

22 'Evacuation from Coventry', in 'Extracts from Daily Police Situation Report dated 15th November, 1940, from Chief Constable of Warwickshire to R.P.S.O. Birmingham', in NA Kew HO 199/178, as above.

23 'Evacuation', in 'Extract from Daily Report No. 56 by Chief Constable of Northamptonshire dated 15th November 1940', also in NA Kew HO 199/178, as above.

24 Interview with Winifred Dales, from 'BtB'.

25 Interview with Doris Dawson, from 'BtB'.

26 Interview with Brian Kelsey, from 'BtB'.

27 Interview with Iris Tune, from 'BtB'.

28 Interview with Harry Anderton, from 'BtB'.

CHAPTER 15: THE MARTYRED CITY

1 Transcripts of BBC and German radio broadcasts at Coventry History Centre in file PA 2815/7.

2 Ibid.

3 See minutes of War Cabinet 289 (40), in NA Kew CAB/65/10/9, p. 63.

4 Morrison's statement from minutes of War Cabinet 290 (40), in NA Kew CAB/65/10/10, p, 75.

5 'Berlin Gloats', in *Sunday Express*, 17 November 1940, p, 12.

6 See Friends' Ambulance Unit, 'Report on the Nightly Exodus from Coventry', p. 4, at HO 207/1069.

7 *The Times*, Saturday, 16 November 1940, p. 5.

8 *Sunday Express*, Sunday, 17 November 1940, p. 1.

9 See report 'Further Notes on the air raid on Coventry, 14/15 November, 1940' (29 November 1940) in NA Kew HO 199/178.

10 GENERAL REPORTS TO THE ADMIRALTY ON R.M.S. OPERATIONS IN COVENTRY, 15–19 NOVEMBER 1940 (20 November 1940), in NA Kew HO 199/178. And for the following details of their mission that weekend.

11 'Telephone Message Received at Home Office' 10.40 on 15.11.1940, in NA Kew HO 199/178.

12 Quoted in Tom Harrisson, *Living Through the Blitz*, p. 134.

13 Ibid., pp. 133–4.

14 Audio interview with Sir Frederick Delve from Imperial War Museum, London, as above.

15 For Beaverbrook's call to Dudley and the setting up of the committee, see Richardson, *Twentieth-Century Coventry*, p. 85.

16 Harrisson, *Living Through the Blitz*, p. 137.

17 Ibid., p. 134.

18 Ibid., p.135.

19 See 17 November 1940, 'HOME SECURITY FROM BIRMINGHAM: Situation Report from 0600 hours to 1800 hours', and also Eric L Bird's Report of 18 November 1940, as above, both in HO 199/178.

20 See Reg Kimber, *Seven Brave Men: The Stories Behind Whitley's War Memorial*, p. 3f. The Whitley Local History Society, whose Honorary Secretary Mr Kimber is, placed a plaque in 2008 at the spot where the tragedy occurred. Mr Laxon, the proprietor of the family-owned business from whose premises the bomb had been removed, was, by tragic mischance, killed while on fire-watching duty there on the night of 14/15 November.

21 See 15 November 1940, 'HOME SECURITY FROM BIRMINGHAM: Situation Report from 0600 hours to 1800 hours', p. 2, in NA Kew HO 199/178.

22 Interview with John Harris, from 'BtB'.

23 Report, 'Military Assistance in Coventry', 22 November 1940, in NA Kew HO 199/178.

24 'Coventry City Police: General Situation Report for the Two Weeks ended 23 November 1940', p.5, in NA Kew HO 199/178.

25 'Prison for Looters', in *Midland Daily Telegraph*, 26 November 1940.

26 'STOLE FROM CATHEDRAL RUINS', in *Midland Daily Telegraph*, 22 November 1940.

27 Gwendoline Holmes, née Rylands, at http://www.familyresearcher.co.uk/Blitz-Victims/Blitz-Stories-part-9.html, as above.

CHAPTER 16: 'ARE WE DOWN-HEARTED?'

1 Longmate, *Air Raid, 1940*, p. 202.

2 Interview with Mayselle Swift, from 'BtB'.

3 Howard, *Ruined and Rebuilt*, p. 20.

4 Longmate, *Air Raid*, p. 202f.

5 Joachim C. Fest, *Hitler*, p. 676f.

6 See http://www.historiccoventry.co.uk/blitz/mayor-with-king.php for the full version, recently related by Jack and Mrs Moseley's great-nephew, Andrew

Ross, and a shorter one, quoted as a 'Coventry legend' in Longmate, *Air Raid*, p. 205.

7 Longmate, *Air Raid*, p. 202 and p. 204.

8 Ibid., p. 205. And for Joyce Moseley's recollections.

9 'Coventry City Police: General Situation Report for the Two Weeks ended 23 November 1940', p. 2, in NA Kew HO 199/178.

10 Transcripts of German radio broadcasts (English translations) at Coventry History Centre in file PA 2815/7. And for the following excerpts.

11 *New York Times*, 16 December 1940. The piece had been filed on 15 November by Raymond Daniell, the paper's highly respected London Bureau Chief.

12 Quoted in Longmate, *Air Raid*, p. 212.

13 Editorial, 'Bombs on Coventry', in *New York Times*, 17 November 1940.

14 'NAZIS CHANGE THEIR TACTICS', in *Midland Daily Telegraph*, 16 November 1940.

15 It seems that the slot had been created as a 'spoiler', due to the authorities' realisation that many listeners would turn over straight after the BBC news to German radio to listen to 'Lord Haw-Haw' (real name William Joyce). The Irish-born German propagandist's caustic view of the war news, delivered in a bizarre upper-class drawl, had, curiously, gained wide popularity with the British public. See Hugh Chignell, *Public Issue Radio: Talks, News, and Current Affairs in the 20th Century*, p. 207.

16 Text of Harrisson's talk at (MO online) SxMOA1/1/5/11/19.

17 Minutes of War Cabinet 290 (40), in NA Kew CAB/65/10/10, p. 76.

18 See Asa Briggs, 'The War of Words', in *The History of British Broadcasting*, Vol. III, p. 304f.

19 Motion, *Philip Larkin: A Writer's Life*, p. 48f.

CHAPTER 17: THE QUICK AND THE DEAD

1 See 15 November 1940, Home Security from Birmingham to London at 0600 hours, in NA Kew HO 199/178.

2 See text of *Deutschlandsender* broadcast at 13:00 on 16 November 1940, among transcripts of BBC and German radio broadcasts at Coventry History Centre in file PA 2815/7.

3 For Saturday's estimate of casualties see (undated) day-by-day summary, beginning with the quotation 'The City of Coventry was attacked last night . . .' p. 3, in NA Kew HO 199/178.

4 'HOME SECURITY FROM BIRMINGHAM: COVENTRY PROGRESS REPORT' 16 November 1940, 11:25 hours, in NA Kew HO 199/178.

5 Ibid.

6 'Civil Defence No. 9 Region: Air Raid on Coventry 14/15 November, 1940' (19 December 1940) p. 3f. And for the following comments of effectiveness of rescue parties and lack of proper equipment, in NA Kew HO 199/178.

7 Handwritten notes from time of the raid appended to le Grand's letter to the Lord Mayor (1962) in Coventry History Centre PA 1781.

8 18 November 1940, Home Security from Birmingham, 'Situation Report to 1800 hours 18/11/1940', p.1, in NA Kew HO 199/178.

9 See handwritten note 10.11.1941 commenting on estimates of the lightly injured at Coventry: '. . . very unreliable because in heavy raiding no count is kept owing to inadequacy of staff in F.A.P. [First Aid Posts]'. 'Comparative Estimate as between East End Boroughs and Coventry', in NA Kew 199/395.

10 Dr Alan Ashworth, quoted in Longmate, *Air Raid*, as above, p. 222f. And for the following description of what happened to the gasometer and the problems with identification of the victims' bodies. Dr Ashworth had spent the night of the raid in charge of casualty operations at the Civil Defence Control Centre adjoining the Council House.

11 'Civil Defence No. 9 Region: Air Raid on Coventry . . .' as above, p. 4, in NA Kew HO 199/178.

12 Longmate, *Air Raid*, p. 223.

13 Interview with Sheila Thornett, from 'BtB'.

14 Longmate, *Air Raid*, p. 224.

15 Interview with Lord Henry Plumb, from 'BtB'. Lord Plumb later became President of the National Farmers' Union, a Conservative MEP, and President of the European Parliament.

16 For Massey's interview when in the US as a guest of the American Public Health Association, see *Brooklyn Daily Eagle*, 5 June 1944, p.11 at http://bklyn .newspapers.com/newspage/52681404

17 See 'HOME SECURITY WEEKLY APPRECIATION NO. 22 FOR THE PERIOD 0600 13TH NOVEMBER TO 0600 20TH NOVEMBER 1940', 'APPENDIX: AIR RAID ON COVENTRY', p. 3, in NA Kew HO 199/178.

18 Interview with Ethel Lucas, from 'BtB'.

19 'Feeding the Homeless', in *Midland Daily Telegraph*, 22 November 1940.

20 Interview with Eileen Rees, from 'BtB'.

21 'Air Raid on Coventry, 14–15 November 1940' (submitted 18 November 1940, by Eric. L. Bird), p. 1, in NA Kew HO 199/178.

22 Longmate, *Air Raid*, p. 187.

23 In sequence interviews with Jesse Smith, Len Dacombe and John Harris, from 'BtB'.

24 See Richardson, *Coventry in the Twentieth Century*, p. 216. For further details see the history of the network at http://www.coventrytramways.co.uk/history .htm. Ironically, the tram network was reprieved during the late 1930s because,

running as it did on electricity, it was considered strategically more reliable, in case of a new war, than the motor bus system, since it did not depend on imported fuel.

25 'Review of Damage', in 'REPORT AND RECOMMENDATIONS OF THE COVENTRY RECONSTRUCTION CO-ORDINATING COMMITTEE', 31 December 1940, p. 1, in NA Kew CAB 89/14.

26 Interview with John Harris, from 'BtB'.

27 General statistics regarding damage to individual lines, see Longmate, *Air Raid*, p. 188.

28 Audio interview from Imperial War Museum, London (2001) with Mary Elizabeth Harrison, former WAAF NCO, reel 1, available from the IWM website at http://www.iwm.org.uk/collections/item/object/80020746.

29 'Recovering the Victims of Coventry Blitz: Denial of a Rumour', in *Midland Daily Telegraph*, 25 November 1940.

30 'Guarding Against Epidemics', in *Manchester Guardian*, 23 November 1940, p. 7.

31 See Longmate, *Air Raid*, p. 228f.

32 'Some air raid shelters were hit and completely demolished. In cases where there were thought to be no survivors the shelters were later sealed and the bodies never recovered . . . it is possible that as many as 1000 innocent people actually died.' See the mostly excellent online information source http://www .familyresearcher.co.uk/Blitz-Victims/Coventry-Air-Raids-Operation-Moonlight-Sonata.html

33 Quoted in Longmate, *Air Raid*, p. 226.

34 *Daily Mirror*, 21 November 1940.

35 *Daily Express*, 21 November 1940.

36 *The Times*, 21 November 1940.

37 *Manchester Guardian*, 21 November 1940, p. 6.

38 'Coventry Dead Laid in One Grave; Air Raid Siren Is Their Requiem', in *New York Times*, 21 November 1940.

39 'MORE COVENTRY FUNERALS', in *Manchester Guardian*, 22 November 1940.

CHAPTER 18: COVENTRATED?

1 *Midland Daily Telegraph*, 26 November 1940.

2 See Longmate, *Air Raid*, reproduction of the document facing p. 174.

3 'Withdraw at the last moment and in a time of crisis as did the trapped British soldiers 29 May to 3 June 1940 with the aid of many small boats from the ports and harbours of southern England'. See P. R. Wilkinson, *Concise Thesaurus of Traditional British Metaphors,* p. 191.

4   Entry for 29 November 1940, in Helen D. Millgate (ed.), *Mr Brown's War: A Diary from the Home Front*, p. 77. See also 'Lord Haw-Haw was able to gloatingly coin a new word – "to Coventrate"', quotation from the article 'Coventry Cathedral, Ruined by German Bombs, To Rise Again', in *Illustrated London News*, 12 May 1945.

5   'Coventry: The Aerial Attack in November 1940', from *Luftwissen*, December 1940, prepared by the Coventry Branch of the Royal Aeronautical Society (their translation), now at Coventry History Centre, as above, in file PA 608.

6   Harrisson, *Living Through the Blitz*, p. 143.

7   See Adrian Smith, *The City of Coventry: A Twentieth-Century Icon*, p. 151. Dr Smith, Coventry-born but a Senior Lecturer at Southampton University, has written about both cities' separate and common experiences during the Blitz.

8   Harrisson, *Living Through the Blitz*, p. 149.

9   Quoted in ibid., p. 145.

10 Harrisson's judgement and Hodsoll's opinions quoted in Smith, *The City of Coventry*, p. 157.

11 Dr Aubrey Lewis, quoted in Jones, Woolvin, Durodie and Wessely, 'Civilian Morale During the Second World War', in *Social History of Medicine*, p. 478. And for the quote from Tom Harrisson.

12 See front page of the *Daily Mirror*, Tuesday, 9 November: 'Blitz's New Turn North'.

13 See Smith, *The City of Coventry*, p. 161.

14 Dr Massey quoted in *Brooklyn Daily Eagle*, 5 June 1944.

15 Longmate, *Air Raid*, p. 161.

16 See Juliet Gardner, *The Blitz: The British Under Attack*, p. 126f.

17 Dr C. W. E. Emmens, quoted in Jones, Woolvin, Durodie and Wessely, 'Civilian Morale During the Second World War', in *Social History of Medicine*, p. 472.

18 See Friends' Ambulance Unit, 'Report on the Nightly Exodus from Coventry', p. 2, in HO 207/1069

19 Cited in Smith, *The City of Coventry*, p. 160.

20 See Jones, Woolvin, Durodie and Wessely, 'Civilian Morale During the Second World War', in *Social History of Medicine*, p. 471.

21 By 20 November, 6,400 unemployed had been registered in Coventry, compared with a pre-raid unemployment total of something close to zero. See 'Coventry: Report on Reconstruction Work Following the Raid on 14/15th November, 1940' (n.d.), p. 3, in NA Kew HO 199/178.

22 'COVENTRY RECONSTRUCTION CO-ORDINATING COMMITTEE: REPORTS AND RECOMMENDATIONS' (31 December 1940), p. 4, in NA Kew CAB 89/14.

23 Interview with Len Dacombe, from 'BtB'.

24 See Len Dacombe's contribution to BBC *WW2* – *People's War*, archived at
    http://www.bbc.co.uk/history/ww2peopleswar/stories/31/a4190131.shtml
25 Ministry of Airport Production to Prime Minister, 19 November 1940, in NA
    Kew PREM 3/108.
26 'HOME SECURITY WEEKLY APPRECIATION NO. 22 FOR THE
    PERIOD 0600 13TH NOVEMBER TO 0600 20TH NOVEMBER 1940',
    'APPENDIX: AIR RAID ON COVENTRY', p. 4, in NA Kew HO 199/178.
27 Ibid., p. 8.
28 Coventry RECONSTRUCTION CO-ORDINATING COMMITTEE:
    REPORTS AND RECOMMENDATIONS', as above, p. 20, in NA Kew
    CAB 89/14.

CHAPTER 19: DEFIANCE

 1 Interview with Vera Miles, from 'BtB'. See also http://www.bbc.co.uk/history/
    ww2peopleswar/stories/18/a4162718.shtml for Mrs Miles' further memories of
    the time.
 2 See 'HOME SECURITY FROM BIRMINGHAM', 17 November 1940, in
    NA Kew HO 199/178.
 3 Gwendoline Matthews, 'Diaries 1939–1943' (handwritten), in Coventry History
    Centre file PA 2928/1.
 4 See 'SHOPS MAKE QUICK RECOVERY: "Business (Nearly) as Usual"', in
    Midland Daily Telegraph, 22 November 1940.
 5 Clitheroe, *Coventry Under Fire*, p. 39.
 6 'Lord Woolton on Food Situation in Coventry', in *Midland Daily Telegraph*,
    22 November 1940.
 7 *Midland Daily Telegraph*, 21 November 1940.
 8 See 'Civil Defence No. 9 Region: Air Raid on Coventry 14/15 November, 1940',
    p.4, in NA Kew HO 199/178.
 9 Included as p. 40 in Clitheroe, *Coventry Under Fire*.
10 Interview with Stan Morris, from 'BtB'.
11 Matthews, 'Diaries 1939–1943', as above, in Coventry History Centre file PA
    2928/1.
12 'Civil Defence No. 9 Region: Air Raid on Coventry 14/15 November, 1940',
    p. 5, in NA Kew HO 199/178.
13 Figures in 'COVENTRY RECONSTRUCTION CO-ORDINATING
    COMMITTEE: REPORTS AND RECOMMENDATIONS', p. 1 (Intro-
    duction), in NA Kew CAB 89/14.
14 Interview with Ethel Lucas, from 'BtB'.
15 Minutes of Council, 'Information to Public after Air Raids', p. 37, in Coventry
    History Centre file PA 170.

16 'Civil Defence No. 9 Region: Air Raid on Coventry 14/15 November, 1940', p. 7, in NA Kew HO 199/178.

17 'COVENTRY RECONSTRUCTION CO-ORDINATING COMMITTEE: REPORTS AND RECOMMENDATIONS', p. 15, in NA Kew CAB 89/14

18 Ibid., p. 8.

19 Ibid., p. 15.

20 'COVENTRY CARRIES ON: NEIGHBOURLINESS', in *Manchester Guardian*, 25 November 1940, p. 6.

21 'COVENTRY RECONSTRUCTION CO-ORDINATING COMMITTEE: REPORTS AND RECOMMENDATIONS', p. 12f, in NA Kew CAB 89/14.

22 See MO Report on Coventry, at Mass Observation Archive, SxMOA1/2/23/8/T.

23 Script of Harrisson's talk at Mass Observation Archive, SxMOA1/1/5/11/19.

24 Tom Harrisson, 'A Public Demand for Reprisals?', in *The Cambridge Review: A Journal of University Life and Thought*, Vol. LXII, No. 1529, Friday, 30 May 1941.

25 See Hilde Marchant, '"Coventry" for "Courage"', in *Daily Express*, 22 November 1940, p. 4.

26 See James Hinton, 'Coventry Communism: A Study of Factory Politics in the Second World War', in *History Workshop*, No. 10 (Autumn 1980), pp. 90–118. The Party was especially influential at Standard in Canley, at the Standard Shadow Factory in Banner Lane, and the Armstrong Whitworth factory at Baginton (p. 93).

27 Account of Gallacher's speech in Parliamentary Reports, *Manchester Guardian*, 22 November, p. 7.

28 'Reprisals', in *Midland Daily Telegraph*, Friday, 22 November 1940.

29 Audio interview with Ernest Rex Chuter, recorded 1994, accession no. 14592, reel 2, available from the IWM website at http://www.iwm.org.uk/collections/item/object/80014196

30 Overy, *The Bombing War*, p. 239ff.

31 Minute from Stevenson, 20 November 1940, in Miscellaneous Papers: Director of Home Operations, NA Kew AIR 20/2765. And for the following.

32 CAS's scribbled response (21 November) and Harris's Minute (25 November) also in Miscellaneous Papers: Director of Home Operations, NA Kew AIR 20/2765.

33 Overy, *The Bombing War*, p. 257.

34 Quote from the post-war autobiography of Marshal of the RAF Sir Arthur Harris, *Bomber Offensive*, p. 83.

35 From *Britain Under Fire (With a Foreword by J. B. Priestley)*, published by Country Life Publications, c. 1941, p. 12.

36 Sir Arthur Harris, *Bomber Offensive*, p. 51f.

CHAPTER 20: 'THANK GOODNESS YOU'RE ALRIGHT'

1   See 'Additional Notes to Narrative of the Raid of 14/15 November 1940', in NA Kew HO 192/1167.

2   Overy, *The Bombing War*, p. 109.

3   See Misha Glenny, *The Balkans 1804–1999: Nationalism, War and the Great Powers*, p. 474.

4   See Gerhard Schreiber, Bernd Stegemann and Detlef Vogel, *Germany and the Second World War*: Vol. 3, *The Mediterranean, South-East Europe, and North Africa 1939–1941*, p. 498f, and Glenny, *The Balkans 1804–1999*, p. 477.

5   For the still unclear estimates of deaths resulting from Operation Retribution, see Schreiber, Stegemann and Vogel, *Germany and the Second World War*: Vol. 3, p. 498, n. 7. Glenny, *The Balkans 1804–1999*, estimates 17,000.

6   'LUFTWAFFE IN THE BALKANS: ABOUT 1,000 MACHINES', in *The Times*, 8 April 1941, p. 6.

7   See Richardson, *Twentieth-Century Coventry*, p. 87f.

8   Longmate, *Air Raid*, p. 254.

9   Dr George Forrest as earlier (Interview 5), transcript available at http://www2.warwick.ac.uk/fac/arts/history/chm/outreach/cwhp/sitesofmemory/interviews/interview85/. For other details see Warwick University, *Coventry and Warwickshire Hospital Project*, at http://www2.warwick.ac.uk/fac/arts/history/chm/outreach/cwhp/events/onelastlook/sites/blitz. The *Manchester Guardian* (10 April 1940) mentioned the nurses and doctors passing by, the bomb crater, and the explosion, but omitted the fact that several people had been killed.

10 Interview with Adrian and Howard Macey, from 'BtB'.

11 Interview with Hilda Bruce, from 'BtB'.

12 Author's interview with John and Thelma Green, Coventry, 22 March 2012.

13 Matthews, 'Diaries 1939–1943', in Coventry History Centre file PA 2928/1. And for the following.

14 A bomb did go off in Hollis Road after the 10 April raid, though only one death – that of a fifty-four-year-old man who worked at Morris Motors – is recorded in the admittedly incomplete record. See http://www.familyresearcher.co.uk/Blitz-Victims/Coventry-Blitz-Victims-details-F.html entry for David Stanley Fish.

15 Figures based on those given at the diligently kept website http://www.familyresearcher.co.uk/Blitz-Victims/Coventry-Blitz-Resource-Centre.html. These figures are generally very useful for indicative purposes but are incomplete.

16 Richardson, *Twentieth-Century Coventry*, p. 88.

17 See 'DOUBLE ATTACK ON COVENTRY', in *The Times*, 10 April 1941, p. 4. For report of the 11 April raid see 'HEAVY DAMAGE IN MIDLANDS: WIDESPREAD ATTACKS: RAIDS ON BIRMINGHAM AND COVENTRY RENEWED', in *The Times*, 12 April 1940, p. 2.

18 'BURIAL OF COVENTRY AIR RAID VICTIMS: A COMMON GRAVE', *The Times*, 16 April 1941, p. 2.

19 '5 NURSES KILLED BY A D.A. BOMB: IN WRECKED HOSPITAL AT COVENTRY', in *Daily Express*, 10 April 1941, p. 3, and 'THE GOOD FRIDAY MIRACLE OF COVENTRY: PRAYER AMID RUINS', in *Daily Express*, 12 April 1941, p. 3.

20 'BRIDE DIED SHIELDING PATIENTS', in *Daily Mirror*, 10 April 1941, p. 2. 'HUN KILLS BRIDE – "IS PLANE BURNT"?', 'PROVOST'S HOSPITAL', and 'THOUSANDS OF HUN HOMES HIT', in *Daily Mirror*, 12 November 1940, p. 2. 'AMID RUINS THEY PRAY FOR VICTORY', in same edition, p. 5.

21 'CITY'S RAID DEAD LIE IN ONE GRAVE', in *Daily Mirror*, 16 April 1941, p. 3.

22 In Norman Longmate's otherwise excellent and comprehensive *Air Raid*, the April attacks are dealt with in a single paragraph (see p. 254).

CHAPTER 21: *RESURGAM*

1 These details and the following taken from Middlebrook and Everitt, *The Bomber Command War Diaries*, p. 111.

2 Overy, *The Bombing War*, p. 113f.

3 Taylor, *Dresden*, p. 116f.

4 See ibid., p. 60.

5 Gavin Stamp, *Britain's Lost Cities*, pp. 45–53, except where otherwise indicated.

6 See Jeremy and Caroline Gould, *Coventry Planned: The Architecture of the Plan for Coventry, 1940–1978*, p. 13, online at the city council website: http://www.coventry.gov.uk/download/downloads/id/5895/gould_report_-_coventry_planned_april_2009_revision

7 Stamp, *Britain's Lost Cities*, p. 51. And for the newspaper quote below.

8 'SITE SPECULATION: REPORT SHORTLY', in *Manchester Guardian*, 9 April 1941, p. 3.

9 'Resurgam', in *Midland Daily Telegraph*, 18 November 1940.

10 See Richards, *Twentieth-Century Coventry*, pp. 167ff.

11 Provost Howard's recollections of criticisms of the new Cathedral, quoted in Longmate, *Air Raid*, p. 255.

12 Sir Henry French (Ministry of Food) to Sir George Gater (Ministry of Home Security), 20 November 1940, in HO 207/1169 ('Coventry: Shopping difficulties and other factors affecting morale').

13 Stamp, *Britain's Lost Cities*, p. 53.

14 See Tom Donnelly, Jason Begley and Clive Collis (all Coventry University), SURGE Working Paper Series Working Paper no. 6, *The West Midlands Automotive Industry: The Road Downhill*, p. 4.

BIBLIOGRAPHY AND RESEARCH GUIDE

Secondary Sources

Coventry

Adams, T. Ian, *The Sabotage Plan*, Raleigh, 2011

Cameron, Jacqueline, *Coventry Through Time*, Stroud, 2010

Coventry Evening Telegraph, 'Coventry's Blitz', Coventry 1990

Douglas, Alton, Gordon Stretch and Clive Hardy, *Coventry at War: A Pictorial Account 1939–45*, Studley, 1996

Fairfield, Letitia, CBE, MD (ed.), *The Trial of Peter Barnes and Others (The IRA Coventry Explosion of 1939)*, London and Edinburgh, 1953

Goddard, Richard, *Lordship and Mediaeval Urbanisation: Coventry, 1043–1355*, London, 2004

Howard, R. T., *Ruined and Rebuilt: The Story of Coventry Cathedral 1939–1962*, Coventry, 1962

Kimber, Reg, *Seven Brave Men: The Stories Behind Whitley's War Memorial*, Coventry, 2010

Lewis, Tim, *Moonlight Sonata: The Coventry Blitz, 14/15 November 1940*, Coventry, 1990

McGrory, David, *Coventry: History and Guide*, Stroud, 1993

— *Coventry at War*, Stroud, 2011

O'Donoghue, David, *The Devil's Deal: The IRA, Nazi Germany and the Double Life of Jim O'Donovan*, Dublin, 2010

Page, William (ed.), *A History of the County of Warwick*, vol. 2 (Religious Houses of Warwickshire), London, 1965

Richardson, Kenneth, assisted by Elizabeth Harris, *Twentieth-Century Coventry*, London and Basingstoke, 1973

Smith, Adrian, *The City of Coventry: A Twentieth-Century Icon*, London, 2006

Smith, Albert, and David Fry, *The Coventry We Have Lost*, Coventry, 1991

Stamp, Gavin, *Britain's Lost Cities*, London, 2007

Biographies and Memoirs

Clitheroe, Dr G. W., *Coventry Under Fire: An Impression of the Great Raids on Coventry in 1940 and 1941*, Coventry, 1942

Dudley, Lexa, and Reg Kimber, A. C. Wickman, *A Life Diary*, privately published 1990s (courtesy of Reg Kimber)

Gibson, Hugh (ed.), introduction by Sumner Welles, *The Ciano Diaries, 1939–1943*, London, 1947

Humbert, Agnes, *Resistance: Memoirs of Occupied France*, translated by Barbara Mellor, London, 2008

Millgate, Helen D. (ed.), *Mr Brown's War: A Diary from the Home Front*, Stroud, 1998

Motion, Andrew, *Philip Larkin: A Writer's Life*, London, 1993

Priestley, J. B., *English Journey*, London, 1934

Britain's War

Briggs, Asa, 'The War of Words': *The History of British Broadcasting*, Vol. III, Oxford, 1995

Cave Brown, Anthony, *Bodyguard of Lies*, London, 1975

Chandler, Malcolm, *Britain in the Age of Total War*, London, 2002

Clayton, Aileen, *The Enemy Is Listening*, London, 1980

Country Life Publications *(With a Foreword by J. B. Priestley)*, *Britain Under Fire*, London, 1941

Edgerton, David, *Britain's War Machine: Weapons, Resources and Experts in the Second World War*, Oxford, 2011

Irving, David, *Churchill's War*, Melbourne, 1987, and online at http://www.fpp.co.uk/History/Churchill/Coventry_1411940/summary_1984.html

Johnson, Brian, *The Secret War*, London, 1979 (paperback)

Jones, R. V., *Most Secret War: British Scientific Intelligence 1939–1945*, London, 1979 (paperback)

Lukacs, John, *The Duel: Hitler vs Churchill*, Abingdon, 1990

— *Five Days in London: May 1940*, London, 1999

Winterbotham. F. W., *The Ultra Secret*, London, 1975 (paperback)

War in the Air

Bungay, Stephen, *The Most Dangerous Enemy: A History of the Battle of Britain*, London, 2000 (paperback)

Gardner, Juliet, *The Blitz: The British Under Attack*, London, 2010

Hanson, Neil, *The First Blitz*, London, 2008

Harris, Sir Arthur, *Bomber Offensive*, London, 1947

Harrisson, Tom, *Living Through the Blitz*, London, 1990 (paperback)

Kurki, Allan W., *Operation Moonlight Sonata: The German Raid on Coventry*, Westport, 1995

Longmate, Norman, *Air Raid: The Bombing of Coventry 1940*, London, 1976

Middlebrook, Martin, and Chris Everitt, *The Bomber Command War Diaries: An Operational Reference Book 1939–1945*, Leicester, 2000

Overy, Richard, *The Bombing War: Europe 1939–1945*, London, 2014 (paperback)

Robinson, Derek, *Invasion 1940: The Truth About the Battle of Britain and What Stopped Hitler*, London, 2006 (paperback)

Taylor, Frederick, *Dresden, Tuesday 13 February 1945*, London, 2004

Germany's War

Balke, Ulf, *Kampfgeschwader 100, 'Wiking': eine Geschichte aus Kriegstagebüchern, Dokumenten und Berichten 1934–1945*, Stuttgart 1981

— *Der Luftkrieg in Europa: Die operativen Einsätze des Kampfgeschwaders 2 im Zweiten Weltkrie, Teil 1, Das Luftkriegsgeschehen 1939–1941: Polen, Frankreich, England, Balkan, Russland, Koblenz*, 1989

Verbrannt bis zur Unkenntlichkeit: Die Zerstörung Dresdens 1945 (Begleitbuch zur Ausstellung im Stadtmuseum Dresden, Februar–Juni 1995), Dresden, 1994

Boelcke, Willi A., Herausgegeben und Ausgewertet von, *Wollt Ihr den totalen Krieg? Die geheimen Goebbels-Konferenzen 1939–1943*, Munich, 1978

Fest, Joachim C., *Hitler*, London, 1982 (paperback)

Glenny, Misha, *The Balkans 1804–1999: Nationalism, War and the Great Powers*, London 2012

Goebbels, Josef, *Tagebücher* (Band 4: 1940–1942), Munich, 2000

Maier, Klaus, Horst Rohde, Bernd Stegemann and Hans Umbreit, *Die Errichtung der Hegemonie auf dem Europäischen Kontinent*, Band 2 of *Herausgegeben vom Militärgeschichtlichen Forschungsamt, Das Deutsche Reich und der Zweite Weltkrieg*, Stuttgart, 1979

Schreiber, Gerhard, Bernd Stegemann and Detlef Vogel, *Germany and the Second World War*, Vol. 3: *The Mediterranean, South-East Europe, and North Africa 1939–1941*, Oxford, 1995

Taghon, Peter, *Die Geschichte des Lehrgeschwaders 1, Band 1, 1936–1942*, Zweibrücken, 2004

Verhandlungen des Reichstages 4. Wahlperiode 1939, Sitzungen 1–8 (also available at www.Reichstagsprotokolle.de)

Wakefield, Ken, *Pfadfinder: Luftwaffe Pathfinder Operations Over Britain, 1940–44*, Stroud, 1999

Articles

Boog, Dr Horst, 'A Luftwaffe View of the Intelligence War', in *Air Intelligence Symposium, Bracknell Paper No. 7* (March 1997)

Donnelly, Tom, Jason Begley and Clive Collis (all Coventry University), SURGE Working Paper Series Working Paper no. 6, *The West Midlands Automotive Industry: The Road Downhill*, at http://www.coventry.ac.uk/Global/05%20 Research%20section%20assets/Research/SURGE/Working%20papers/ SURGE%20WPS%20Working%20Paper%206.pdf

Gould, Jeremy and Caroline, *Coventry Planned: The Architecture of the Plan for Coventry, 1940–1978*, pub. Coventry City Council, online at http://www.coventry.gov.uk/download/downloads/id/5895/gould_ report_-_coventry_planned_april_2009_revision

Harrison, Tom, 'A Public Demand for Reprisals?', in *The Cambridge Review: A Journal of University Life and Thought*, Vol. LXII, 30 May 1941

Hinton, James, 'Coventry Communism: A Study of Factory Politics in the Second World War', in *History Workshop*, No. 10 (Autumn 1980)

Jones, E., R. Woolvin, B. Durodié, and S. Wessely, 'Civilian Morale During the Second World War', in *Social History of Medicine* 2004, Vol. 17, No. 3

Primary Sources

Newspapers
Daily Express (UK Press Online)
Daily Mirror (UK Press Online)
Manchester Guardian (online archive)
Midlands Daily Telegraph (History Centre, Coventry)
New York Times (online archive)
Sunday Express (UK Press Online)
Sunday Times (online archive)
The Times (online archive)
Völkischer Beobachter (British Library)

National Archives and Records Office, Kew

AIR 2/5238	German Operations 'Moonlight Sonata' (Bombing of Coventry) and Counter-Plan 'Cold Water'
AIR 2/7415	Raid on Coventry on Night of 14/15 November 1940. Report
AIR 20/2070	Possible German Courses of Action and Distribution of Attack
AIR 20/2765	Miscellaneous Papers: Director of Home Operations (Air Ministry)
AIR 40/2336	Radio Counter-Measures: 80 Wing Periodical Reports (to 31 December 1940)
AIR 40/2401	Air Intelligence AI 1(k) Prisoners of War Reports: nos 702–901; vol. 8
AIR 40/3072	CSDIC (UK) reports SRA 900–1199 (incomplete): information obtained from German Air Force POWs
AIR 40/3127	Air Intelligence AI 1(k) Prisoners of War Reports: nos 902–986, vol. 9
AIR 8/352	Operations 'Moonlight Sonata' and 'Cold Water'
CAB 65/10/10	Cabinet Minutes 18 November 1940
CAB 80/22/17	CAB 80. Memoranda: nos 901–950 (October 30 to 18 November 1940)
CAB 89/14	Coventry Reconstruction Coordinating Committee: Report and Recommendations
HO 187/1780	Administration and Organisation: Emergency fire brigade measures in case of concentrated air attack
HO 192/1167	Ministry of Home Security: Research and Experiments Department, Registered Papers, Surveys of Damage in Great Britain, Coventry. Effects of Raiding
HO 207/1069	Coventry: Shopping Difficulties and Other Factors Affecting Morale
HO 199/395	Comparative Estimate of Damage as Between East End Boroughs & Coventry
HW 14/9	Government Code and Cipher School: Directorate: Second World War Policy Papers
HW 5/6	Government Code and Cipher School: Reports of German Army and Air Force High Grade Machine Decrypts (26 October to 2 December 1940)
PREM 3/108	Coventry defence of and damage to

Table   Continued

WO 166/2143	Anti-Aircraft Command: Anti-Aircraft Divisions: Headquarters 4 Anti-Aircraft Division, Signals (HQ)
WO 166/2261	Anti-Aircraft Command: Anti-Aircraft Brigades: Headquarters 34 Anti-Aircraft Brigade, General (HQ G)
WO 166/2385	Anti-Aircraft Command: Heavy Anti-Aircraft Regiments: 95 Heavy Anti-Aircraft Regiment (HAA)

History Centre, Coventry
'Diary of Air Raids in Coventry' by Betty Bokes (handwritten), August–November 1940, File PA 2516
'Douglas Hancox Reminiscences', File PA 2837
Letter, Captain le Grand to Lord Mayor of Coventry, 28 April 1962, File PA 1781. Plus handwritten enclosures
Transcripts of BBC and German radio broadcasts, 1940, File PA 2815/7
'Coventry: The Aerial Attack in November 1940', translation of article from the German magazine *Luftwissen*, December 1940, prepared by the Coventry Branch of the Royal Aeronautical Society, File PA 608
Minutes of Council, 'Information to Public after Air Raids' (1940), File PA 170
Gwendoline Matthews, 'Diaries 1939–1943' (handwritten), File PA 2928/1
Coventry City Records, Air Raid Precautions Committee 1938–1939, File CCA 1/4/45
'Beyond the Blitz', CDs of used and unused interview material donated to the History Centre by BBC Radio Coventry and Warwickshire, File PA 2815/3/7 (for details see eyewitness accounts)

Eyewitness Accounts

Interviews recorded by the author
Edwards, Mike, and Annie, Ashurst, New Forest, 16 May 2014; Fountain, Heather, Coventry, 12 May 2014; Green, John, and Thelma, Coventry, 21 March 2012; Kimber, Reg, Coventry, 22 March 2012

Archive Interviews Recorded for the BBC Radio Coventry and Warwickshire Documentary Beyond the Blitz *(broadcast 2010)*
Adler, Dennis; Anderton, Harry; Barnes, Thomas Arthur; Bees, Eileen; Brooks, Ann; Brown, Beryl; Bruce, Hilda; Buckley, Roma; Cook, Gladys; Dacombe, Cecilia; Dacombe, Len; Dales, Winifred; Dawson, Doris; Evans, Mary; Harris, John; Hartley, Alan; Howes, Sheila; Huthwaite, John; Huwson, Brian; Keen,

Hazel; Logan, Michael; Lucas, Ethel; Macey, Adrian and Howard; Miles, Vera; Morris, Stan; Penton, Geoff; Plumb, Lord Henry; Swift, Mayselle; Thornett, Sheila; Tucker Family; Tune, Iris; Ward, Bill.

Archive Eyewitness Recordings Made by Imperial War Museum, London
(year of interview in parentheses)
Chuter, Ernest Rex (1994); Cunningham, John (1989); Cunningham-Boothe, Thomas Ashley (1999); Delve, Sir Frederick (1990); Leverton, Bertha (née Engelhard) (1997); Mitchell, Richard Ronald (1990); Sadan, Ingeborg (née Engelhard) (1997); Thompson, Donald Frederick (1999); Winterbotham, Group Captain F. W. (1984); Winterbotham, Mrs Petrea (1984).

Mass Observation Archive, University of Sussex
(online access at the British Library, London)
Comparison of Savings Between Coventry and London Borough of Islington (SxMOA1/2/57/3/D)
Script of Tom Harrisson's Talk for BBC European Service (SxMOA1/1/5/11/19)
Mass Observation, 'Report on Coventry, 18.11.40' (SxMOA1/2/23/8/T)

Acknowledgements

Like so many recent works of history, this book owes a great deal to the ever-burgeoning quantity of information and resources that are available online. If, years ago, one felt obliged to be a little apologetic about this, it is no longer the case.

These resources include digitised copies of newspapers from the period. The days are over when, for a historian, consulting the contemporary press involved a trek out on the Northern Line to the London suburb of Colindale and hours of lonely leafing through often fragile, decades-old original newspapers. Searchable newspaper databases alone can save a researcher many hours of unnecessary labour, and for this author they undoubtedly did.

The same goes for websites. Much valuable and fascinating local history still appears in printed form, as books or pamphlets, but a substantial amount of reliable information is now available on the internet. In the case of Coventry, two outstanding online resources are Rob Orland's Coventry History website (www.historiccoventry .co.uk) and the Coventry-based genealogist Jane Hewitt's Coventry Blitz Resource Centre (http://www.familyresearcher.co.uk/Blitz-Victims/Coventry-Blitz-Resource-Centre.html). At the latter, most victims of the German raids are listed by name and address with any biographical details that Ms Hewitt has managed to gather during her tireless work to keep their memories alive. As readers will see, this proved invaluable to me, and I am especially grateful to her. It was also through Ms Hewitt that I was able to contact Dr J. M. Holmes, former Chaplain and Life Fellow of Queen's College, Cambridge, who gave permission for me to quote from his late mother, Gwendoline Holmes's, account of her experiences during the November 1940 bombing, which is also found in full on the Coventry Blitz Resource Centre website. I am, finally, thankful to Richard Hargreaves for his invaluable advice on finding German accounts of the raid.

In more praise of the internet (and our increasingly hard-pressed museum and archive sector), I was also able to access and listen to a great deal of the Imperial War Museum's collection of historic eye-witness recordings online. I thank the IWM for permission to transcribe and quote from these recordings in my account of the Coventry raid and its politico-military context.

Three-quarters of a century has passed since 'Moonlight Sonata', the big Luftwaffe attack on Coventry. Inevitably, the number of eye-witnesses who can be interviewed about their experiences has diminished. I have therefore had to draw, for the first time while writing about the Second World War, mostly on the kindness of strangers when it comes to quoting from the experiences of Coventrians, born or adopted, who were there on the night of the bombing. An extraordinarily rich seam of survivor reporting exists in the form of the many hours of recordings made by BBC Radio Coventry and Warwickshire before 2010 for its marvellous radio documentary, *Coventry: Beyond the Blitz*. This outstanding, award-winning, one-hour programme was broadcast to coincide with the seventieth anniversary of the 'Coventry Blitz'. DVDs containing the seventy audio interviews conducted – much of which material had perforce to remain unused in the actual broadcast – were donated to the Coventry History Centre, where I first encountered them. Siobhan Harrison of BBC Coventry and Warwickshire has kindly granted me permission to transcribe and quote extensively from those interviews, for which I am immensely grateful.

The number of interviews I conducted personally was, as a result, quite small (had I done more, many could, of course, have been more or less duplications of those already recorded by the BBC).

I am nonetheless grateful to those other survivors who did allow me to talk with them, including Reg Kimber, who is both an eyewitness and a distinguished local historian; John and Thelma Green; Mike and Annie Edwards, who now live in the New Forest; and to Heather Fountain. Mrs Fountain also gave me a whirlwind 'insider's' tour of Earlsdon, including the parts that were once internationally famous factories but are now somewhat bland industrial and retail parks.

My thanks, as ever, to the staff of the National Archives at Kew for their helpfulness and efficiency. Like all public bodies that do not make much in the way of immediate profit, the NA has been presented with the choice of 'monetise or be cut', and now closes on Mondays. For the Coventry History Centre, the archive and resource centre housed in the Herbert Museum and Gallery complex near the Cathedral, the situation is even more serious. Cuts and staff shortages have made it hard for them to open more than a few hours, on four – and I think now three – days a week, or to deal with more than a certain number of document requests per day. My thanks to the archivist, Mr Hinman, for his help in enabling me to get as much work done as I did, and my wish is that one day our government will once again recognise the value, and not just the price, of our country's historical resources.

My warmest thanks, as ever, to my patient editor at Bloomsbury, Bill Swainson, and his team, and to my friend and agent, Jane Turnbull, whose occasional impatience was probably also a good thing. I also wish to acknowledge the help of the arts organisation Literature Works, which awarded me a grant that enabled me to extend my visit to Coventry.

The late Mike Murphy and his wife, Marian, were extremely generous in their hospitality during my first stay in Coventry. Mike also chauffeured me around his native city and provided the benefit of his local knowledge. His loss, just weeks after my last visit, was sudden and very sad.

Another recent loss was that of my friend Götz Bergander, to whom this book is dedicated. It may seem odd that I would dedicate a book about an attack by the German Luftwaffe on a British city to a German. All I can say in reply is that he, a teenage survivor of the bombing of Dresden and also author of the first book (written in the 1970s) that began the process of demythologising that tragedy, has always been an example to me of objectivity, decency and fairness – not forgetting courage, for his urge to write what he saw as the truth made him enemies. Reconciliation comes about through such people and the risks they take. It seems appropriate for all these reasons that a native of Dresden, a city that was also a victim of the air war but now enjoys warm relations with the new Coventry, should appear in this place, in this book.

Lastly, heartfelt thanks to my wife, Alice. As ever.

Saint Keverne, Cornwall
April 2015

INDEX